D0450936

THE ULTIMATE ASSIST

THE RELATIONSHIP AND BROADCAST STRATEGIES OF THE NBA AND TELEVISION NETWORKS

THE HAMPTON PRESS COMMUNICATION SERIES
Mass Communications and Journalism
Lee B. Becker, supervisory editor

THE ULTIMATE ASSIST

THE RELATIONSHIP AND BROADCAST STRATEGIES OF THE NBA AND TELEVISION NETWORKS

John A. Fortunato
St. Peters College

HAMPTON PRESS, INC.
CRESSKILL, NEW JERSEY

Copyright © 2001 by Hampton Press, Inc.

All rights reserved. No part of this publication may be reproduced, stored in a retrieval system, or transmitted in any form or by any means, electronic, mechanical, photocopying, microfilming, recording, or otherwise, without permission of the publisher.

Printed in the United States of America

Library of Congress Cataloging-in-Publication Data

Fortunato, John A.
   The ultimate assist : the relationship and broadcast strategies of the NBA and television networks / John A. Fortunato.
      p. cm. -- (The Hampton Press communication series)
   Includes bibliographical references and indexes.
   ISBN 1-57273-407-8 (cl) -- ISBN 1-57273-408-6 (pb)
      1. National Basketball Association. 2. Television broadcasting of sports. I. Title. II. Series.

GV885.515.N37 F67 2001
070.4'4979632364'0973--dc21

                                                              2001039539

Cover design: Robin Malik/Buddy Boy Design
Cover photo: © 1996 NBA Entertainment. Photo by Dick Raphael

Hampton Press, Inc.
23 Broadway
Cresskill, NJ 07626

To Mary-Louise, Rosanne, Angela, and Diane
Your inspiration and never ending support
are on every page of this book

CONTENTS

ACKNOWLEDGMENTS

This book would not have been possible without the tremendous help of many people. I recognize their assistance and express my great appreciation to them all. At the earliest stages and through every step of this project was Dr. Ronald E. Rice from Rutgers University. Dr. Brent D. Ruben, Dr. Shannon E. Martin, Dr. Hartmut Mokros from Rutgers University, and Dr. James W. Carey from Columbia University were also instrumental in helping this project become better every step of the way. The careful review and suggestions from Dr. Lawrence Wenner, Dr. Donald Shaw, and Dr. Lee Becker were of immense help.

I would like to acknowledge the people who helped me coordinate interviews and offered assistance in providing data: Tina Bucciarelli, Steve Jenkins, Daniel Kerber, Fred Kerber, Joyce Kostrinsky (NBA), Peter Marion, Michael Mastando, Mike May (Sporting Goods Manufacturers Association), Neil McDonald (NBA), John Morsillo, Tricia Morsillo, Nielsen Media Research, Mary Beth Weber (ESPN/Chilton), and Anthony Yacullo.

I would finally like to thank the people who volunteered their time and allowed themselves to be interviewed, many of whom are people whose work I have admired for many years: John Andariese, Mike Breen, Chris Brienza, Hubie Brown, Mike Burks, P.J. Carlesimo, Dave Checketts, Dave Coskey, Vincent Costello, Chuck

Daly, Ed Desser, Ricky Diamond, Ian Eagle, Mike Francesca, Tom Fox, Joe Gangone, Tom Heinsohn, Fred Kerber, Brian McIntyre, John Mertz, Mike Pearl, Tommy Roy, Bob Ryan, Ted Shaker, Adam Silver, Howie Singer, Kevin Smollon, David Stern, Kelly Tripucka, Stephen Ulrich, and Greg Winik.

INTRODUCTION

In the game of basketball an assist occurs when one player sacrifices his or her own opportunity to shoot by passing the ball to a teammate who is in a better position to score. The assist simply enables a partner to score a basket for the benefit of the entire team involved in the game. An assist takes a tremendous amount of coordination in understanding the teammate's and opponents' thoughts, strengths, and weaknesses. Each individual, however, must also possess skills and characteristics independent of a teammate to better the partnership. In basketball, the point guard is often the assist leader and responsible for handling the basketball and being able to pivot and pass around opposing defenders to open teammates. The players without the basketball must move to free themselves from their defenders to be in a position where they can receive a pass and score, maximizing the success of the partnership. If neither performs his or her individual assignments, nor understands the role of a teammate, the opportunity for an assist and a successful partnership is decreased.

In the sport of basketball the highest professional level is the National Basketball Association (NBA). A top NBA point guard will deliver over 10 assists per game; however, the ultimate NBA assist does not even take place on a basketball court, but at negotiating tables in meeting rooms, in television studios and production trucks, and eventually on television sets all across the United States. The ultimate assist is the way a television network can enable a sport to grow through utilizing certain framing methods. In this book *framing methods* are defined as broadcast strategies used to televise the sport and the terms are used interchangeably. The ultimate assist is created by the relation between the NBA and the broadcast networks that televise the games. The relation between the NBA, or any other professional sports league, and a television network might be better characterized as a partnership because when a network signs a contract with a league it too now has a vested interest in that league and must present that league in the best possible light. When operating at its optimal efficiency, the partnership benefits the NBA, television networks, advertisers, and the audience.

Networks and leagues sign a contract in which the network pays the league a certain dollar amount over a certain number of years for the right to broadcast that league's games. Networks can then offer this programming to attract advertisers, while providing the league with a source of revenue and exposure that cannot be attained through any other mechanism. Advertisers benefit in being associated with sports television because they get the opportunity to have their product exposed to a difficult-to-reach demographic audience. The audience should benefit from this partnership by seeing a game at a convenient day and time that is enhanced through camera replays, announcer analysis, the providing of storylines which help hook the audience, player and coach interviews which personalize the participants in the game, and statistical information about the individual players and teams which help keep the viewer more informed and entertained.

The over-the-air national television network partner for the NBA is the National Broadcasting Company (NBC). The annual showcase event for the NBA and NBC partnership is the broadcasting of the NBA Finals. On Friday, June 25, 1999, game five of the NBA Finals was played at Madison Square Garden between the San Antonio Spurs and the New York Knicks with the Spurs holding a three-games-to-one advantage in the best-of-seven series. I was sitting down in section 209 of the Garden for the first NBA Finals game that I had ever attended and holding an orange towel that had been given to all fans in attendance courtesy of Dodge Automotive with the phrases "Go NY Go" and "I Still Believe." The crowd at the Garden was at a level of excitement that I had rarely witnessed.

As the players were going through their pregame warmup, so too were the television personnel. Near mid-court, NBC announcers Bob Costas and Doug Collins rehearsed their opening on-camera segment. In the upper level of the Garden, NBC's *NBA Showtime* crew of Hannah Storm, Bill Walton, Isiah Thomas, and Peter Vescey were preparing for their pregame program. Assisting the announcers, but often unseen were several producers, directors, production assistants, camera operators, and technical personnel. Sitting together a few rows from the center of the basketball court were the top executives and chief officers of this partnership: NBA Commissioner David Stern and NBC Sports President Dick Ebersol.

The back-and-forth contest featured a tremendous individual duel as the 31 points of the Spurs Tim Duncan were answered by 35 points from the Knicks Latrell Sprewell. The game was not decided until the final 47 seconds when Spurs guard Avery Johnson connected on a 16-foot baseline jumper with an assist from Sean Elliot and a last second shot by Sprewell fell short giving San Antonio a 78-77 victory and its first NBA championship. On this night in Madison Square Garden, I was one of the 19,763 fans in attendance. For the rest of the country and the world, television and NBC became the next best alternative. The television audience did, however, at least get the opportunity to see this game live.

Today the broadcasting of the NBA Finals live on television is a certainty, but that was not always the case. This partnership between the NBA and the television networks was not always successful, and television exposure was a problem for the NBA, particularly through the late 1970s and early 1980s. The NBA Finals were not a prominent sports event in the view of television networks, advertisers, and the audience. For example, four of the six games of the 1981 NBA Finals between the Boston Celtics and the Houston Rockets were broadcast on tape delay at 11:30 p.m., while, since 1991, every NBA Finals game has been televised in primetime. It was not that the 1981 NBA Finals matchup lacked a prominent team or a star player. The Celtics have won the most championships in NBA history, (16, 13 prior to 1981) and Larry Bird was in his second NBA season.

Television networks undoubtedly play a vital role in the operation of any successful professional sports league because of the revenue and exposure they provide the league; however, I chose the NBA because this league has grown the most over the past 25 years and the extent of television coverage has drastically changed in comparison with other sports. One of the reasons for the prior lack of success was that the NBA was poorly "framed" on television. Thus, the assumption is television networks have been influential in the emergence of the NBA and there have been new broadcast strategies behind the way the NBA is covered to help grow the sport. Based on this assumption of television networks influencing the NBA, this book does not question *if* television networks can influence sports leagues, but offers an explanation *how* this influence occurs.

Attempts to explain how media influence can occur for sports leagues have been previously stated, particularly from an economic perspective. Parente (1977) claims that "once a sport, league, or team has had its 'product' bought by television for use as programming that entity can seldom exist thereafter, at least in the same style or manner, without the financial support of television" (p. 128). Bellamy (1989) points out that "television could survive without professional sports, but professional sports could not exist in their present form without television monies" (p. 120). In terms of audience popularity, Bogart (1995) contends that "while talk about sports teams and players has long made up an important part of American conversation, its decibel level has been raised by the commercially induced influence of television" (p. 107). McChesney (1989) focuses on the amount of exposure that television networks can provide a sports league, claiming that "virtually every surge in the popularity of sport has been accompanied by a dramatic increase in the coverage provided sport by the media" (p. 49).

Although McChesney makes a valid claim, it must be clearly noted that the amount of television coverage is not the only broadcast strategy that caused league growth. There are multiple factors as this book demonstrates. For example, the nature of the coverage is viewer-dependent as well as producer-dependent. Other television factors that contribute to league growth that have occurred over the last 20 years have been the exposure that the NBA receives from television networks in terms of where games are placed in the program schedule and broadcast strategies in the way the game is being framed, produced, and presented to the audience. The changing of NBA telecasts from CBS to NBC, and the rise of cable outlets TNT and TBS, are other directly related television developments that have influenced the NBA as an industry.

Other factors include initiatives from the NBA itself, particularly advertiser recruitment, media relations, and marketing strategies which reveal how the NBA helped to better frame itself and obtain a level of economic and popular culture status previously not attained. Also influential were strategies systematically promoting more notable players such as Larry Bird, Magic Johnson, and Michael Jordan into celebrity status beyond the realm of sports, and the tenure of David Stern as NBA Commissioner.

The assumption here is that all these are contributing factors to a complex web of simultaneously interacting influences in growing the leagues' fan base and advertising appeal, and although none of these alone is the direct cause of the growth of the NBA, television broadcast strategies must be included near the top of any list. In this light, McChesney's (1989) claim may not have been an indication of direct causality, but more a recognition of the potential that television networks have in influencing the public, and the power of advertising revenues. McChesney's claim also relates this area of study to the more theoretical communication issues of mass media power, mass media effects, and agenda setting.

Mass communication approaches assist in understanding the NBA strategy. In response to the issue of how television influence occurs, one theoretical framework that provides an explanation is agenda-setting research inspired by McCombs and Shaw (1972, 1993). Agenda-setting serves as a guide of how communication theory can be used to explain the growth of the NBA. Through the assumption of television network influence and the study of how television networks influence through broadcast strategies, a connotation of direct and powerful media effects can be inferred. The broadcast strategies, however, must exist in conjunction with the needs of the audience and the needs of advertisers. Both of these key constituency groups could still reject any type of programming despite television network strategies.

The role of the audience thus mitigates direct media effects approaches and lends credence to the indirect media effects perspectives. A theoretical framework that focuses on the connections between television networks and the audience is the uses and gratifications approach inspired by Blumler and Katz (1974). A theoretical framework that explains the relationship among television networks, advertisers, and the audience is the media dependency research as described by Ball-Rokeach and DeFleur (1976, 1986). The rationale behind utilizing multiple theoretical frameworks is to create an integrated model that could provide a more complete evaluation of mass communication. The integrated model provides a better guide to describing and explaining broadcast strategies in the situation of the NBA and television.

This book begins with an examination of the unique characteristics of the sports television industry and how these characteristics elevate the position of sports within the corporate culture. Chapter One also includes a brief description of how the NBA has grown in terms of the amount of product available to the audience and the increase in television revenue that the NBA has enjoyed. Demonstrating that there has been this growth is imperative if arguing that television strategies are one of the factors. Chapter One concludes with audience motivations toward sports programming and how these motivations differ from other types of programming. Chapter Two demonstrates how a communication approach can assist in understanding the NBA television strategy focusing on agenda setting, uses and gratifications, and media dependency leading to an integrated model of mass communication. Chapters Three, Four, and Five explicitly examine the NBA broadcast strategies implemented to grow the NBA. Chapter Three focuses on the exposure strategy, chapter Four on the portrayal strategy, and chapter Five examines how the NBA manages the quality of its own product. Chapter Six explains the connections between the NBA strategy and the integrated communication approach. Chapter Seven offers a concluding analysis of the necessity and value of implementing the proper communication and television broadcast strategies that led to the growth of the NBA.

The overall goal of this book is to identify and describe the broadcast strategies television networks used to better present the NBA and help influence the growth of the league. This book also provides: a description of the characteristics of the relationship between the NBA and the television networks who broadcast games, a description and explanation of the network personnel and NBA perceptions of the effects the broadcast strategies used for NBA broadcasts have on an audience, and a contribution to the theoretical research question through the development of an integrated theoretical model of direct and indirect mass media effects perspectives through an intensive explanation of the influence dynamic in the single, complex context of broadcasting NBA basketball.

This book hopes to achieve these objectives and provide insight about this topic for many different groups. Sports fans who have the majority of their experience with professional sports occur through television can learn how leagues and broadcast networks interact with one another from the perspective of the people who produce sports television. Sports fans can learn which broadcast strategies are employed, why these strategies are used for televising a NBA game, and how they benefit from these strategies when watching a game on television. Insights for other sports or non-sports organizations will be to learn the influence that the proper strategic usage of communication and television can provide in growing an industry. Hopefully, this book also provides a reflective summary for the many people involved in the broadcasting of NBA basketball. For the television network and NBA personnel interviewed, this book provided an opportunity and a forum for them to systematically discuss and analyze their role in the broadcasting of the NBA. Many people interviewed commented on the fact that often they do not think about their role, how it is performed, and its impact in the large-scale presentation of the league. Often in television, due to time constraints, there is no opportunity for lengthy debate about procedures and strategies utilized for event coverage.

   Overall, this book hopes to demonstrate how television networks have been an influence in the growth of the NBA through new broadcast strategies, and more importantly, how the NBA utilizes television as a major part of its overall business strategy for revenue and exposure to the audience. This book is not only a study of a transfer of an agenda, but of the strategic decision making of the people who have the ability to understand what television is able to provide to a sports league. This strategic decision making has been a major impetus in creating the public perception of NBA basketball as an extremely entertaining product played by highly skilled professionals. The growth in audience behavior of viewing games, attendance, and purchasing of NBA-related products does allow for the simple conclusion that people enjoy watching and being associated with NBA basketball.

   People know the names of the NBA superstars such as Larry Bird, Magic Johnson, or Michael Jordan. Most fans even know the names of the stars who have announced games and presented these NBA stars to us, such as Brent Musburger, Dick Stockton, Marv Albert, and Bob Costas. This book introduces people to a new set of superstars who have helped frame and explain the story of NBA basketball and bring the game into our living rooms. People from the NBA: Chris Brienza, Ed Desser, Brian McIntyre, Adam Silver, and Gregg Winik; from NBC: Ricky Diamond, Tommy Roy, Kevin Smollon, and Vincent Costello; from CBS: Mike Burks and Ted Shaker; and from Turner Sports: Mike Pearl. This book identifies and explains the broadcast strategies these people utilized to help grow the sport of NBA basketball. These are the architects who can offer an explanation as to how and why the growth of the NBA occurred and to explain the role that television networks played in creating this growth—creating THE ULTIMATE ASSIST.

1

TELEVISION SPORTS, CULTURE, AND THE GROWTH OF THE NBA

Sports television is the coming together of two of the most prevalent elements of society: sports and television. Individually, each consumes large amounts of hobby and leisure time activity. Combined in the form of watching sports on television, this activity is a major part of the American culture. Sports maintain a continuous presence in the national dialog because there is always a new and different game or event available with no repeats. It is not only one sport in particular, but often many people are fans of all sports, with favorite teams in each sport. Often fans must deal with sports seasons running simultaneous to one another. For example, a Spring evening in the New York area could hypothetically feature three teams in the NHL playoffs, two teams in the NBA playoffs, and two baseball games. These fans' loyalties are divided only by a matter of which game is *more* important, as any sports fan will attest that *all* games are important. So in the Spring a fan would probably watch the NBA or NHL playoff game rather than a regular season baseball game. However, in the Fall, the baseball playoffs would trump an early season NBA or NHL game. The fanaticism goes beyond team sports, incorporating an interest in individual sports special events such as golf, tennis, boxing, or horse racing. For many sports fans it is not a decision of whether watching sports is going to be the leisure-time activity, but rather which sport and which game. The way for most of these fans to experience these sports is through television, with the sports fan having the uncanny ability to navigate from channel to channel to keep abreast of the action in all games and not miss a critical play in any of the games.

Mass communication research examines the role of television and sports within the American culture. Wenner (1991) contends that "watching television is something one has to do to understand our culture. To not watch is like sticking one's head in the sand. Our cultural sense of what is new and important—our cultural agenda—comes largely from what plays on television." He emphasizes that "with such wide play, television's stories matter more than others told in America" (pp. 388-389). Regarding sports, Tutko (1989) comments,

> many see athletic events and sports contests as the backbone of America and that what we see displayed on the playing field stands for, and represents all of the virtuous characteristics that make this country great. In a philosophical sense the sporting scene does represent a slice of this country's culture. If it didn't it could not survive, let alone thrive, in this nation. (p. 112)

In putting sports and television together as one entity, Zillmann, Bryant, and Sapolsky (1989) claim that

> the enjoyment people all over the world apparently derive from watching sport contests is worthy of investigation, regardless of other benefits or the lack thereof. If spectatorship produced no effects other than enjoyment, and even if such enjoyment were branded as "superficial," it would still be an experience of some value and preferable to many others. (p. 254)

THE CORPORATE STRUCTURE OF SPORTS

It is more than the mere enjoyment of watching sports, but the economic structure that is created around sports television that has given this industry its prominent place in American culture. The pervasiveness of sports within American culture can be grounded in its corporate appeal from ownership of teams, to purchasing of tickets and luxury boxes, to sponsorship of arenas and advertisements on sports television programs. The appeal of the corporate culture for sports exists because these corporations can reach a sports audience that possesses the critical characteristics of a difficult-to-reach demographic who is loyal and does not often miss their favorite team play or other key games. While competition exists on the courts and playing fields, another strategic competition for corporate support and access to the sports audience gets played out.

The competitive nature of the corporate culture is addressed in detail by Schiller (1989), who wrote extensively about the emergence of the American corporation and its influence in the societal culture. The competition goes beyond that of simple economic support, into the domain of support for ideas and images, and importantly, who controls these ideas and images. In understanding the corporation's overall philosophy, Schiller (1989) states that, "the main objective of the American corporate economy is to maximize profits in whatever are the given circumstances. This requires being in charge of key levers of power" (p. 28). Schiller claims that there are only two main choices for control of ideas and images—either "big government" or "big business." He contends that corporations have emerged as the proliferators of culture and images, largely through advertising and the media, particularly television. Schiller states that "the private corporate sector in the American economy has widened its economic, political, and cultural role in domestic and international activities" (p. 3). He simply claims that corporate speech, advertising, is the "loudest in the land" (p. 4).

Corporations must find a way to influence or control the culture and how it is achieved through advertising and supporting what Schiller refers to as the culture industries—publishing, the press, film, television, radio, recordings, photography, and sports. Schiller points out that "the industries whose main function is the production of messages and imagery—those that can be seen as cultural industries in their own right—continue to be the main centers of symbolic production" (p. 30). He claims that "all economic activity produces symbolic as well as material goods. In fact, the two are generally inseparable" (p. 01). Schiller continues, "a community's economic life cannot be separated from its symbolic content. Together they represent the totality of a culture" (p. 31). To a large extent, according to Schiller, economic support becomes support for that entity and its existence within the culture. The interesting component, however, is that industries of cultural messages are not unlike any other business enterprise designed to maximize profits. Companies produce different types of products all designed to be sold for profit, so Coca-Cola produces soft drinks; General Motors produces cars; Disney produces television programs, books, and films; and the NBA produces games, other television programming, and merchandise.

The corporate power as a cultural influence is as an agenda setter or gatekeeper in validating certain performers, or even entire industries through their form of economic support, sponsorship, and advertising. Validation occurs not solely based on talent, but perhaps more importantly on marketability. Schiller states that "if a creative project, no matter what its inherent quality, cannot be viewed as a potential money-maker, salable in a large enough market, its production is problematic at best" (p. 43). This distinction is critical in the analysis of the NBA as it can be argued that the game has changed very little (in fact, some critics might argue that through expansion the product is diluted with less talent), however, the marketability and revenue generating of the NBA as a league, its teams, its coaches, and its players is an unprecedented success.

Teams and athletes with the combination of skill and marketability become the ultimate scenario for themselves, the sponsor, and the sport. For example, the Chicago Bulls of the 1990s had this tremendous combination of skill with Michael Jordan, Scottie Pippen, and Dennis Rodman, but Jordan was also the most marketable player in the NBA—much the way golfer Tiger Woods is now. Contrast this combination of skill and marketability with a player who is extremely talented, but does not have a huge marketing appeal, such as tennis great Pete Sampras, who has won more singles grand slam championships than any other player in the history of tennis, or the player who is an initial marketing phenomenon, but cannot maintain the skill level to sustain this lofty position, such as former NFL linebacker Brian Bosworth, who prematurely retired due to injury.

Individual expression and creativity is only available to those who can afford it and have the means to put out their messages on their own. With the channels for expression certainly limited, other individuals need the support of corporations and the market to get out their messages. The influence of corporations goes beyond that of financial support to the individual or industry, to the public as a whole, who sees their advertising as a degree of validation in that there will be continued exposure of those ideas and images. Schiller (1989) operates from a "strong assumption that social imperatives channel individual expression" (p. 6). He explains:

> Individual expression occurs each time a person dresses, goes out for a walk, meets friends, converses, or does any of a thousand routine exercises. Expression is an inseparable part of life. It is ludicrous to imagine that individual expression can be completely managed and controlled. Yet, no matter how integral to the per-

son, it is ultimately subject to social boundaries that are themselves changeable but always present. These limits have been
created by the power formations in society, past and present. I
have tried to trace how some of these defining conditions have
been established or reinforced in recent decades and what impact
they have. The growth of private corporate power is seen as the
prime contractor in the construction of contemporary boundaries
to expression. (p. 6)

In acting as a validation for cultural ideas and images, personalities and industries, Schiller explains that "the corporate history machine has at its disposal the means by which it becomes the
national narrator of record. Television, which takes its screening
orders from corporate marketing furnishes the history (such as it is)
that is seen by millions, be it through the news, drama, sports, or historical narratives" (pp. 7-8). He claims that

television is now one of the most influential, largely unacknowl-
edged educators in the country. One reason why television is
heavily discounted as a powerful educational force is the distinction made between "educational" and "entertainment" programming. This artificial separation seems to mesmerize many into
believing that entertainment shows are not educational. (p. 106)

For television networks and professional sports leagues the
recruitment of sponsorship and advertising, and therefore validation
of their programming content, is a never-ending endeavor as it
remains the only revenue source for broadcasters, who in turn are
the major revenue source for a professional sports league. Individual
teams also seek sponsorship and advertising for their stadiums or
arenas. In this regard, it would appear that corporations have all the
power and there is a dependency from broadcasters and professional
sports leagues on sponsors and advertisers. However, sponsors and
advertisers also have a dependency on the media to reach their
potential customers, in particular their target market, and to let
them learn about their available products and services. In this
regard, television networks regain some power in the relationship as
they could ask for a higher price for commercials during their better
programming. The nature of this relationship is therefore interdependent. Once this interdependency is realized by both broadcasters
and corporations, mutual support and relationships, or at this point
what is better characterized as partnerships, are fostered.

The specificity as to types of television programming in which sponsors attempt to connect to audiences creates a powerful position on the side of the networks. This is especially true for sports programming, which delivers a specific target audience to the television screen. Schiller (1989) states that "the transnational corporate order's use of commercialized and privatized media to increase sales, create consumers, and transmit to a mind-set supportive of the system is especially evident in the sphere of sports" (p. 129). Schiller deems the sports audience as a fertile area for cultural influence by corporations. He states:

> With the capture of sports for corporate promotions, the audience is targeted in its most vulnerable condition, relaxed yet fully receptive to the physical action and the inserted sales pitch. It is the ideal ambiance for the penetration of consciousness by a wide variety of ideological images. (p. 130)

Validation, in the form of sponsorship, guarantees a continuing presence (exposure) of that industry. However, validation does not guarantee, nor equate to, public acceptance of the endorsed industry. Audience behavior regarding attendance at events, watching a television program, or the purchasing of products serves as the ultimate validation and acceptance and might be the ultimate indicator of continued sponsorship support. Wenner (1989) points out that "the symbiotic economic relationship between sports organizations and media organizations has created a large marketplace for mediated sports" (p. 38). He claims that, "not only is mediated sport content designed to be pleasurably consumed, it is packaged as a vehicle that carries messages promoting the consumption of products. Whether there is control in that is in the eye of the beholder" (p. 21).

SPORTS TELEVISION: GENERAL CHARACTERISTICS

It is not every industry that receives corporate support, and few obtain the large amounts of money given to sports entities, either at the stadium and arena event or through television. In what it can provide to the corporate market, sports television is unique in comparison to other programming genres. As Gantz (1981) points out, "uses of sports programming merits investigation because such programming offers sharp contrasts with other media entertainment" (p. 263). The pervasive element of sports plays a major role in the influence of the corporate culture. Wenner (1989) adds that "whether a sports fan or not, every individual in America is to some degree influenced by the communication of sports culture. Mediated sports culture is an inescapable reality, forming part of the context of every American's life" (p. 16).

In terms of sports being a mediated event, Williams (1977) points out that "at the point of the telecast, the event, the audience, and the medium all intersect, with the media imposing their own structures and emphases" (p. 133). Although writing about professional football, Williams contends that in actuality there are three events coexisting at the time of live coverage: (a) the game event, which features "the action on the field plus directly related activities taking place on the sidelines" (p. 135); (b) the stadium event, which describes "the total sequence of activities occurring in the stadium, both perceived and participated in by the fans and including the game event" (p. 135); and (c) the medium event, which describes "the total telecast of which coverage of the game event is part" (p. 135). Comisky, Bryant, and Zillmann (1977) explain that "whereas the viewers in the stadium perceive the event as it is, the home viewers are exposed to a 'media event' that is the product of a team of professional gatekeepers and embellishers" (p. 150).

The major tool of mediation is obviously the visual content available through the camera. Lever and Wheeler (1993) focus on the power of the camera's ability to bring fans closer to the game action than is experienced by the fan actually attending the game. They point out that the "use of slow motion coupled with a second technological device, instant replay, allows an appreciation of the intricate and speedy moves that often represent the best of sport in action" (p. 136). The camera can show the emotion of the athletes involved. Lever and Wheeler state, "the fan at home is able to see the action from the perspective of the immediate participants, thanks to cameras on the level of the field that also provide close-ups of athletes on the sidelines" (p. 137). They contend that:

> With the use of multiple cameras, television can give the viewer a sense of the totality of action that may never be achieved by the eye witness seeing the event from only one angle of vision. By the use of close-ups of other fans, distant shots of the stadium, and officials wired for sound, the fan may become a part of the event in a way that he or she cannot when actually attending. (p. 137)

In contrasting the stadium and television event, it is imperative to point out that a small percentage of people participate in the

NBA or see NBA games live in comparison to the large numbers of people who view the games on television. Regarding sports events, Wenner (1989) points out that the most common involvement people have is through viewing them on television, and Lever and Wheeler (1993) claim that "the single most dominant influence on the way in which sport is experienced in American society is that of the mass media, particularly television" (p. 125). Overall, the greatest similarity between sports and all other types of program genres is that the mass media organization attempts to provide programming that will reach a large audience and thus creates advertising interest and revenues. Wenner (1989) points out that "media organizations buy and sell sport much as they do any other news or entertainment commodity. The content per se is not what is being sold; rather it is the audience for that content that is being sold to advertisers" (p. 22).

Although the necessity to attract an audience and advertisers is similar, there are major differences between sports television and other programming genres. Foremost is that a league and a network sign a multiyear contract for broadcast rights. A television organization pays a certain fee to the league for the rights to broadcast a certain number of games for a certain number of years on their network. The network then hopes this type of programming will compel viewers to watch its network because they sell these viewers and the commercial time during these games to advertisers. Wenner (1989) describes this relationship as "a sports organization directly markets a product—its team's playing abilities—to spectators who pay for the privilege of watching the team play. The organization indirectly markets this product to broadcast media organizations, who repackage and embellish the product as the lure for the audiences advertisers seek to reach" (p. 22). Although rights fees have now reached in excess of $1 billion (beginning with the 1998-99 season the NBA will receive a combined total of $2.4 billion for the broadcast rights over four years from NBC and Turner Sports), networks continue to pay because sports television offers an opportunity for the networks to provide programming with consistent ratings and thus consistent advertisers.

Parente (1977) points out that "television was relatively unimportant to sports until the end of the 1950s when organized professional team sports began to look at television as a potential major source of revenue" (p. 129). Professional sports franchises combine as a league and sell the broadcast rights of their games to a national network who packages the games. Horowitz (1974) describes network packaging in terms of hiring announcers, providing technical crews and equipment, and selling commercial time to sponsors. The revenues from the national broadcasting contracts are then shared equally among all franchises.

The selling of rights fees for games to television broadcasters was originally a major point of contention between both league and television executive personnel. Horowitz (1974) explains the conflict and that "the prospect of significant broadcast revenues, and the threat that broadcasts would adversely affect attendance, led to the adoption of rules in each sport that restricted inter-team competition for the sale of broadcast rights" (p. 279). These rules became a force behind several antitrust suits surrounding laws of broadcast policy. The first time antitrust issues were raised was in 1946 when Major League Baseball adopted a rule prohibiting one team from broadcasting a game into another team's home territory or from another stadium without the home team's consent in order to protect the interests of the local team's ticket sales. Fearing the creation of a system that would not permit open competition, the Department of Justice became involved in trying to settle this antitrust issue.

Many of the early sports broadcast suits dealt with the televising of the National Football League (NFL), and on October 9, 1951, the Department of Justice filed suit against the NFL. In *United States v. National Football League* (1953), Judge Allan K. Grim decided to uphold the legality of the NFL bylaw which prevented the telecasting of an outside game in a third team's home territory when that team had a home game. This ruling would in effect allocate marketing territories for the purpose of restricting competition. Horowitz (1974) explains that "the court found that such a restraint was reasonable because of the adverse effects that competitive outside telecasts would be likely to have on the home club's attendance" (p. 281). The court also ruled that because of the mutual interdependence of the franchises, by protecting the home attendance of the weaker teams, the restriction would help preserve the league. The court did find two illegal restrictions on broadcasts: (a) the prohibition against telecasts by another team when the home team was also telecasting an away game in its home territory, and (b) all restrictions on outside radio broadcasts. Through these two restrictions the court, in essence, confirmed that ticket sales were the major economic enterprise not to be infringed on and validated the power of television as opposed to radio.

The professional sports leagues did not feel the ruling of the court interfered with the situation in which all the teams could collectively bargain as a cartel in negotiations for broadcast rights. Thinking the collective selling of broadcast rights to be legal, the NBA and NBC signed the first professional sports league-wide television agreement in 1954, and in that year the first nationally televised game between the Boston Celtics and the New York Knicks was broadcast on NBC (Staudohar, 1996). Following television contracts between the American Football League (AFL) and ABC in 1960 and the NFL and CBS on April 24, 1961, a petition seeking an interpretation of the 1953 ruling was brought again in *United States v. National Football League* (1961). Judge Grim ruled that by pooling television rights the franchises eliminated competition among themselves in the sale of these rights. Horowitz (1974) explains that "the court also held that by granting to CBS the right to determine which games would be telecast and where, the agreement violated the 1953 judgement enjoining the league from entering into any agreement that could tend to restrict broadcast areas" (p. 283). The court thus deemed the NFL-CBS contract to be in violation of the 1953 ruling.

Having failed in the judicial branch of government, the leagues and the networks petitioned Congress for permission to pool and sell their broadcast rights to television networks. The result of hearings before the House of Representatives was the Sports Broadcasting Act (public law 87-331) approved by Congress on September 30, 1961. The new law simply granted clubs in professional sports an antitrust exemption allowing them to pool their broadcast rights for the purpose of selling those rights to the highest bidder. The purpose of the Sports Broadcasting Act is different from that of the Sherman Act, which is designed to ensure free market competition.

The Sports Broadcasting Act established the legality of the practice employed by a professional sports league which tends to restrain competition by packaging its league games to a network and not allowing teams to individually sell their broadcast rights. The Sports Broadcasting Act is, however, a "special interest legislation, a single-industry exception to a law designed for the protection of the public" (*Chicago Professional Sports Limited Partnership and WGN Continental Broadcasting Company v. NBA*, 961 F. 2nd 667, p. 671 (7th Cir. 1992). Section 1291 of the Sports Broadcasting Act amended antitrust laws so that they

> shall not apply to any joint agreement by or among persons engaging in or conducting the organized professional team sports of football, baseball, basketball, or hockey, by which any league of clubs . . . sells or otherwise transfers all right or any part of the right of such league's member clubs in the sponsored telecasting of the games. (75 Stat. 732)

Individual sports franchises also engage in the selling of the rights to broadcast their games for local telecasts. Horowitz (1974) points out that "the local rights of a team include all broadcasting possibilities not subsumed under the national contract or proscribed by league rules" (p. 277). Although teams receive local broadcast rights fees, a majority of their broadcast revenues come from the league's major network broadcast package. Teams from larger cities and media markets may receive a lucrative broadcast contract from a local cable network that accounts for a larger percentage of total revenue than the national television contract shared among all of the leagues' franchises.

The signing of a contract between a sports league and a television network has two distinct advantages for the league: revenue and exposure. Television contracts not only provide the largest vehicles for revenues, but also opportunities for sports leagues to televise and promote their product—not only games, but merchandise as well. Television networks pay for the rights to broadcast sports because there are characteristics inherent to sports television that are advantageous to the network and cannot be obtained through televising other programming genres. Four distinct advantages are: (a) the ability to influence the program schedule, (b) the potential advertising possibilities, (c) the potential promotion possibilities, and (d) the real-life qualities of sports television.

Unlike major news events, a television network can control or at least have some input into when major sporting events will occur. A sports television schedule is structured temporally in accordance with the league so the network can schedule its other programming around league games and its league games around other programming as it so desires in attempting to reach the largest audience and greatest advertising revenues for the network as a whole. Developing the proper exposure is a major framing method for both a league and a network. The ability to carefully place sports in the programming schedule is similar to other entertainment programming as the sport becomes another source of the entire network programming inventory. From the network perspective, another attractive characteristic of sports television involves its exposure attributes to the audience. Sports programming provides the networks with programming at spots (days and times) not occupied by other major programming genres. In the mid-1950s, much of the weekend programming was devoted to religion and politics, and ratings were not high (e.g., Lever & Wheeler, 1993). Sports programming helped fill this time slot and created another opportunity to attract advertisers. Parente (1977) summarizes that "television has become dependent upon sports to fulfill many of its programming needs" (p. 128).

The companies that advertise for the NBA have the advantage and the opportunity to reach the NBA audience, a desirable demographic for certain companies, particularly sneaker, car, and beverage manufacturers. Wenner (1989) points out that sports programming is a good proposition because this type of programming caters to the desirable, and relatively hard-to-reach, male audience between the ages of 18 and 49. He also claims the sports programming demographic tends to be well-educated with considerable disposable income and "advertisers are willing to pay top dollar for this audience because they tend to make purchase decisions about big-ticket items such as automobiles and computers" (p. 14).

Horowitz (1974) points out that the sponsor-league-network relationship "assures the sponsor," first, "of an advertising monopoly for the league. Second, it permits the telecasting of either the most attractive game available, or else a game of regional interest" (p. 300). This is a win-win situation for the sponsor: whatever game is televised in this scenario is either the most attractive game, which will reduce the dependency on a local appeal, or a game of regional interest that takes advantage of it. Ideally, viewers are seeing the game that should be of the most interest to them and simply attracts the largest audience, which is the vital criterion for an advertiser. Horowitz (1974), however, points out that the disadvantage of the system of buying advertising for a league package is that "unsuccessful bidders and firms too small even to consider sponsorship may well find themselves at a competitive disadvantage. Thus, network broadcasts will tend to be sponsored by the largest national firms" (pp. 300-301). It is important to recognize the disadvantage as explained by Horowitz is not a disadvantage to the league or the network who would prefer the largest companies with the largest advertising budgets as the sponsors.

Corporations can support a sport through purchasing spot advertising on television or event sponsorship. McAllister (1998) makes a distinction between sponsorship, and spot advertising, or buying a single commercial within a program. He defines sponsorship as "the funding of an entire event, group, broadcast or place by one commercial interest in exchange for large amounts and special types of promotion connected with the sponsored activity" (p. 358). McAllister claims that

> from the sponsors' point of view, advertisers have been continually frustrated with the viewer's ability to "zap" ads, with the fragmentation of the media audience, and with the high cost of spot advertising in different media, and they have turned to sponsorship as a corrective to these problems. (p. 359)

One of the positive benefits of a sponsorship agreement with a league is the exclusivity of a particular product genre that a company receives. McAllister (1998) describes exclusivity as a promotional incentive for sponsors: unlike spot advertising or commercials, sponsors can now be the exclusive voice of an event. Exclusivity eliminates any competition that one corporation might receive from a rival for a sponsored event. For example, Visa has been the exclusive sponsor of horse racing's "Triple Crown Challenge," which features the Kentucky Derby, Preakness Stakes, and Belmont Stakes, eliminating American Express from advertising at any of these events. McAllister focuses on the role of sponsorship in college football bowl games claiming, "by being the 'signature sponsor' of an event these corporations hope their name will be strongly tied to the event, and will receive most of the promotional benefit" (p. 363).

Another unique characteristic of sports television related very strongly with attracting advertisers is that of promotion. Unlike sports television, most other programming—prime-time dramas, movies, news magazine shows, or situation comedies—can only offer commercial time to advertisers. In addition to commercial time, sports programming offers the opportunity for the network to generate advertising revenue within the framework of the program content itself. The sports format allows networks to sell to advertisers' billboards, still shots (when coming out of commercial of a company logo) with a voice-over announcing the company name and slogan against the backdrop of the live event, sponsored pregame or halftime shows, scoreboards, starting lineups, player of the game, and halftime statistics, all serving as extra forms of advertising revenue within the context of the actual program itself.

In addition to product advertising during the framework of its content, the network can promote its other programming while people are watching a game, rather than during a commercial break when viewers might be switching to other channels. Or if the network chooses, because of sponsorship within the program content, the network could use commercial time that was previously needed for revenues to promote some of its other programming. Anderson (1995) claims that "probably the most commercialized sector of popular entertainment is the result of the merger between sports and product promotion" (p. 36). Regarding the large dollar figures necessary to acquire sports broadcasting rights, Lever and Wheeler (1993) point out that "astronomical costs (rights fees) can be justified by giving valuable exposure to new series and entertainment specials through promotional spots" (p. 135).

Another major difference for sports television is the nature of the programming itself and the real-life element of the content and the people involved. This characteristic is also obviously present in news; however, news lacks some of the other positive characteristics of sports television. The real-life competition with real people and not fictional characters combined with the opportunity to see this event with the outcome unknown live on television creates the drama that intrigues the audience. Wenner and Gantz (1989) explain that "athletes' careers hinge on their performances, and outcomes are uncertain, with the 'drama' later reported as news. Reality and uncertainty in sports give its viewing a unique flavor" (p. 242). Wenner (1989) adds that "what makes the sports contest on television so appealing to advertisers may be the relative intensity with which sports fans view the game. The sporting event is unscripted and live. Dramatic things may happen at any moment" (pp. 14-15).

THE OPENING TIP: A BRIEF HISTORY OF NBA PRODUCT GROWTH

In order to explain television's influence on the growth of the NBA, it is necessary to demonstrate that the NBA has grown in terms of the number of teams, the number of markets, and the number of games, all of which create more product of NBA basketball to be consumed. The fact that economically the NBA has grown in terms of broadcast rights fees, demonstrating the increased investment and positive attitude that the networks have toward the NBA, must also be expressed.

On June 6, 1946, Walter Brown of Boston, Al Sutphin of Cleveland, Ned Irish of New York, Mike Uline of Washington, and seven other owners from the cities of Chicago, Detroit, Philadelphia, Toronto, Providence, Pittsburgh, and St. Louis, met at the Hotel Commodore in New York City to discuss the organization of a professional basketball league. Many of these owners, including Brown, Sutphin, Irish, and Uline, owned arenas and professional hockey franchises in those cities and needed events to fill their buildings on nights their professional hockey teams were not playing or were playing on the road. In addition to filling their arenas, owners, driven by the success of attendance at college basketball games, were looking to transform this popularity into a professional league.

The Basketball Association of America (BAA) was then born. Eleven franchises paid the $10,000 fee and were formed to compete in two divisions (see Table 1.1).

The franchise fee was used for league operating expenses and a salary for Maurice Podoloff, whom the owners were familiar with as the President of the American Hockey League. He was chosen to become the first BAA President.

Table 1.1. The Inaugural Basketball Association of America 1946-47 Season.

The East	The West
Boston Celtics	Pittsburgh Ironmen
Philadelphia Warriors	Chicago Stags
Providence Steamrollers	Detroit Falcons
Washington Capitols	St. Louis Bombers
New York Knickerbockers	Cleveland Rebels
Toronto Huskies	

(Source: NBA)

Owners looked at the success of college basketball at Madison Square Garden in New York and in other cities and felt a professional basketball league that would continue to feature established stars from the college game should succeed. In building off the success of college basketball many professional franchises featured players from the same geographic region (e.g., Goldaper, 1996). For example, 13 of the 20 players who saw game action in the 1946-47 season for the New York Knickerbockers had also played college basketball in New York or New Jersey (see Table 1.2). The Knickerbockers also tabbed Manhattan College coach Neil Cohalan to be their first head coach.

While similar in rules and style to the college game, professional basketball owners wanted to differentiate their game from that of collegiate basketball. Professional games would be 48 minutes rather than 40 minutes and played in four 12-minute quarters rather than two 20-minute halves so that ticket buyers would receive two hours of entertainment. Less than three months after the season began the zone defense permitted in college basketball would also not be allowed in the professional game because it slowed the game down.

Although basketball is America's game in terms of its origin, with Dr. James Naismith inventing the game in 1891 in Springfield, Massachusetts, the first game of the BAA was played on November 1, 1946, at the Maple Leaf Gardens in Toronto, Canada, when the home team Huskies lost 68-66 to the Knicks before a crowd of 7,090 (Goldaper, 1996). Fifty years later on November 1, 1996, the New York Knicks and the Toronto Raptors would tip off the golden anniversary of the NBA, with New York beating Toronto 107-99 before 28,457 in attendance at the SkyDome in Toronto.

Table 1.2. The 1946-47 New York Knickerbockers with College Affiliation.

Player	College
Sonny Hertzberg	CCNY
Stan Stutz	Rhode Island
Tommy Byrnes	Seton Hall
Ossie Schectman	Long Island
Bud Palmer	Princeton
Leo Gottlieb	no college
Robert Cluggish	Kentucky
Ralph Kaplowitz	New York
Lee Knorek	Detroit
Nat Militzok	Cornell/Hofstra
Hank Robertson	CCNY
Frido Frey	Long Island
Bob Fitzgerald	Fordham
Bob Mullens	Fordham
Aud Brindley	Dartmouth
Dick Murphy	Manhattan
Butch Van Breda Kolff	Princeton/New York
John Murphy	no college
Jake Weber	Purdue
Frank Mangiopane	New York

(Source: New York Knickerbockers)

The BAA was in a constant state of flux during its early years. In its second season only eight franchises continued to play, with teams located in Pittsburgh, Detroit, Cleveland, and Toronto dissolving, but a new franchise starting in Baltimore (Bullets). In its third season, the league moved up to 12 franchises by adding four teams from the National Basketball League (NBL), a Midwestern basketball league. For the beginning of the 1949-50 season, the BAA absorbed the remaining six survivors from the NBL and changed its name to the National Basketball Association (NBA). Seventeen franchises (the Providence Steamrollers folded after three seasons), however, were impractical and weaker franchises folded. By the start of the 1954-55 season, the shakedown was complete and the NBA consisted of eight very strong franchises to form a viable major sports league (see Table 1.3).

The stability that was started with the 1954-55 season is important. Although several teams have changed their home locations, no NBA franchise has folded and the league has continuously added teams. Since the 1954-55 season, the NBA has never started a season with less franchises than the previous year. The NBA has also experienced growth in the number of teams which now stands at 29 (see Table 1.4).

Table 1.3. The NBA 1954-55 Season.

East	West
Syracuse Nationals	Fort Wayne Pistons
New York Knickerbockers	Minneapolis Lakers
Boston Celtics	Rochester Royals
Philadelphia Warriors	Milwaukee Hawks

(Source: NBA)

Table 1.4. NBA Team Expansion.

Year	# of NBA Teams
1946	11
1947	8
1948	12
1949	17
1950	11
1951	10
1953	9
1954	8
1961	9
1966	10
1967	12
1968	11
1970	17
1974	18
1976	22
1980	23
1988	25
1989	27
1995	29

(Source: NBA)

A major development of NBA growth was its merger in 1976 with the rival basketball league, the American Basketball Association (ABA). The term merger might be misleading as only four franchises, the Denver Nuggets, Indiana Pacers, New York Nets, and San Antonio Spurs, paid the $3.2 million entrance fee into the NBA to bring the total number of teams to 22. The ABA existed for nine seasons, beginning with the 1967-68 season and ending after the 1975-76 season. The ABA had a tumultuous run as 28 different franchises existed at one point or another. The inaugural ABA season featured 11 teams, but only teams in Denver, Indiana, and Kentucky had not moved in the 9-year history of the league, and only seven teams competed in the final season (see Table 1.5).

The most distinguishing characteristic of the ABA was its red, white, and blue basketball. NBA legend and first ABA Commissioner George Mikan insisted on the red, white, and blue ball "because it is easier to see" and "kids will love it" (Pluto, 1996, p. 23). The economic operations of the ABA were also unstable and although the red, white, and blue ball was a popular selling item, the ABA did not have a patent on the ball and received no money from these sales. The ABA had features that were later adopted by the NBA, such as

Table 1.5. The 1967-68 and 1975-76 ABA Seasons.

1967-68	East	West
	Pittsburgh Pipers	New Orleans Buccaneers
	Minnesota Muskies	Dallas Chaparrals
	Indiana Pacers	Denver Rockets
	Kentucky Colonels	Houston Mavericks
	New Jersey Americans	Anaheim Amigos
	Oakland Oaks	
1975-76	ABA	
	Denver Nuggets	
	Indiana Pacers	
	Kentucky Colonels	
	New York Nets	
	San Antonio Spurs	
	St. Louis Spirits	
	Virginia Squires	

(Source: NBA)

the dunk contest and the three-point shot, but when the league folded its greatest gifts to the NBA were star players such as Julius Erving (Dr. J), George Gervin, Artis Gilmore, Dan Issel, and Moses Malone, as well as coaches Hubie Brown and Larry Brown (see Pluto, 1991, for a detailed history of the ABA).

Expansion into Dallas in 1980, Charlotte and Miami in 1988, Minnesota and Orlando in 1989, and Toronto and Vancouver in 1995 completed the NBA growth into a 29-team league. The NBA is divided into the Eastern and Western Conference and separated into four divisions; the Atlantic and Central in the East, and the Midwest and Pacific in the West (see Table 1.6).

More teams allow more games to be played. Only twice has the NBA originally scheduled fewer games than the previous season (the NBA Lockout for the 1998-99 season reduced the number of games played to 50). Sixty games were played in the original BAA season, but only 48 in the 1947-48 season before a return to 60 for the 1948-49 season. In the 1951-52 season only 66 games were scheduled, fewer than scheduled in the 1950-51 season. All teams in 1950-51, however, did not play the same number of games. For example, the Boston Celtics played 69 games, but several teams only played 66. This happened when the Washington Capitols disbanded on January 9, 1951, with a 10-25 record, and their players were assigned to other teams. The folding of the Washington franchise was indicative of the league's early instability. Since the 66-game 1951-52 season, the league schedule has steadily grown and every season since 1967-68 the NBA has scheduled an 82-game campaign (see Table 1.7).

More teams allow an expansion of the playoffs, when the NBA has the opportunity to showcase its top teams and players. The playoff expansion is two-fold as more teams have been added to the competition and the length of a playoff series has been expanded. The initial season had six teams qualify for the playoffs, with the winners of the Eastern and Western Divisions meeting in a best of seven series and the winner advancing to the Finals. The second and third place teams respectively from each division would play in a best-of three series. The winners would then meet in another two-out-of-three playoff for the right to advance to the Finals. The Philadelphia Warriors, led by the league's leading scorer Joe Fulks (23.2 avg.), won the first championship by defeating the Chicago Stags four games to one (see Figure 1.1).

As the league was in an early transition period, so too were its playoffs due to the varying number of teams. Different playoff formats were tested, such as in the 1949-50 season when the NBA had three divisions and the winners of the divisional playoff would leave

Table 1.6. The 2000-01 NBA Season.

Eastern		Western	
Atlantic	*Central*	*Midwest*	*Pacific*
Boston Celtics	Atlanta Hawks	Dallas Mavericks	Golden State Warriors
Miami Heat	Charlotte Hornets	Denver Nuggets	Los Angeles Clippers
New Jersey Nets	Chicago Bulls	Houston Rockets	Los Angeles Lakers
New York Knicks	Cleveland Cavaliers	Minnesota Timberwolves	Phoenix Suns
Orlando Magic	Detroit Pistons	San Antonio Spurs	Portland Trail Blazers
Philadelphia 76ers	Indiana Pacers	Utah Jazz	Sacramento Kings
Washington Wizards	Milwaukee Bucks	Vancouver Grizzlies	Seattle SuperSonics
	Toronto Raptors		

(Source: NBA)

Table 1.7. NBA Games Growth.

Year	# of NBA Games
1946	60
1947	48
1948	60
1949	64
1959	68
1951	66
1952	70
1953	72
1959	75
1960	77
1961	80
1966	81
1967	82

(Source: NBA)

(Source: NBA)

Figure 1.1. 1947 playoffs

three teams remaining. The team with the best regular season record did not have to play a semi-final playoff round and received a bye into the Finals. The 1953-54 season utilized a complicated round robin playoff format. Once the league reached stability in the 1954-55 season, so too did its playoff format. This stability marks a period of continuous growth in the playoff structure in terms of the number of games needed to decide a playoff series and the number of teams that qualify for the postseason.

The years beginning with the 1954-55 season had six of the eight teams qualify for the playoffs, with the second and third place team from each division facing off in a best-of-three series, and the winner facing the regular season champion in a best-of-five series before advancing to the best of seven NBA Finals. In 1957-58 the divisional finals became a best-of-seven series and in 1960-61 the preliminary playoff series expanded to a best-of-five. In 1966-67 a fourth playoff team from each division was added to the playoff format, and in 1967-68 the preliminary playoff series expanded to a best-of-seven. A fifth playoff team from each conference was added in 1974-75 with the fourth and fifth seed from each conference meeting in a best-of-three series before the best-of-seven conference semi-finals.

Two years later in the 1976-77 season, after the ABA merged with the NBA, a sixth team from each conference was added to the playoffs. The division winners would then receive a bye in the preliminary playoff round, with conference finishers three through six meeting in a best-of-three series. This format remained unchanged until the 1983-84 season when the NBA expanded to a playoff structure of eight teams from each conference with all rounds except the best-of-five preliminary round being a best-of-seven series (see Figure 1.2).

What is significant in this continuous growth is that at the very least an argument can be made that there was an increased demand for the product of NBA basketball into different markets. The increase in the number of teams means an increase in the number of players, but also an increase in the number of markets for advertising. Having more teams also leads to a greater number of games so that all teams compete against one another. The NBA scheduling format allows every team to play each opponent, even those in the other conference, at least twice. This ensures that each NBA superstar will visit every NBA city at least once. Michael Jordan and the Bulls played each team from the Western Conference away at least once so that cities such as Vancouver and Seattle got the opportunity to see him play. Overall, the growth of the number of teams, the number of games, and the length of the playoff schedule represents an increase in the inventory of the NBA product that is available for public consumption.

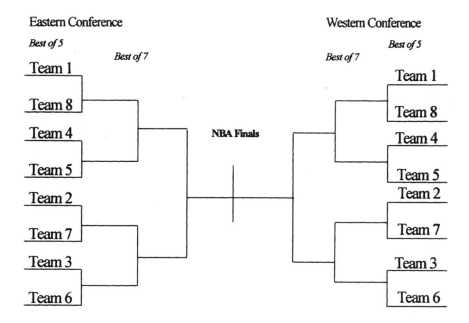

Figure 1.2. The NBA playoff structure, 1984-present

The essential issue is what role did the television industry play in helping to present this inventory and enable growth to occur? The question is legitimate because it was not long ago that the league did not enjoy the economic and popular status to which it currently has risen. One of the major problems for the NBA in the late 1970s and early 1980s that is indicative of its substandard status in the entire schema of important issues and events, sports or otherwise, was its lack of exposure and the nature of its coverage on television. The number one vehicle of exposure for a professional sports league is its placement and coverage on network television. The game of basketball at its core remains unchanged, even at the highest level of the NBA. There are still 10 players and the rim remains 10-feet high. Subtle changes like the shot-clock, the three-point basket, and others have been implemented by the NBA to improve the game, but the television coverage, marketing, and framing of the NBA have drastically changed during this period of growth and have a far greater impact than any rule changes.

Despite the advantageous characteristics of the relationship between a professional sports league and a sports broadcasting network, the NBA and television organizations were not able to capitalize on the exposure benefits and the initial relationship was not a tremendous success for either entity. One glaring example of the NBA's lack of exposure and prominence is that at probably the greatest individual performance in a NBA game—Wilt Chamberlain scoring 100 points on March 2, 1962—there was not one single television camera present. The only visual record of that accomplishment are still photographs. Early television contracts with the Dumont Network for 1952 and 1953 had each team receiving approximately $130,000 for broadcasting rights, accounting for 8% of total basketball revenues. The early Dumont contracts and the contract with NBC from 1954 to 1962 produced only minimal revenues for the league, and overall promotion and sponsorship continued to be a problem; in 1962 NBC dropped its coverage of regular season games.

In light of its inability to market the league and its product, in 1963 the NBA hired Walter Kennedy, who previously had worked in the publicity field for the Harlem Globetrotters, as its second commissioner. At the time of Kennedy's hiring there was heated competition between ABC's *Wide World of Sports* and *CBS Sports Spectacular* for Saturday and Sunday viewers. It was Roone Arledge at ABC who suggested putting live sports against the taped events that CBS was using. In 1964, Kennedy was able to sell the rights to a package of regular season Sunday afternoon games for $650,000 to ABC. Ratings for NBA basketball on ABC were higher than *CBS Sports Spectacular* and, although ratings climbed from 20.2% in 1965 to 27.1% in 1968, they did not meet the expectations of advertising agencies (Rader, 1984). Rader claims that "the NBA owners blamed ABC, arguing that the network did not adequately promote the games" (p. 125).

In 1973 CBS won the broadcast rights to the NBA, and in 1974 CBS paid each franchise $535,000 annually. ABC's Arledge was upset that the NBA had violated what he believed to be a gentlemen's agreement between ABC and the league whereby ABC was permitted to match any offer from another network for the NBA broadcasting rights (Rader, 1984). ABC countered CBS by adding *Wide World of Sports* to its Sunday schedule. Soon, the Sunday *Wide World of Sports* program was defeating the NBA in the ratings. The broadcasting of the NBA for CBS produced a 26% share of the Sunday afternoon audience for the 1976-77 season (compared to the 43% that CBS had received that same year for its coverage of the NFL). By the 1980-81 season, the share had fallen to 18% (Rader, 1984).

The NBA was suffering from a poor perception of the game itself. The perceptions of the NBA included being a league that was drug-infested, featured too many African-American players, was boring until the last two minutes of the game, and only featured one-on-one play. This poor perception and its status in comparison to other available sports programming to which CBS had broadcast rights dictated the poor exposure the NBA was receiving. CBS was the preeminent sports network during the late 1970s and early 1980s and the NBA was in competition with the network's other sports programming such as the NFL, the Professional Golf Association Tour (including the Masters), the Daytona 500, U.S. Open tennis, as well as college sports. Ed Desser, President of NBA Television, says that the NBA "literally was shoe-horned in between other things and it wasn't the center piece, it wasn't a focal point and they didn't put the resources into it. When it came time to decide things like who would get the slot after the Daytona 500 show, there was a college sports faction and a professional sports faction and for quite a long time the college sports guys got that slot" (E. Desser, personal communication, August 26, 1998).

One of the major events in the growth of the NBA was the awarding of its network broadcast rights to NBC on November 9, 1989, after being with CBS since the 1973-74 season. NBC signed a 4-year contract for the broadcast rights beginning with the 1990-91 season, agreeing to pay the NBA $600 million. CBS had an exclusive negotiation period with the NBA that was a condition of its contract with the NBA, but on October 31, 1989, that period had ended. The NBA made a final proposal to CBS and also the same proposal to ABC and NBC. While CBS and ABC rejected the proposal, NBC agreed. At the time of the contract President of NBC Sports Dick Ebersol stated, "we were shocked we even got this opportunity." Ebersol also claimed that "what's even more amazing is that the figure is one that our people in sales say will allow us to make a profit or break even. NBC is the number one network. We were not looking to sports to promote a dying prime-time lineup. This deal makes good business sense to us" (cited in Stewart, 1989, p. C11). Ebersol estimated that CBS had been earning an annual profit of $40 to $50 million in broadcasting the NBA. NBC renewed its contract with the NBA for the 1994-95 season with another 4-year deal, this time increasing the rights package to $750 million. The total rights fees paid to the NBA including revenue sharing of advertising came to $900 million (McClellan, 1997).

In addition to the network money, the broadcast rights for the NBA were increasing substantially through cable television contracts. For the 1981-82 season the NBA received less than $23 million for both its network and cable television contracts. In 1984 Turner Networks became the exclusive cable partner for the NBA, replacing ESPN and the USA Network. Turner paid $20 million for a two-year contract beginning with the 1984-85 season. This was a considerable increase from the NBA's first venture into the cable television industry—the USA Network which paid the league only $400,000 in 1979. The Turner contracts grew to $75 million in 1986. For the 1990-91 season, in addition to the switch to NBC, the NBA benefitted from an increase from Turner to $275 million for a 4-year contract. The two contracts represented a 241% increase in television revenues from the previous broadcast contracts.

On November 12, 1997, the NBA once again substantially increased its broadcast rights packages to a total of $2.64 billion; both NBC and Turner had doubled their payments to $1.75 billion (up from $750 million) from NBC and $890 million (up from $350 million) from Turner for another 4-year contract starting with the 1998-99 season. Commenting on the NBA and NBC and Turner television agreements, Steve Grubbs, media buyer at BBDO advertising agency, states, "the track record with the NBA and David Stern is that they are very loyal to their broadcast partners." Grubbs also claims, "if the NBA had gone to Fox or ESPN, it probably could have made more money. But it is looking to create a solid relationship by keeping its partners happy" (Associated Press, 1997). NBC sources claimed that the network had earned approximately $200 million under the previous NBA contract, including half a $300 million pot the network split with the league in the revenue sharing agreement after NBC reached a certain sales threshold (McClellan, 1997).

NBC will now attempt to pass this increase in rights fees to advertisers. Ebersol points out that "a 30-second spot in the Finals now costs just under $400,000, up from $200,000 when NBC first picked up the NBA" (cited in McClellan, 1997, p. 14). Ebersol believes that a 10% increase for NBA Finals and regular season games, which were approximately $100,000, is very reasonable (McClellan, 1997; Stroud, 1998). NBC also receives broadcast rights to more games to help defray the increase, including more prime-time and playoff games. Ebersol points out that NBC had already sold "considerably more than half" of the next four years of advertising inventory (cited in Stroud, 1998, p. 50). The increases in advertising are inevitable because the NBA is, without question, the best second-quarter sports vehicle on television for reaching younger males with spending power (McClellan, 1997).

Much of the growth of the NBA can be traced back to audience behavior, therefore a key question may be, what are the needs or motivations of the sports audience? And, are these needs different for audiences who view other types of programming? Wenner (1989) developed a transactional model to assist in explaining the sports, media, and audience relationship. He states "four systems—society, the production complex, mediated sport content, and the audience experience with that content—transact with each other over time. The suprasystem—or containing frame—is the society that brings about a subsystem of sports media production organizations" (p. 25). The transactional model examines the relationship with a primary focus on audience experience. Wenner explains, in the transactional view, "the audience's perceptions are as much 'cultural indicators' as the content material to which they respond. Although its point of departure is audience experience, a transactional approach to mediated sport also entails assessments of content in conjunction with the forces that have led to the production of that content" (p. 27). Therefore, in Wenner's view, the audience is active, but its experience is taking place within a cultural context.

Differing from the transactional model of Wenner, the approach of this book examines the broadcast strategies of the content producers, both the NBA and television networks, as the primary focus. These strategies are thought of in relation to the needs of the audience. Because of all the characteristics offered through sports programming that are attractive to a network, the sports league draws power in this interdependent relationship in that they have a product—broadcast rights—that the networks will compete against one another for. Sports leagues can now ask for and receive large fees for the rights to broadcast their games. It should also be noted that most broadcast rights are only for a relatively short term of perhaps three or four years. If the NBA is dissatisfied with the current network, once the contract expires the league can offer its games to another network.

AUDIENCE MOTIVATIONS TOWARD SPORTS TELEVISION

The greatest difference between a sports television audience and audiences of other programming genres might be the attitude and motivation toward sports programming in terms of both what fans receive from watching sports events and the purposeful behavior toward this activity. Sloan (1989) believes the term *fan*, short for fanatic, is more descriptive for people who watch sports, rather than spectator or viewer, stating "if people who do watch sporting events do so to satisfy a particular desire, then it is likely that only a few are merely spectators in its strict sense (i.e., watchers, observers)" (pp.

176-177). In watching sports, Gantz (1981) claims that "viewers also appear to be far more vocal and interactive with others while watching" (pp. 273-274).

In studying sports television audiences, Gantz (1981) claims that the underlying dimensions of television sports viewing are generalizable across sports rather than unique to each sport. He identifies four dimensions in order of their perceived importance: (a) to thrill in victory, suggesting that people watch sports to root for participants, and vicariously participate and experience the emotional satisfactions associated with winning; (b) to let loose, indicating a sense of rowdiness and letting off steam or pent-up emotions; (c) to learn, involving the acquisition of information about the players and the game itself; and (d) to pass time, suggesting a last resort when no other activity seems worthy of pursuing. In relation to the hierarchy as described by Gantz, the primary objective of the broadcast in engaging the audience should be the development of a rooting interest on the part of the viewer. The broadcast might obviously try to tap into all four of these dimensions to ensure the behavior of viewing without any true preference as to which viewing dimension the audience member might emphasize.

Tutko (1989) would agree with the audience motivations as described by Gantz, particularly the two most important motivations: to thrill in victory and the emotion involved in watching sports. He claims that

> there can be little doubt that the athletic area has become a center for taking care of our emotional needs. We participate in and are spectators of the emotional charge. If athletics did not provide excitement it would be gone in a short period. We look forward to indulging in the joys of victory but all too often steep in the agony of defeat. Without the occasional emotional charge, life would be a little bit duller—a little bit less alive and perhaps even have less meaning. (p. 113)

He describes the emotion and character associated with sports stemming from two sources: (a) personal encounters with athletics and (b) the observation of contests where we have been able to witness exceptional performances. Tutko (1989) explains that

> when we see an athletic contest, we are able to see in the performer certain characteristics that are a reminder of trials, tribulations, and pressures that we have. Because of our experience we are able to empathize with this position. The athlete (or team)

and ourselves become one. To see a performance where the athlete does well is tied to the good feeling inside of us—that feeling
of trying and doing well. (p. 115)

Tutko is describing two key personal reactions in the idea of
encounters with athletes. The first is that of the similarity of sports
to our everyday life. The competition, the decision making, and the
pressures to achieve are real for every working individual. In most
occupations, however, there is not a scoreboard. The second
encounter is the personal connection and the feelings of togetherness
and community through rooting that fans forge with players and
with other fans. Tutko (1989) emphasizes the entertainment and
sociability aspect of watching sports. He describes "a bunch of people
crowded together in a common cause where they can laugh, cry, kib-
itz, exchange, and get the emotional high during the tense moments
of the game or the 'on the edge of your seat' tension and we can see
how athletics provide a unique charge" (p. 122). Zillmann, Bryant,
and Sapolsky (1989) agree with the recreational and communal value
of sports spectatorship, claiming that "if spectators indeed share (to
some degree) the apprehension, the anguish, the joy, the pride, or the
humiliation of the teams they affiliate with, the experience should
bond together those who confess to the same affiliation" (p. 251).
    Zillmann et al. (1989) see a similarity to the emotion of the
spectators and the actual players, claiming

> sportsfanship is principally not different from actual participa-
> tion. Differences of degree may well exist, however. It is conceiv-
> able that winning or being defeated in sport contests produces
> degrees of cohesion for the players that the spectators' feelings of
> solidarity cannot match. But it appears that sportsfanship can
> unite and provide feelings of belongingness that are beneficial to
> individuals and to the social setting in which they live. (p. 251)

The point of Zillmann et al. is amplified in that teams in every sport
are constantly striving during the regular season to win the home
court or home field advantage during the playoffs. For example, in
the NBA Finals the home team has won 61% of the games between
the years 1977 and 2000. The emotion of the crowd is thought to
motivate the players and influence the outcome of the game in favor
of the home team.
    It is not only the emotional characteristics but the actual
physical activities of sports that people can relate to. In addition to

the similarity of pressures and the sense of community connection, Zillmann et al. (1989) introduce a third characteristic of sports: fans can relate because they are watching people participate in sports that they have often played. Their appreciation of the skill they are watching is enhanced because they know its difficulty. The "weekend golfer" is amazed at the skill of professional golfer, so he or she can relate and have more of an interest in watching them perform. The appreciation of skill is not only sports related; a person who plays a musical instrument as a hobby also appreciates the talent of a professional because of his or her knowledge of the difficulty of the task. Zillmann et al. (1989) explain that

> popular sports feature highly developed but nonetheless basic motor skills: speed, agility, balance, accuracy, strength, and endurance. The most popular sports (e.g., baseball, football, basketball, soccer, and tennis) are, in fact, built around skills that nearly everybody masters: carrying, throwing, kicking, catching, or hitting a ball. In general, then, sports spectatorship appears to pay homage to commonly practiced skills. (p. 249)

For team sports, the outcome, however, still remains the objective rather than the appreciation of skill. This is the difference, and it is significant, between appreciation and viewing of sports and other forms of entertainment. If examined with the findings of Gantz, which claimed that thrill in victory is the number one motivation for sports viewing, Zillmann et al. (1989) describe a disposition theory of sportsfanship. Their disposition theory claims that enjoyment of watching sports contests and athletic excellence,

> depends to some extent at least, on the particular person displaying such excellence, and on the particular team to which this person belongs. People applaud great play on the part of their favorite athletes and teams. The same excellence, the same mastery of skills, seems to be far less appreciated, possibly even deplored, when it is exhibited by disliked athletes or resented teams. (p. 256)

Fans in New York appreciate and cheer the skills of Latrell Sprewell but deplore the similar ability of Philadelphia 76ers guard Allen Iverson.

All these various motivations toward participation in sports and what the viewer actually receives from watching these events lead to the very intentional behavior of media use on the part of the audience. *Intentionality* is described as the extent to which viewing is purposive and planned (e.g., Rubin & Perse, 1987). In addition to describing audience motivations in terms of what the audience can receive from watching sports, Gantz (1981) characterizes viewing as purposeful behavior on the part of the audience member, claiming "viewing rarely is the default option selected when there is nothing else to do; it appears to meet a variety of needs rather than simply relieve boredom" (p. 273). He states that "there appears to be a certain amount of pre-program preparations for sportscasts not documented for other entertainment programming" (p. 273).

In speaking of media use as purposeful behavior, Rubin (1983, 1984) identifies two media-use orientations toward a medium and its content that are based on motives, attitudes, and behaviors. The ritualized and instrumental uses of media as identified by Rubin are not static or discrete characteristics of individual users. Ritualized media use focuses on a particular medium, rather than on content. It is a less intentional and nonselective orientation with a tendency to use the medium regardless of the content. In this situation people are turning on the television and randomly going through different channels during their leisure time attempting to find a program worthy of taking the time to view, as "watching" is the ritual activity. Instrumental media use focuses on purposive exposure to specific content and is more intentional and selective on the part of the individual audience member (e.g., Rubin & Perse, 1987). In this situation people are constructing their day so they have the availability to attend to a certain program. Media organizations attempt to tap into both orientations by aligning certain programs with the leisure time of their desired audience and desired advertisers.

NBA personnel would like to believe they produce a product whose audience participates in instrumental viewing. The audience members are behaving with a purpose and have altered their schedules. They are watching television to specifically view a NBA game. However, also understanding that television viewing can be based on leisure or disposable time, the NBA and the television network might create a consistent game programming schedule that capitalizes on the ritualized nature of television viewing, giving the networks an opportunity for one or both media-use orientations to be exercised by the audience. Gantz's (1981) argument that audience behavior toward television sports is more instrumental than ritualistic is that of the perspective of a fan—people are watching because they know a game is on and watching sports is a purposeful behavior. For example, a Knicks fan purposely watching a Knicks game is a more plausible scenario than a person clicking through channels and deciding at random to watch the game. Through this example, the specific content does matter. Still, the network would be foolish not to schedule a sports event during the leisure time of most viewers to capitalize on the ritualized orientation. This is the rationale behind games being played on weekends, and important games being played in prime-time, to create a combined instrumental and ritualistic orientation and influence the audience behavior of watching sports.

2

THE NBA STRATEGY: A COMMUNICATION APPROACH

A model of integration offers the best explanation into the communication strategy of the NBA. Producers, directors, and announcers must operate under an assumption that they have the power to influence an audience through their broadcast strategies. The overall communication philosophy of this book is that the media have the potential to influence the audience. The use of the term *potential* acknowledges the power of the mass media through their ability to select and frame messages. The term potential also allows for an active audience through their ability to select and interpret messages and translate meanings that guide their behavior. In describing a model of integration, the entire context of the message (producer, content, and medium) and audience (selection, interpretation, and behavior) must be considered in the evaluation of the mass communication process.

AGENDA-SETTING

The agenda-setting function of the mass media assists the integration model in questioning the shaping of public perception of a sports league based on media exposure and the selection of broadcasting

NBA games as opposed to any other type of programming. In addition to exposure characteristics, the agenda-setting function assists in studying the portrayal of coverage by a network and the potential effects of both of these framing methods. The original agenda-setting hypothesis proposed by McCombs and Shaw (1972) tested whether media coverage influences the public's perception regarding the importance of issues. This transfer of issue salience from the media agenda to the public agenda was based on exposure alone and is referred to as Level One of agenda-setting research.

Extending from the original idea of media exposure's singular influence on the public regarding which issues to think about, agenda-setting researchers claim that the media may be successful in indicating to people how to think about an issue. The idea of media coverage not only being able to indicate what the public thinks about, but also how the public thinks about an issue is referred to as Level Two of agenda-setting research. McCombs and Shaw (1993) have reconsidered their original agenda-setting hypothesis and extended the agenda-setting function, describing it as a process that can affect both what to think about and how think about it.

The standard of Level One agenda-setting effects is merely media exposure of the issue to the audience. By simply seeing, hearing, or reading about an issue, regardless of how the content is presented, this media coverage will cause the audience member to at least devote some thought to the exposed issue and ergo the transferring of an issue from the media agenda to the public agenda will occur. Exposure offers the opportunity for an issue to move from the media agenda to the public agenda as the media selection of certain issues heightens the importance of those exposed issues at the expense of other issues that the audience does not receive (e.g., Hunt & Ruben, 1993; Lasorsa, 1997; Wanta & Wu, 1992; Wright, 1986). A key characteristic in the selection process is that the amount of issues that receive coverage is limited by media constraints of time and space (e.g., Lippmann, 1922; Miller, 1956; Shaw & Martin, 1992; Shaw & McCombs, 1977). Protess and McCombs (1991) claim that "placing an issue or topic on the public agenda so that it becomes the focus of public attention, thought, and discussion is the first stage in the formation of public opinion" (p. 2).

Although transfer of issue salience from the media agenda to the public agenda based on the amount of exposure alone was the original claim to come out of agenda-setting studies, agenda-setting researchers have also focused on how an issue gets covered and how the framing of an issue by a mass media organization can affect the public agenda (e.g., Ghanem, 1997; Schoenbach & Semetko, 1992; Semetko & Mandelli, 1997). In addition to exposure alone, media organizations must take advantage of a second opportunity to influence the audience by framing its content to attract an audience and advertisers in transferring an issue from the media agenda to the public agenda. Similar to the selection process in which only certain issues will receive exposure, the framing process also does not permit every issue to be covered with the same standard.

Entman (1993) explains "to frame is to select some aspects of a perceived reality and make them more salient in a communicating text, in such a way as to promote a particular problem definition, causal interpretation, moral evaluation, and/or treatment recommendation for the item described" (p. 52). Although the framing of an issue is recognized in agenda-setting research as a potential influencing factor about how the public thinks about an issue, Ghanem (1997) still emphasizes exposure contending that "the frequency with which a topic is mentioned probably has a more powerful influence than any particular framing mechanism, but framing mechanisms could serve as catalysts to frequency in terms of agenda-setting" (p. 12). It is imperative to recognize that the potential media influence on an audience through portrayal framing methods is an extension and not a replacement for the original agenda-setting idea of exposure alone. Agenda-setting researchers now simply recognize that exposure of an issue and the way an issue is framed can both have an effect on the audience.

Following the agenda-setting model of Level One and Level Two, framing methods can be separated into two distinct types: exposure and portrayal. Exposure framing methods do not only include selection in terms of which stories get aired or printed or even have the opportunity of reaching the public. Exposure becomes a method of framing the issue through characteristics such as frequency, placement, and the amount of time and/or space devoted to an issue within the entire scope of the mass media organization's production. Portrayal framing methods are how the organization's production staff presents the content about a topic to the audience.

The exposure characteristics of selection, frequency, placement, and the amount of time and/or space devoted to a topic are determined by the mass media organization decision makers and can be easily recognized and consistently identified by independent observers. The objective of exposure framing methods is to present the issue in the most convenient and accessible manner to attract and engage the largest audience and reach the program's desired target audience in attempting to earn greater advertising revenues. In understanding the audience is selective, broadcast media outlets offer their programming at a time when exposure is possible, particularly for their target audience. Whether in the print media, where the frequency is in terms of topic selection and its daily or weekly coverage, column inches, and placement of an article; or on television in terms of topic selection and its daily reporting, amount of time, and placement of a story, these ideas that are based on issue exposure to the audience alone are present in every form of mass media.

Although the results of their study indicate a very strong relationship between the emphasis placed on various political campaign issues by the media and by the public, McCombs and Shaw (1972) are quick to point out their findings are not discussed in terms of media causality. Critical in their analysis, McCombs and Shaw (1972) claim the agenda-setting function is "not *proved*" (p. 184, emphasis in original) by their correlation data, but the data presents evidence that agenda-setting does occur. Even in this seminal agenda-setting study there is a maneuverability and allowance for the audience to be factored into the media effects process. McCombs (1976) clarifies any misconceptions regarding direct agenda-setting effects stating, "no one contends that agenda-setting is an influence process operating at all times and all places in all people" (p. 2). McCombs and Weaver (1985) claim that although the original agenda-setting study of McCombs and Shaw (1972) was "a reassertion of powerful media effects, it was not an assertion of universal, undifferentiated effects" (p. 95).

In agenda-setting research, an acknowledgment should be made as to the thought process of the audience. Agenda-setting theorists would point to the idea of the media being successful in telling the public what to think about and how to think about an issue; however, intrinsic in this definition is that there is a thought process by the public receiving the media. The public, ultimately, determines what they will think about the topic. More importantly, the ultimate objective for the NBA and television partnership is beyond the public thinking about the NBA, to their behavior of tuning into the television broadcasts, attending league games, purchasing NBA merchandise, and purchasing products of companies who support the NBA. Sutherland and Galloway (1981) imply a two-step agenda-setting process in which a transfer of salience eventually leads to a behavioral outcome.

In addition to the audience characteristics, the type of issue can be a factor in the agenda-setting process producing an effect. Palmgreen and Clarke (1977) found that the media play very different agenda-setting roles depending on whether the issues are of local or national political origin, with the impact of the media being weaker on local level issues in which the public has firsthand experience with the situation and do not rely solely on the media for information. Consistent with Palmgreen and Clarke, Zucker (1978) claims that agenda-setting effects are stronger for unobtrusive issues, when the public has no direct experience with that issue, because the audience has to rely on the media for information about these issues. Obtrusive issues when the public can personally experience an issue are less susceptible to agenda-setting effects.

In traditional media effects studies, the content is often the independent variable acting as the influencing force on the audience. However, mass media content can also be construed as a dependent variable that is being influenced by a multitude of factors or constituency groups. Agenda-setting should also focus on how agendas are built as the media might not be thought of as the sole agenda-setter (e.g., Carragee, Rosenblatt, & Michaud, 1987; Danielian & Reese, 1989; Roberts, 1997; Rogers, Dearing, & Bregman, 1993; Takeshita, 1997). Issues are constantly placed on the media agenda. Learning which issues, the reasons why, and how these certain issues are transformed to the public agenda is the essence of agenda-setting research. The media may be granted too much power in the media effects agenda-setting process. For example, advertising in all media also has the ability to set the agenda. McAllister (1998) would agree with the ideas of corporate power as expressed by Schiller (1989), and states that, "sponsors have an agenda-setting power, as they may chose which cultural and social programs exist, and which do not, through their selective funding" (p. 359). In addressing the agenda-building question, Roberts (1997) summarizes, "it is highly doubtful given the growing complexities of contemporary political communication environments that any single medium or entity can solely serve as the agenda-setter. Instead, the individual influence of any particular entity must participate as an agenda builder" (p. 95).

Other groups that need to be considered in the agenda-building process are organizations or individuals who act as an impetus in promoting their own agenda. In a political situation as originally studied by McCombs and Shaw (1972), politicians are constantly promoting the agenda of their candidacy and their ideas by holding press conferences or events to obtain the media's attention. The political understanding of how to utilize the media to gain exposure is the same as that used by the NBA. There is an agenda or a message that needs to reach the audience and the mass media, particularly television, is the best vehicle for this message transfer to occur.

The transferring of the NBA agenda began with initiatives developed by the NBA itself. As president of NBA Television, Ed Desser's primary responsibilities are dealing with how the NBA is positioned on television and the strategic planning and business development of the NBA's television product. Desser contends that the NBA is a factor in the agenda-setting process and the league is very much an originator of many agenda-setting initiatives. He explains that media attention

> doesn't just happen in a vacuum and our job is to be an advocate for the NBA and to push the NBA agenda and to try and get the media's attention so that they will talk about, pay attention to, and highlight the NBA. It's not just the media deciding on their own; oh well, let's focus on the NBA today. It didn't just happen. It's true that you could make all of the noise in the world that you want and that's not going to make them pay attention if they don't want to, if they don't think it's interesting. We always thought we had something interesting to tell people, but we weren't getting the message out and so we spent many years working towards getting the message out. (E. Desser, personal communication, August 26, 1998)

Once a contract is signed between the NBA and NBC (or any other network), the NBA has been placed on the media agenda and a partnership in which both entities need to assist the other for profit and promotion of their mutual agenda to the audience is established. The network now has a vested interest in the league through their rights fees investment and is no longer an objective organization in claiming the importance of the league. The broadcast partner is very subjective in attempting to set the public agenda by putting NBA programming in a favorable scheduling position and positively framing its coverage to increase the opportunity of generating high ratings and advertising revenues or risk losing millions of dollars on its investment.

USES AND GRATIFICATIONS

Another media theory that can assist in explaining the NBA-television relationship, but from a more audience-centered perspective, is the "uses and gratifications" literature inspired by Blumler and Katz (1974). In terms of how mass communication is thought about, uses and gratifications represents a movement away from direct and powerful media effects. The uses and gratifications approach examines what is it that people do with, and what gratifications they find in, mass-produced news and entertainment (e.g., Carey & Kreiling, 1974). Katz, Blumler, and Gurevitch (1974) claim that uses and gratifications "simply represents an attempt to explain something of the way in which individuals use communications, among other resources in the environment, to satisfy their needs, and to achieve their goals" (p. 21). The uses and gratifications approach contends that individual audience members use their own experience to select media and interpret the meaning of these messages to satisfy their own experience, needs, attitudes, values, and beliefs (e.g., Blumler, 1979; Blumler, Gurevitch, & Katz, 1985). This approach argues for an understanding of audiences as active in their involvement and thereby questions models of media influence that see the audience as loyally passive customers.

The notion of an active audience is the essential uses and gratifications characteristic and the distinguishing characteristic that necessitates its inclusion along with the agenda-setting model in helping to explain the relationship among the NBA, television networks, advertisers, and the audience. The active audience devalues media power as the uses and gratifications approach contends that the gratifications experienced by the audience are not dictated by the message content, the message producer, or the message conduit, but can be interpreted by individual audience members. Kline, Miller, and Morrison (1974) claim the "uses and gratifications model suggests that individual uses for media content act as an intervening variable: mitigating or enhancing the ultimate effects of a media message" (p. 113).

At its extreme, theorists of the uses and gratifications approach who claim that there is an active and selective audience would contend that any effect can be obtained by any message at any time. Budd, Entman, and Steinman (1990) claim that "whatever the message encoded, decoding comes to the rescue. Media domination is weak and ineffectual, since the people make their own meanings and pleasures" (p. 170). They continue "we don't need to worry about people watching several hours of TV a day, consuming its images, ads and values. People are already critical, active viewers and listeners, not cultural dopes manipulated by the media" (p. 170). Ang (1990), however, cautions that "audiences may be active, in myriad ways, in using and interpreting media . . . it would be utterly out of perspective to cheerfully equate 'active' with 'powerful'" (p. 247). The comment by Ang points out that audience members are never totally autonomous because they are limited not only by their own psychological and sociological situations or their predispositions to the content, but by the choices they are presented in the media. The idea of the mass media selecting and framing content confers power to the media that must be recognized.

Even though the audience is thought to be active, media use must coincide with individual availability. The unequivocal active audience does not explain media phenomena and gratifications that might be based on the content. Swanson (1987) argues that if message content is not considered in uses and gratifications approaches then we will not be able to explain why particular gratifications are sought in various types of content, or link gratifications sought to effects through attributes of the type of message. Content should, however, be positioned to operate in conjunction with the media use of the audience. Sports networks select their content by broadcasting certain games and events, and then carefully situate it in their program schedule to ensure their desired target audience the opportunity to be exposed. The understanding of the audience is thus essential to the producers of media messages so they can select and frame the content to meet these needs and achieve audience gratification through their production—perhaps not the total audience, but more importantly the target audience that the content is designed to reach and that can be delivered to advertisers.

In analyzing media use and content, Gantz and Zohoori (1982) claim that accommodation to television changes may be a function of two factors: type of time and activity involved, and television content and gratifications associated with it. The element of time could refer to exposure framing methods, whereas the presentation of the content alludes to portrayal framing methods. The element of time is separated into "non-disposable time for required activities such as work or sleep vs. disposable time for leisure activities such as watching TV" (p. 265).

Gantz and Zohoori (1982) summarize their position claiming:

> The likelihood of accommodation for television is maximized when it involves the rearrangement of leisure activities during disposable time for content sought out and uniquely associated with desired gratifications. The likelihood of accommodation for television is minimized when it involves the rearrangement of non-leisure activities during non-disposable time for content of little interest or value to the viewer or for which there are functional alternatives available. (p. 265)

The consideration of program content leading to gratifications provides a justification for a more integrated model of mass communication. Some early uses and gratifications research began integrating effects research by examining the potential for effects not caused or controlled by the audience itself. McLeod and Becker (1974) write of an integration between direct and indirect media effects perspectives. They caution "if the receiver can get anything he or she wants out of any message, then the content of the media does not really matter" (p. 137). Their transactional model, however, calls for a reasonable synthesis in which "the exposure characteristics of the message *combine with* the orientations of the audience member in producing the effect" (p. 141, emphasis in original). The transactional model includes the essential uses and gratifications characteristics of being audience-centered, but also incorporates and examines the role of the message producer. More recently, Becker and Kosicki (1995) presented another position of integration, describing the relationship between audience members and media institutions as a transaction, stating that "audience members bring much to the communication situation, and what they bring alters what they take away" (p. 33). They claim through viewing media effects as a transaction that neither audience members nor message producers are fully dominant.

Integration is also a goal of McQuail and Gurevitch (1974). They introduced a structural/cultural perspective that includes the message or message producer. McQuail and Gurevitch (1974) describe the structural/cultural perspective as

> audience expectations and satisfactions derived from the media should be explained primarily in terms of: (1) the patterns of media materials that are made available and (2) the customs, norms, and conventions—defining what counts as appropriate ways of using and reacting to media provision—that prevail in particular social settings. (p. 291)

In the structural/cultural perspective media exposure by the audience is predictable and regular, similar to the ideas of ritualized viewing as described by Gantz and Zohoori (1982). Similar to the transactional model, exposure characteristics are critical: exposure characteristics not only of the message—for example, the programming schedule—but also the exposure characteristics of the audience and when they have the ability to attend to mass media messages.

Although simple exposure to television, or participating in a medium, might produce audience gratifications, NBA personnel are most hopeful that it is the program content of their games that produce the gratification sought and obtained by their target audience. Before the NBA and television could draw on the audience motivations and gratifications that exist through sports broadcasts, an agenda-setting function had to be performed. In bringing together agenda-setting and uses and gratifications models there are dual intentions regarding the message content, that of the message producers and that of the audience. These dual intentions can compete against each other, but the feeling here is that the message producers attempt to select and frame messages that will comply with the gratification expectations that audience members, particularly that of the target audience, bring to media content.

AN INTEGRATION OF AGENDA-SETTING AND USES AND GRATIFICATIONS: MEDIA DEPENDENCY

An attempt to integrate the theoretical perspectives of agenda-setting, with the implications of the mass media's ability to select and frame messages, and the uses and gratifications approaches, with the audience being able to interpret messages, is motivated mainly because these characteristics from each framework make a valid contribution to the relationship among the NBA, television networks, advertisers, and the audience. An integrated model utilizing characteristics from both perspectives provides a clearer understanding of the media producer, content, and audience relationship. Livingstone (1990) succinctly summarizes the problem and the necessity for a more integrated approach, stating:

> If we see the media or life events as all-powerful creators of meaning, we neglect the role of audiences; if we see people as all-powerful creators of meaning, we neglect the structure of that which people interpret. The important questions concern the interrelation between the two: how do people actively make sense of structured texts and events; how do texts guide and restrict interpretations. The creation of meaning through the interaction of texts and readers is a struggle, a site of negotiation between *two* semi-powerful sources. Each side has different powerful strategies, each has different points of weakness, and each has different interests. It is this process of negotiation which is central. And through analysis of this process, traditional conceptions of both texts and readers may require rethinking, for each has traditionally been theorized in ignorance of the other. (p. 23, emphasis in original)

In addition to the transactional model and the structural/cultural perspective, the media dependency theoretical framework provided by Ball-Rokeach and DeFleur (1976) integrates mass media effects research perspectives because it examines both the message producer and the message user. Ball-Rokeach and DeFleur define dependency as "a relationship in which the satisfaction of needs or the attainment of goals by one party is contingent upon the resources of another party" (p. 6). From a mass media perspective these resources include the capacity to: create and gather, process, and disseminate information (e.g., Ball-Rokeach, 1985). According to this definition, media dependency occurs on many levels from both an organizational and individual standpoint. Dependencies occur for an organization who has content to disseminate to an audience and needs the media as the vehicle to reach the consumers necessary for its industry to thrive. Individuals are dependent on mass media organizations and various types of product or service organizations, as well as other individuals, to provide the amenities for everyday life.

Regarding organizational media dependency, Ball-Rokeach and DeFleur (1986) recognize that organizations depend on the mass media for communication links. For a sports league there is dependence from the league on television networks for economic stability, promotion, and exposure of its product, games, and merchandise to its consumers. Media organizations are also dependent on content producers, people and organizations who actually make the news, entertainment, or sports events, creating a relationship of interdependence (e.g., Ball-Rokeach & DeFleur, 1986; Curran, Gurevitch, & Woollacott, 1982). The interdependent relationship and the need for content evaluation is developed with the idea that a certain type of content will bring a certain type of audience and a certain type of advertiser (e.g., Ball-Rokeach & DeFleur, 1986; Cantor & Cantor, 1986). Grant, Guthrie, and Ball-Rokeach (1991) summarize the relationship among broadcasters, merchandisers, and the public, stating:

> Commercial broadcasting in the United States has been built on dependency relationships between broadcasters and merchandisers. In this system television programs are produced to attract large audiences, with merchandisers buying access to those audiences so they can air advertisements designed to entice viewers into buying their products. Broadcasters depend on the proceeds from the advertising sales to produce their shows. Merchandisers depend on television to reach consumers. (p. 773)

One mass communication model that continuously emphasizes advertising as the connection between message producers and consumers is the $P <\!\!-\!\!> I <\!\!-\!\!> C$ model of Hunt and Ruben (1993). They take the reconciliation of direct and indirect effects a step further as the $P <\!\!-\!\!> I <\!\!-\!\!> C$ model accounts for consumer influence on the message producer. In this model the P represents *Information*

Producers, *I* represents *Information Products and Services*, and *C* represents *Consumers*. Hunt and Ruben describe producers as mass communication organizations that create and distribute information products and/or services. These products and services are distributed to an audience, where they compete for the attention of, acceptance, and use by audiences. Product manufacturers and service providers are dependent on the mass media to reach potential customers. The public is also dependent on the mass media to learn about and simply be exposed to the available products and services.

A key distinction between this model and other theories is that the *P* <—> *I* <—> *C* approach offers an interactive nature of mass communication in which influence can be exerted by the consumer as well as the producer. From a uses and gratifications approach, the consumer would be determined as active in selecting products and services to fulfill his or her needs. This interactive nature is key to understanding the approach of network television as consumer-driven ratings that dictate advertising revenues are an essential element of programming strategies and economic stability. In explaining media effects, Hunt and Ruben (1993) conclude "the effects that occur between mass communication producers and consumers are *mutually causal*, or *mutually controlling*" and are "the result of particular *patterns of consumption in relation to product characteristics and availability*" (p. 84, emphasis in original).

The interdependence between a sports league and a television network and the link to the public through advertisers can now be examined in terms of the second level of dependence: individual dependence on the mass media. Ball-Rokeach, Rokeach, and Grube (1984) attempt to explain individual media dependency and how these dependencies can relate to potential media effects by offering five conditions that can lead to media effects. They claim: (a) the greater the media dependency, (b) the greater the level of attention during exposure, (c) the greater the level of affect toward the message and its senders, (d) the greater the likelihood of postexposure communication about the message, and thus (e) the greater the probability of message effects intended or unintended. Ball-Rokeach and DeFleur (1986) identify three needs for which audience members are dependent on the media system: (a) the need to satisfy information goals to understand one's social world, (b) the need to act meaningfully and effectively in the world, and (c) the need for play, exposure satisfaction, or escape from daily problems and tensions.

These media-dependent needs are magnified when the media are the only plausible option for an audience member to experience an event such as a NBA game. Dependency relies on the notion that the mass media, particularly television, for many topics and audience members, are the only vehicle available for an audience to experience or learn about events or people that they do not come into contact with through everyday experience, but which might impact their everyday lives. For sports events, the media provide firsthand exposure and information that cannot be attained through face-to-face interaction alone. Other than having a ticket to the game, the media represent the only option to personally experience the game or event, with television being the main option to satisfy the dependency through live visual experience. The structure of the league, with games being played simultaneously all over the continent, makes the NBA dependent on the mass media to provide the necessary information for a consumer to continue to be informed of league happenings and to invest his or her time and money into attending or viewing games on television.

Although the research of McCombs and Shaw (1972) focused on politicians and political issues, the question posed is, do the media perform an agenda-setting function regarding sports television similar to its function in news as claimed by McCombs and Shaw? McCombs and Shaw emphasize some important aspects of media power in that the public has few alternative means of learning about the political arena. In terms of agenda-setting and media dependency, one of the major similarities is that the media in both political and sports situations provide exposure and information that cannot be attained through face-to-face interaction alone. There is a personal (political candidate) or organizational (NBA) dependency on the mass media to provide exposure. There is also an individual dependency on the part of audience members to be exposed to these people and organizations for information or other social desires. Political candidates and NBA games appear before the people through the mass media rather than in person, with information coming from the mass media being the only contact most people have with those entities. In addition to the unobtrusive nature and the desire for attracting an audience and advertisers, another key similarity between news (political stories) and sports coverage (NBA games) is that events are selected and framed by the media (e.g., Jhally, 1989; Kosicki, 1993). The media, as the major primary source for information, construct the reality of either the candidate or the political issue, similar to their construction of the game, the league, its teams, and its players to the public.

Recognition of an organizational interdependence between the NBA and the media, particularly network television, and the incorporation of individual dependence on the media to connect to the NBA, creates two spheres of dependence with both the league and the public being dependent on the media. The media dependency approach does not examine the message producer or the audience as separate entities operating in a vacuum of the mass communication process, but rather the relationship of these components in the effects process. Ball-Rokeach and DeFleur (1986) state "the nature of the tripartite audience-media-society relationship most directly determines many of the effects the media have on people and society" (p. 85).

Mass media dependency provides a strong extension and integration of agenda-setting and uses and gratifications research. If the agenda of the public has been properly set and the subject is acknowledged via gatekeepers, the topic then becomes one with the potential for audience gratification to occur. The mass media then provide the source of gratification for the audience, thus demonstrating a media dependency for an individual. Overall, Ball-Rokeach et al. (1984) attempt to present a perspective that incorporates "a realistic balance between forces that set the conditions for powerful or direct effects and forces that set the conditions for weak or indirect effects" (p. 4). Their main idea is that mass media effects not be viewed as an absolute dichotomy. Such effects can be integrated, with crucial factors such as content selection, framing, and audience context all considered in the evaluation of the mass communication process. Ball-Rokeach (1985) adds, "the powerful audience of the uses and gratifications approach most likely coexists with the powerful media that uses and gratifications rejects" (p. 503).

MASS MEDIA INTEGRATION PERSPECTIVE

An integration of media dependency, agenda-setting, and uses and gratifications is essentially the reconciliation of the mass communication process involving messages from an all-powerful mass media organization to a passive audience and/or messages from media with the potential for only limited effects of their messages on, and creation by, an active audience. Media dependency assists in explaining why relationships between individuals and the media exist and relationships between social organizations and the media exist. Agenda-setting contributes by explaining the role of the media in selecting and framing stories, thus establishing the importance of certain issues and creating or further increasing individual dependency on the media. Agenda-setting speaks to influence over which issues the public think about and how they think about those issues. This cognitive thought process of an audience member relates more closely with the uses and gratifications characteristic of an active rather than a passive audience. The uses and gratifications approach can extend the agenda-setting function of the media by combining the idea of the media telling the audience member what to think about and how to think about it with the active audience member choosing media and interpreting the content to fulfill his or her needs.

The mass media may not have the power to directly control the audience, but the media do have the potential to influence. The audience may not be totally active and autonomous, but the audience can actively select, interpret the meanings of these media messages, and behave based on their needs. Even in the ability of the individual audience member to assign his or her own thoughts about an issue, it is imperative to recognize that the audience is always limited in its choices of topic and the amount of information presented on that topic based on the selection and framing of the media. In setting the public agenda and establishing the importance of an issue, the public then becomes dependent on the media for further needs to be satisfied. The audience members have the capability to indicate their media needs are satisfied through behavioral feedback to the media producer through watching, reading, or listening.

Communication scholars often comment on mass media power in terms of message effects. This debate continues and the model presented here hopes to contribute to this debate (see Becker & Kosicki, 1995, for a succinct overview of the mass media effects debate). The rationale for a complete integration of these mass media effects perspectives is that none of the theories can solely explain the NBA and television relationship. Characteristics from each of these perspectives are needed because they all make a contribution to the overall model, and without any of the characteristics the model is not complete (see Figure 2.1).

One fundamental question the management of the NBA must ask is: How can the league best operate its business? Inevitably, an integral part of that response includes an association with television. The integration model utilized to describe and explain the NBA-television relationship begins with acceptance of the general assumptions from each of the mass media effects perspectives: (a) the media can be successful in telling the audience which issues to think about (agenda-setting level one), (b) the media can be successful in telling the audience how to think about that issue (agenda-setting level two), (c) organizations are dependent on the mass media for communication links (organizational media dependency), (d) individuals are dependent on the mass media for information and social connection (individual media dependency), and (e) audiences actively select and interpret media to satisfy their own needs based on their own experience, attitude, and values (uses and gratifications). There are also the characteristics of the transactional model that focus on the idea

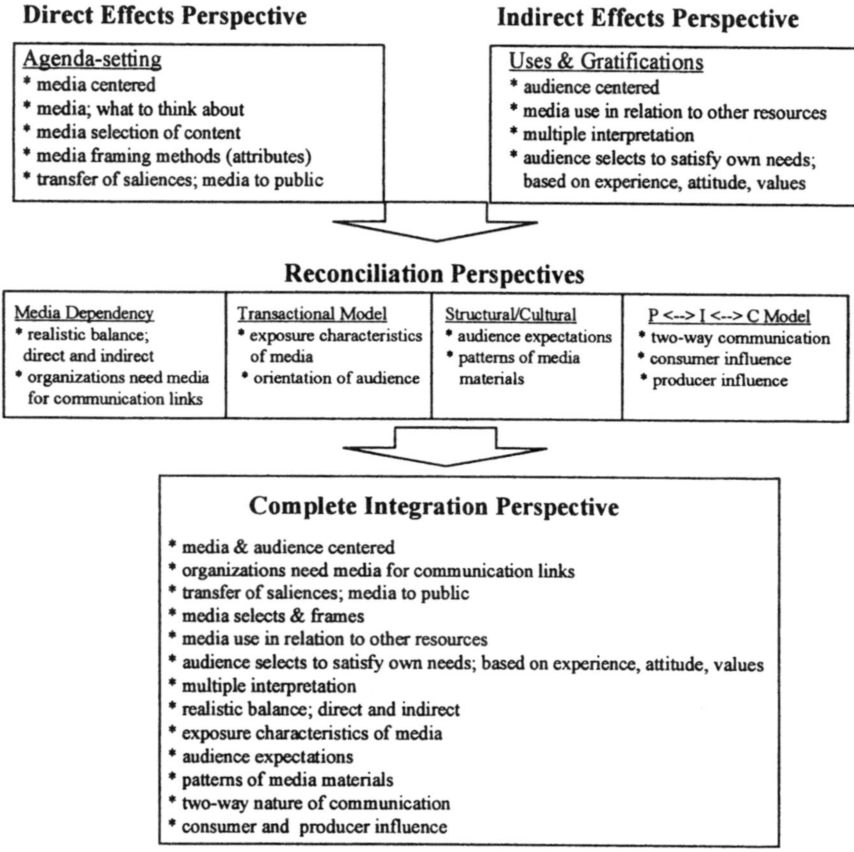

Direct Effects Perspective   **Indirect Effects Perspective**

Agenda-setting
* media centered
* media; what to think about
* media selection of content
* media framing methods (attributes)
* transfer of saliences; media to public

Uses & Gratifications
* audience centered
* media use in relation to other resources
* multiple interpretation
* audience selects to satisfy own needs;
  based on experience, attitude, values

Reconciliation Perspectives

Media Dependency	Transactional Model	Structural/Cultural	P <--> I <--> C Model
* realistic balance; direct and indirect	* exposure characteristics of media	* audience expectations	* two-way communication
* organizations need media for communication links	* orientation of audience	* patterns of media materials	* consumer influence
			* producer influence

Complete Integration Perspective

* media & audience centered
* organizations need media for communication links
* transfer of saliences; media to public
* media selects & frames
* media use in relation to other resources
* audience selects to satisfy own needs; based on experience, attitude, values
* multiple interpretation
* realistic balance; direct and indirect
* exposure characteristics of media
* audience expectations
* patterns of media materials
* two-way nature of communication
* consumer and producer influence

Figure 2.1. Mass media integration model

of exposure characteristics of the media (constituency groups), the idea of media patterns contributed from the structural/cultural model, and the idea of the consumer having the ability to influence the message producer and the critical role of advertising emphasized in the $P <\!\!-\!\!> I <\!\!-\!\!> C$ model. The integration model is needed for sports television because there are characteristics of this type of broadcasting genre that are unique in comparison to other types of programming.

The integration model applied to sports can be explained beginning with an organization that has a product that needs revenue and exposure to its potential customers. The mass media, particularly network television, satisfy both of these criteria. Through this dependency, in the broadcasting of NBA games, neither the league nor the television network are autonomous, and both organizations exist in relation to one another. The relationship between television and the NBA appears to be one of co-evolution from which emerges an organizational structure that itself becomes an entity.

The descriptive factors of this relationship are simple as a network enters into an agreement with the league in which they pay a certain fee for the broadcast rights to their games. In accordance with the league, the television network will now select which games and frame its coverage to attract the most viewers, generating higher ratings and higher advertising revenues, and eventually higher rights fees being paid to the NBA. The reasons for profit and promotion are easy to recognize in this relationship (see Figure 2.2).

The issue that remains is: What are the broadcast strategies that were implemented to help grow the NBA? The integration of characteristics from several theories and the description and explanation of the NBA and television relationship is investigated utilizing two primary approaches: First, key informant interviews that provide the perspective of the people involved in the NBA and television network relationship and help in the identification and explanation of the network selection and framing methods, as well as the analysis and interpretation of data trends. The rationale for interviewing NBA and television personnel and obtaining their perspective is explained by Ball-Rokeach (1985), who claims "that the average individual, as opposed to groups and organizations, does not come into direct contact with media information creators, gatherers, or processors" (p. 487). Second, unobtrusive measures, such as the playoff programming schedule, and audience behavior including television ratings, game attendance, merchandise purchases, and survey data demonstrating trends about television and NBA fans, will describe the changes of the NBA and its relationship with television networks and the audience.

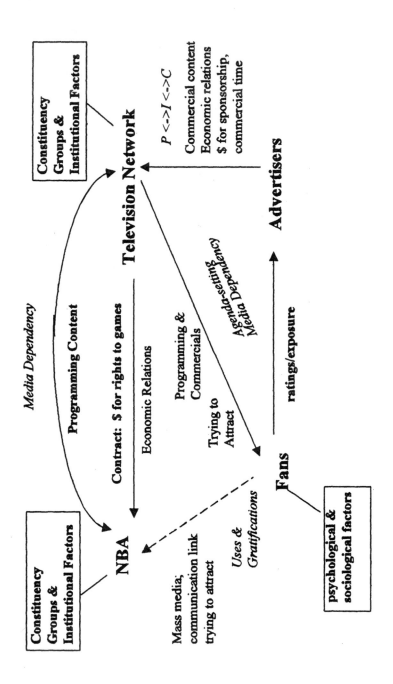

Figure 2.2. NBA-television relationship

Ratings data for these programs is a major unobtrusive measure that can demonstrate some trends as to the number of people who watch NBA games and NBA-related programming. Webster and Lichty (1991) define ratings as "estimated percentages of the population that see a program or listen to a station" (p. 3). The rating estimation is based on the number of television households watching the NBA in comparison with any other activity in which people might be involved. Ratings data provide the network with the number of people who watch the program and their demographic characteristics, such as geographic location, income, race, and gender.

Ratings data are vital because these numbers have such a tremendous impact on the economics of the network and the league. Webster and Lichty (1991) describe ratings as "a fact of life for virtually everyone connected with the electronic media. They are the tools used by advertisers and broadcasters to buy and sell audiences" (p. 3). Whether correctly or not, network personnel, NBA personnel, and advertisers treat ratings as the ultimate feedback measure. These ratings numbers are so accepted in the practical industry that they are often the basis for decision making by the partnership of both the league and television network. Ratings data are a revealing statistic, as much of the growth of the NBA hinges on more people watching the games on television. The amount of money paid to a league in rights fees is dictated by the potential rating level the network feels it can charge and the subsequent price for advertising it can achieve. The more viewers, the more the network can charge advertisers and the more the league can charge the network for rights fees. Increased revenue directed into the league and its franchise owners subsequently increases player and coach salaries.

Another unobtrusive data measure that demonstrates the growth of the league is the program schedules for the NBA playoffs. Indications as to when games are telecast on television today in comparison to previous years demonstrate exposure characteristics needed for the structural/cultural and transactional perspectives. The playoff programming schedule is used because this is the most crucial opportunity for the NBA to showcase its best players and teams, and establishes a change in the attention given to the NBA by the television networks. The playoff programming schedule indicates the value the network places on the NBA in relation to its entire stock of television programming inventory. The television programming schedule for the playoffs from the 1977 to 2000 season was gathered as this time frame incorporates the advent and proliferation of cable television, the shift of the NBA broadcast rights from CBS to NBC, and NBA expansion to 29 teams.

3

THE NBA EXPOSURE STRATEGY

Regarding the NBA, a network decides to purchase the rights for the NBA instead of using economic and personnel resources for other programming endeavors (selection). This forming of a partnership through the signing of a contract circumvents the notion of the television network solely determining where to place its newly acquired product. Even though the league is its broadcast property, the network and the league jointly determine how often games will be broadcast. A second level of selection occurs when the network televises the NBA instead of any other program to which it has broadcast rights, sport or any other genre type.

In sports television, the second level of agenda-setting framing involves the topic's portrayal to the audience. The portrayal framing is dictated through the creative process of the network producers, directors, and announcers. In addition to being broadcast live to an audience at the most convenient time, games and events are often telecast in the most compelling manner to viewers and enhanced by promotions, produced player features, produced teases, instant replays, announcer commentary, player and coach interviews, word graphics, and music.

The relationship between a professional sports league and a television network appears to be an ideal situation for both due to their interdependency on one another and the advertising and audience dependency on their combined entity. Despite the multiple dependencies, these relationships between professional sports leagues and television networks are not a guaranteed success for either. The signing of a broadcast contract puts the professional sports league on the media agenda, creating a partnership or mutual agenda. This partnership then has the challenge to move this agenda to the public. Protess and McCombs (1991) claim that "agenda-setting is about the transfer of saliences, the movement of issues from the media agenda to the public agenda" (p. 3). The NBA and television network partnership had not been a successful one and together they tried to grow the sport through television and other media-related strategies. The strategy very much followed a communication approach of agenda-setting as described through exposure (Level One) and portrayal (Level Two). The initial change of the NBA broadcast strategy focused on television exposure.

Tommy Roy is the co-Executive Producer for the NBA on NBC and is responsible for the content and the look—that is, where cameras are placed around the court, the format for graphics, and how the show comes back from commercial—of a NBA broadcast. He describes the partnership between NBC and the NBA as a cycle: If the NBA does well, more people watch the games, which provides higher ratings and advertising and eventually leads to higher rights fees for the league.

EXPOSURE: SUPERSTATIONS AND THE WGN LAWSUIT

Exposure was a major problem for the NBA in the late 1970s and early 1980s with few regular season games, not all of the playoff games on national television, and even some of the NBA Finals broadcast on tape delay. The NBA also had the problem of individual teams having their own national television broadcast contracts, minimizing the value of the television rights the NBA as a collective could sell to networks. The NBA took several measures to limit the rights of individual teams to sell games. One of the first broadcast initiatives the NBA executed in trying to grow its sport was for the league as a whole to take greater control of its television exposure, particularly control over individual teams that had the capability of having their games broadcast on national television Superstations. The NBA defined a Superstation as "any commercial over-the-air television station whose broadcast signal is received outside of the local designated market area" (*Chicago Professional Sports Limited Partnership and WGN Continental Broadcasting Company v. NBA*, 1991, p.

1345). The Atlanta Hawks (TBS), Chicago Bulls (WGN), and New Jersey Nets (WOR) were the three teams involved, as some of their games were broadcast on cable systems that carried these Superstations throughout the nation. In addition to damaging national television revenue and exposure, the NBA felt that Superstation broadcasts of teams hindered the ability of local teams to sell their games, including both rights fees and advertising. For example, if the Chicago Bulls were consistently being broadcast into the Dallas market, the Dallas Mavericks might not get as much money selling their local broadcast rights because of the constant competition. Their ratings and subsequent advertising opportunities would suffer as viewers might be more compelled to watch the Bulls against the Lakers on WGN, rather than the Mavericks versus the Clippers. In addition to the competition with the national broadcasts, the NBA received no revenue from an independent rights contract of this nature; only the Bulls, Hawks, and Nets profited.

The NBA adopted a "less is more" strategy in which the league would restrict the number of games available to viewers, thus limiting competition with the NBA's national television contracts. The NBA would then better attempt to control the exposure positioning of the NBA on television and not saturate the market with games. In 1979, the NBA made its initial attempt to legislate the exposure of its game telecasts when the NBA's Board of Governors adopted a resolution that all future television contracts entered into by the teams would be made "subject to the Constitution, Bylaws and all other rules and regulations" of the league, "as they presently exist and as they may from time to time be amended," subject to "the terms of any existing or future television contracts entered into by the league and subject to review by the Commissioner to guarantee compliance" (*Chicago Professional Sports v. NBA*, 1991, p. 1342). The Board of Governors also passed a resolution providing the league with "the exclusive right to enter into contracts for the direct tele- casting of NBA games by cable systems located outside the territory of all members" (*Chicago Professional Sports v. NBA*, 1991, p. 1342). The new resolution voided a national contract the New York Knicks had signed with the USA Network that was to pay the Knicks $1.5 million for the broadcast rights to their games for three seasons from 1979-80 to 1981-82.

The NBA continued with its "less is more" strategy of restricting exposure. For the 1980-81 season teams were limited to 41 over-the-air telecasts because, for example, the Atlanta Hawks in the 1979-80 season, had broadcast all 82 of their regular season games on Superstation TBS. Teams were still permitted to sell the other 41 games (if they were not on CBS) to a local cable outlet only and keep all the revenue from whatever contracts they signed. The NBA, however, agreed to broadcast their games on national cable outlets, signing contracts for the 1982-83 and 1983-84 season with both ESPN and USA for 40 games, with ESPN televising on Sunday night and USA televising on Thursday night. Of the 41 games still permitted by teams for over-the-air broadcast, the NBA would also not allow any of these games to be broadcast opposite its new cable partners.

The NBA continued to impose restraints on its teams' ability to broadcast independently on a national network by limiting the number of Superstation games to 25 for the 1985-86 season. In October 1989, the NBA passed a resolution "blacking out Superstation games on nights when a NBA game is shown nationally on cable as part of the league's national cable package" (*Chicago Professional Sports v. NBA*, 1991, p. 1343). Although individual teams are not permitted to broadcast a game on a Superstation opposite a TNT or TBS game, teams can air a game head-to-head with a TNT or TBS game, but strictly on a local over-the-air or local cable channel. For example, if the New York Knicks were playing the Chicago Bulls on TNT, the game could not be broadcast nationally on WGN because it is a Superstation, but it could be televised on the Madison Square Garden (MSG) Network, the local carrier for the Knicks. Games are, however, blacked out on TNT or TBS in the local area of the home team. For example, if the Knicks were playing the Bulls at Madison Square Garden, the game would be blacked out on TNT or TBS in the New York area and only available on the MSG Network. If the same two teams played in Chicago, the game could be seen on either MSG or TNT (TBS) in the New York area. Games that are televised on NBC are not permitted to be broadcast by an individual team carrier at all, not even on tape delay. For example, if the New York Knicks were playing the Chicago Bulls on NBC, neither WGN nor MSG would be permitted to broadcast that game live or at a later time.

The attempt to control the television packaging of its product was eventually challenged by WGN and the Chicago Bulls, when in 1990 the NBA again decided to reduce the number of games on Superstations from 25 to 20. WGN and the Bulls sued the NBA to have the number remain at 25, citing the antitrust exemption provided in the Sports Broadcasting Act of 1961 did not apply and this limit was an unreasonable restraint of trade. The Bulls had approved the Board of Governors' resolutions for earlier reductions to 41 and subsequently 25 games, but moved to block this further restriction. At the time WGN reached 34% of all the television households nationwide, and 31% of those homes were outside the Chicago area. WGN received

no money from cable subscription, and relying on advertising sales for
98% of its revenues, was losing money by not having their games
broadcast to the entire nation. The Bulls and WGN also had a successful ratings and advertising commodity with the broadcast rights
to the most talented and marketable player, Michael Jordan.

WGN and the Bulls at the time were not even taking advantage of a tremendous advertising opportunity. Due to microwave
transmission technology, a Superstation could generate two signals,
one for local over-the-air and another to send out to the rest of the
nation. Ted Turner had been using this technology of splitting the
feed with TBS in Atlanta, and thus for one program had the ability to
double the advertising revenues with two feeds to sell two different
sets of advertising: local spots for Atlanta viewers only, and national
spots that would be seen throughout the country. Although WGN had
not been splitting the feed for its Bulls telecasts, the Superstation
had been using this transmission technology for its broadcasts of
Cubs and White Sox baseball games. For its baseball telecasts, WGN
offered advertisers three possibilities: over-the-air Chicago only,
national cable only, or both.

The positioning of the NBA in this legal matter and its rationale behind the need to limit the number of national broadcasts on
Superstations reverts directly back to the main benefits a league
achieves when it signs a national television contract: revenue and the
proper exposure. In the contract between the Bulls and WGN, the
NBA was not receiving any revenue nor creating the proper exposure. The beliefs of the NBA were clearly spelled out in the Proposed
Findings of Fact and the Proposed Findings of Law that were filed by
the NBA and cited in the case. The extensive rationale of the NBA's
argument is:

> The reduction protects the teams grant of exclusivity in their
> local markets, and enhances the value of the teams' local televi-
> sion contracts by protecting the exclusivity of those contracts
> from dilution caused by the importation of games from other NBA
> cities by reason of Superstation telecasts. It also promotes the
> teams media and sponsor relationship. It also protect(s) the value
> of the market extension agreements pursuant to which cable sys-
> tems pay a fee shared equally by all NBA teams for the right to
> telecast local cable games in a team's extended market. It
> enhances the ability of the NBA to grant exclusive and lucrative
> national broadcast contracts and protects the value of those con-
> tracts. It ensures the league is compensated for all national expo-
> sure of its games. It preserves the price sponsors pay for national
> exposure on NBA national cablecasts and broadcasts. It promotes

the NBA's relationship with the national broadcast and cable networks. It enhances the perception in the marketplace that the NBA offers a unique product and has control over that product. It fosters the development by the NBA of new technologies. It improves the level of competition in the television market and benefits consumers by making the NBA a stronger competitor and by providing greater national network coverage of NBA games. And in the long run, if the NBA as a league has no right to regulate the national distribution of NBA games by individual teams, the attractiveness of the league's national television product will be undermined, its national and local revenues will decline, the weaker teams will face financial difficulties, and the league's future will be threatened. (*Chicago Professional Sports v. NBA*, 1991, pp. 1358-1359)

The NBA also believed that its position was viable under the Sherman Act: Although the reduction of games would hinder the potential competition in the television market for NBA games among individual teams, the reduction of games would actually promote competition "between the NBA's network packages and other network programming and between local NBA broadcasts by the teams and other local programming" (*Chicago Professional Sports v. NBA*, 1991, p. 1359).

Seven weeks after the complaint was filed by WGN and after a five-day trial, Judge Hubert Will, a federal district court judge in Chicago, ruled in favor of WGN and the Bulls because the 1961 Sports Broadcasting Act is clearly worded to mean transfers (of games) by a league. Judge Will ruled that "because the games sold to WGN were owned and transferred by the Bulls rather than the league, the SBA does not, by its terms, cover this case" (*Chicago Professional Sports v. NBA*, 1991, p. 1351). Judge Will continued, "the Bulls and the other teams still own and control the rights to the games not included in the league's contracts with NBC and TNT, and therein lies the NBA's vulnerability to this lawsuit" (*Chicago Professional Sports v. NBA*, 1991, pp. 1351-1352). The Court ruled that the NBA produced no credible evidence, anecdotal or statistical, that inclined the Court to believe that Superstation broadcasts steal viewers from another team's local telecasts, thereby damaging ratings and revenues. The Court also found the arguments of the NBA, which attempted to describe its intentions and beliefs under the Sherman Act, not to be valid, as the Sherman Act in Section One prohibits every contract, combination, or conspiracy in restraint of trade.

The ruling in favor of WGN and the Bulls did not end the dispute between the NBA and WGN, as the parties have revisited the issue in court. The original ruling was reaffirmed on appeal in *Chicago Professional Sports Limited Partnership and WGN Continental Broadcasting Company v. NBA*, 961 F. 2nd 667 (7th Cir. 1992). In 1993, the NBA attempted to adopt rules that would ban Superstation telecasts, but in 1995, Judge Will ruled that the NBA plan was an antitrust violation and WGN and the Bulls would pay the NBA $40,000, rather than the $100,000 the NBA had sought, for each game the Bulls broadcast outside of Chicago. The ruling by Judge Will was largely based on the fact that the NBA was already receiving more than $2 million a year in copyright payments for Bulls games on WGN. On September 10, 1996, a three-judge appellate court, however, banned WGN from airing Bulls games nationally, claiming that the federal judge had overstepped his bounds in his favorable 1995 ruling for WGN (McConnville, 1996).

One of the more interesting aspects of the original lawsuit and its appeals is that it is indicative of the NBA's attempts to properly administer and control the exposure of its product. The league was not anxious for any competition among individual teams for its national broadcasts. The NBA also did not want games being broadcast nationally without the league receiving any of the revenue. Because the Hawks had reduced their TBS schedule to 20 games (TBS signed an agreement with the NBA not to challenge any reduction in the number of Superstation telecasts provided the rules applied equally to all Superstations in attempting to acquire the national television contract from ESPN and USA to TNT, also owned by Ted Turner), and because the Nets were well below that figure with only six games on Superstation WOR, the entire WGN lawsuit on the surface amounted to a dispute over the broadcasting of five games; but the message of the NBA's need for the proper exposure of the product, its games, and the need to protect the largest revenue source—national television money—was clear. The willingness of the NBA to litigate to a great extent also sent a clear signal to all the other NBA teams who might attempt to challenge the league's national television contract structure.

Ed Desser describes the NBA response to the WGN lawsuits, stating "we (the NBA) have an overall strategy, an overall arrangement where teams exploit local rights and the league exploits national and international rights on behalf of all the teams collectively" (personal communication, August 26, 1998). Brian McIntyre, NBA Senior Vice President of Communications, summarizes the problems when there is a system in which Superstations are broadcasting at their own volition and not that of the league. McIntyre states, "it is our property, how do we best position it? How do we best project our image? There is no doubt that television plays a major role in this.

You had no money coming into the league, going right to one team, and killing any kind of national exposure you could do" (personal communication, December 16, 1998).

EXPOSURE: NETWORK POSITIONING

In conjunction with the control of the Superstation broadcasting of games, the change in television exposure as a broadcast strategy was prevalent at the major network level, with a continuation of the "less is more" strategy for the NBA and CBS. Through this strategy, instead of constantly putting game after game on television and saturating the viewing market, the partnership decided to put fewer games on, but in a better position in the program schedule. Ted Shaker was the Executive Producer of the NBA on CBS from 1983 until CBS lost the broadcast rights to the NBA after the 1989-90 season. He describes the NBA's positioning on television and the "less is more" philosophy, stating:

> My first year there were four regular season games or five, a very small number. We coined the phrase "less is more," and what we would do is literally sit and figure when are we going to have a good window where we have a good chance of four or five opportunities. Where are the best opportunities to put these games? We could kind of pick off these things and use them as kind of tent poles to build a story of the NBA on CBS. So we put a game on Christmas Day, at the time on Christmas Day there was a college football game then the NBA game. I don't think there was any other competition for sports then, now there is because everybody else saw the same thing we saw. We put a game on Super Bowl Sunday, even if we didn't have a Super Bowl, early in the afternoon when everybody else was kind of getting away from the Super Bowl. What we figured, there could be a bunch of people that day they are going to be spending the day around the TV. There was a window from 1:00 to 3:30, so we put a NBA game there. All of these sound like pretty obvious things, but at the time no one else was looking at them. (personal communication, October 9, 1998)

Shaker describes the results of this strategy, stating "we would get great ratings and they became these tent poles and all of a sudden the NBA, even though it's only four games, the ratings are up and everybody banged the drum and we created a sense of momentum and we never let it go. It would go into the post-season on an upward trend of four or five games, but we wouldn't say it's four or five games, we'd say the NBA in regular season is up" (personal communication, October 9, 1998).

From the league perspective, NBA Commissioner David Stern explains:

> If truth be told I suppose when your ratings are not strong and your product is not secure in its identity, a lot of exposure is not a good thing because the worst thing for a bad product is a lot of exposure. So we were trying to shape up our product at the same time that we were trying to define exposure. As the product got better, by better I mean not just the players, but the stability of teams, relationships among teams in the league, relationships between the league and its players, relationships having to do with collective bargaining, and marketing strategies as well. When all of that got in place it was time to accelerate our exposure because we felt a lot more comfortable with the overall product. (personal communication, April 14, 1999)

Ed Desser also explains the rationale behind the "less is more" philosophy. He states:

> The market was only ready to accept so much, and one of the strategies that we were fond of talking about for a long time was "less is more." And "less is more" was really all about what the 80s were, which is let's not overexpose ourselves, let's try to make each telecast special. We are fighting for ratings, we want our ratings to be as high as possible on average, and therefore there is potentially too much exposure. If you are in a battle for your lives and what defines being on network television is a 20 share, how do you get a 20 share? You do a variety of things designed, you don't put too many games on, you promote the hell out of the games you do put on, you make sure you schedule each game in a logical way, you've good matchups, you produce it well, you have certain consistency of scheduling so people can know to expect it. Maybe you don't have wall-to-wall games so that people have to choose, I'll watch this game as opposed to that game. You try and have measured amounts of it in the marketplace and therefore that tends to push up the average. At a time when you are a second-class citizen, increasing your average is more important than increasing the total. What's better, what's a more attractive thing for a television network, one game that gets a 10 rating, or five

games that get a 2 rating? The answer is one game that gets a 10 rating and so we had to control the amount of product in the marketplace in order to garner enough eyeballs that people would pay attention. Now things have changed somewhat today. We are much more established and so it doesn't any longer make sense to starve the market in order to inflate the rating, but that was a very important part of the strategy for a long time. (personal communication, August 26, 1998)

Exposure and placement in the programming schedule are most vital during the NBA Playoffs when the league has a two-month showcase of its best teams and best players. The idea was that more people would watch the more important playoff games, increasing the ratings and advertising revenues for the NBA broadcast partners. Mike Pearl, Senior Vice President and Executive Producer for Turner Sports, explains that Turner promotes and broadcasts the playoffs with a major advertising campaign of 40 games in 30 nights. Exposure during the playoffs was a major problem for the NBA as television networks did not view the NBA Playoffs as a high priority and did not adjust their regular program schedule to televise the playoff games.

Consider the following examples:

- Friday, May 8, 1970, is the greatest day in the history of the New York Knicks as an injured Willis Reed limps onto the court at Madison Square Garden for game seven of the NBA Finals, prompting the famous radio call of "Here Comes Willis" by Marv Albert. Reed hit the first two shots of the game and with the addition of 36 points from Walt Frazier helps propel the Knicks to their first-ever NBA Championship by defeating the Lakers, 113-99. This game was not televised live in the New York area, but rather broadcast by ABC on tape delay at 11:30 p.m.
- Game six of the Eastern Conference Finals in 1977 between the Houston Rockets and the Philadelphia 76ers was not televised nationally.
- Game four of the NBA Finals in 1979 between the Washington Bullets and the Seattle SuperSonics and games two and five of the 1980 Finals between the Los Angeles Lakers and the Philadelphia 76ers were broadcast at their west coast starting time of 8:30 p.m., but 11:30 p.m. eastern.
- Game six of the 1980 NBA Finals between the Los Angeles Lakers and the Philadelphia 76ers was broadcast on tape

delay in many areas of the country. The game is one of the most memorable in NBA history as Ervin "Magic" Johnson fills in for an injured Kareem Abdul-Jabbar at center for the Lakers and scores 40 points, 15 rebounds, and 7 assists. Jamaal Wilkes adds 37 points in the 123-107 victory, and the Lakers win their first of five NBA Championships in the decade. NBA Commissioner David Stern would call this game not being on live television "the low point" for the NBA (Hubbard, 1984).

- Four of the six NBA Finals telecasts in 1981, all games during the week, were broadcast on tape delay at 11:30 p.m. In the first NBA Final of Larry Bird's career, instead of game six with the Boston Celtics, who were holding a three games to two advantage over the Houston Rockets, being televised live at 9:00 p.m., CBS elected to broadcast "Magnum P.I.", followed by a special at 10:00 p.m. titled "Ladies and Gentleman, Bob Newhart" with guests Don Rickles, Dean Martin, and Dick Martin.
- Game six of the Eastern Conference Finals in 1982 between the Boston Celtics and the Philadelphia 76ers was broadcast on tape delay with CBS broadcasting a repeat of "Dallas" and the drama "Nurse" in the 9 and 10 p.m. time slots, respectively.
- Game one of the 1987 Eastern Conference Finals between the Boston Celtics and the Detroit Pistons was not televised nationally.
- Not all NBA playoff games were televised nationally in 1994.

Throughout the late 1970s and into the 1980s the NBA Playoffs had only two time slots on CBS: Sunday afternoon, which occasionally featured a double header, and 11:30 p.m. on Friday night, which either featured a live game from the west coast or a game on tape delay. During these years, less than half of the entire NBA Playoff inventory was broadcast on national television. The advent and proliferation of cable television helped the NBA receive more exposure, but it was still not until 1995 that all of the NBA Playoff games were televised by one of its national broadcast partners (see Table 3.1 and Appendix).

The shift of the broadcasting contract from CBS to NBC represented two other changes in the televising of the NBA Playoffs: the majority of playoff series decisive games (game 5 or 7) would be televised on NBC, and NBC would began showing triple headers of playoff games on Sunday, utilizing the 5:30 p.m. time slot. The shift to a

Table 3.1. NBA Playoff Programming Schedule.

	1977	1978	1979	1980	1981	1982	1983	1984	1985	1986	1987
# of NBA teams	22	22	22	22	23	23	23	23	23	23	23
Possible # playoff games	61	61	61	61	61	61	61	89	89	89	89
Actual # playoff games	53	51	53	48	53	47	43	79	68	68	71
# playoff games on tv	21	22	19	19	29	31	30	48	44	41	43
# playoff games-network	21	22	19	19	29	31	30	23	22	21	20
# playoff games-cable	—	—	—	—	3	9	11	25	22	20	23
% playoff games on tv	**40**	**43**	**36**	**40**	**55**	**66**	**70**	**61**	**65**	**60**	**61**
1st round playoffs on tv	3/11	3/9	1/10	2/11	4/10	3/10	7/10	14/37	15/32	12/29	15/31
1st round playoffs- network	3	3	1	2	3	2	2	2	3	3	5
1st round playoffs- cable	—	—	—	—	1	1	5	12	12	9	10
Conference finals on tv	5/10	6/12	6/14	7/10	8/12	10/11	10/11	10/11	10/10	7/9	10/11
Conference finals-network	5	6	6	7	8	7	8	6	7	5	5
Conference finals-cable	—	—	—	—	—	3	2	4	3	2	5

Table 3.1. NBA Playoff Programming Schedule (cont'd).

	1988	1989	1990	1991	1992	1993	1994	1995	1996	1997	1998
# of NBA teams	23	25	27	27	27	27	27	27	29	29	29
Possible # playoff games	89	89	89	89	89	89	89	89	89	89	89
Actual # playoff games	80	62	72	68	73	76	77	73	68	72	71
# playoff games on tv	56	46	56	58	65	66	74	73	68	72	71
# playoff games-network	25	20	26	24	28	30	31	28	28	28	28
# playoff games-cable	31	26	30	34	37	36	43	45	40	44	43
% playoff games on tv	70	74	78	85	89	87	96	100	100	100	100
1st round playoffs on tv	18/35	15/29	21/32	23/32	24/31	26/35	29/31	30/30	31/31	31/31	34/34
1st round playoffs- network	6	5	7	7	6	9	7	6	7	8	8
1st round playoffs- cable	12	10	14	16	18	17	22	24	24	23	26
Conference finals on tv	3/13	10/10	13/13	10/10	12/12	13/13	12/12	13/13	11/11	11/11	11/11
Conference finals-network	6	6	8	7	8	9	7	8	8	6	8
Conference finals-cable	7	4	5	3	4	4	5	5	3	5	3

later Sunday tip-off time enabled more games to be televised by a major network and allowed the game to extend into the prime-time programming schedule of NBC. All NBA Finals games, including those on Sunday (which had previously been afternoon telecasts on CBS), also moved to a prime-time start. The shift to starting games in prime-time on Sunday is important when considering that the NBA Playoffs are during the months of April, May, and June when people might be more apt to enjoy the better weather than sit inside and watch a NBA game. Stephen Ulrich, NBC Director of Talent and Promotion, explains that

> sports has so many variables in terms of what determines the rating. You've got the skill and abilities of the players and teams, plus you've got how that team is functioning. You've got the weather, you have a nice day and you can kiss that rating good-bye. You can have the best promos and have the best games and scoring and be exciting, but if it is a beautiful day and there are a lot more compelling things, it is awfully hard to keep people in front of their TVs. (personal communication, October 21, 1998)

The shift to a Sunday 5:30 p.m. start time, or even later for the NBA Finals, allows people to spend a greater portion of their day outside, but still be home in time to watch the game. The 5:30 p.m. time slot is where the NBA would showcase its best game. Of the nine first- and second-round Sunday broadcasts on NBC at 5:30 p.m. between 1996 and 1998, eight of the telecasts featured the Bulls and Michael Jordan. Starting with the 1999 playoffs, Ed Desser and the NBA created an even greater shift for more coverage on NBC: the first round of the playoffs, which usually began in the middle of the week, now begin on the weekend, and the majority of the game ones of the first-round playoff series begin on NBC. Playoff coverage on NBC also expands in the early playoff rounds to a triple header on Saturday by including the 5:30 p.m. time slot (see Table 3.2).

The "less is more" philosophy begins to speak to Level One of agenda-setting and the idea of exposure framing methods. Although it might seem that the best approach for recognition in other business situations is to be as visible as possible, for the NBA there was a much different approach emphasizing not only the amount, but the proper position in the program schedule. The original study of McCombs and Shaw focused on the amount of coverage; however, the NBA as an organization of study is perhaps beginning to provide evidence for an extension of agenda-setting at Level One in which exposure can be expanded to include not only the amount, but the exposure character-istic and framing method of the placement of the product.

Table 3.2. NBA Playoff Programming Schedule: Comparison 1998, 1999, and 2000.

	1998	1999	2000
# of NBA teams	29	29	29
Possible # playoff games	89	89	89
Actual # playoff games	71	66	75
# playoff games on tv	71	66	75
# playoff games—network	28	29	36
# playoff games—cable	43	37	39
% playoff games on tv	**100**	**100**	**100**
1st round playoff on tv	34/34	33/33	33/33
1st round playoffs—network	8	11	12
1st round playoffs—cable	26	22	21
Conference finals on tv	11/11	10/10	13/13
Conference finals—network	8	8	10
Conference finals—cable	3	2	3

Positioning in the program schedule is only one of the criteria for improvement of game exposure as a broadcast strategy. The proper selection of the content in the form of which teams and which players to televise is equally important for both the regular season and the playoffs. Through the "less is more" strategy, the fewer games would not only be located at the best possible position in the program schedule, but would also feature the best teams and best players that the NBA had to offer in helping to advance its agenda.

Shaker describes the approach of utilizing the best teams and players that the NBA had to present to viewers:

At the time there were three franchises that were really working well and they were all built around personalities about those franchises. It was Julius Erving in Philadelphia, Larry Bird in Boston, and Magic Johnson and Kareem Abdul-Jabbar out in Los Angeles. So we had big name stars and we began talking about the players as much or more than teams. We wanted people to tune in to see the players more than tune in to see anything else. So that was kind of the way it began and that was kind of what I did. We had our first meeting with the NBA, Ed Desser was there, we had lunch at a place called Joe's Pier 52 and I remember that was where we kind of sat down and said, we are going to play up these three guys, or these three teams and these guys on these teams and we are going to have them playing each other, and we are never going to have a game where one of them is not playing on either side. So there was a lot of Philly-Boston and Boston-L.A. and L.A.-Philly, all of those combinations, and then we would introduce somebody else with one of them, the Detroit Pistons or whatever the team. (personal communication, October 9, 1998)

Brian McIntyre claims that showing the best teams worked in conjunction with the "less is more" television exposure philosophy the NBA had adopted. He explains, "we took our best properties, put them forward to the public who didn't even know us well, and they saw the best of the best." McIntyre adds, that "we made each event kind of special so if you didn't catch this national game today, you were not going to catch another one for X number of days and it worked" (personal communication, December 16, 1998).

In its understanding of television as an agenda-setting vehicle, the league had to be accommodating to CBS in terms of scheduling. The preference of network television in scheduling league games is still a prevalent strategy by the NBA. The scheduling process is, however, complicated because there is not only the programming schedule of the network to consider, but also the game schedule requirements of the 29 teams and their arena availability, many of which are shared with that particular city's professional hockey team or local college basketball team.

The process begins with teams submitting approximately 80 dates that their arena is available for their 41 home-game schedule. Teams are allowed by the league to obtain two "must have" dates when they are guaranteed the home game. Madison Square Garden, which in addition to the Knicks in the winter is also the home of the NHL's Rangers; a slew of college basketball including St. John's, the Big East Tournament, the pre- and post-season National Invitational Tournament, and the ECAC Holiday Festival; as well as the Westminster Kennel Club Dog Show; in the fall a women's tennis tournament and the Milrose Track and Field Games; and in the spring the Ringling Brothers Barnum and Bailey Circus is an excellent example. Dave Checketts, the President and CEO of Madison Square Garden, describes the scheduling process as a balancing act and summarizes the difficulty of scheduling the "World's Most Famous Arena," including trying to provide some consideration to the interests of the NBA and its broadcasting partners at NBC:

It is a negotiation all of the time. We submit dates that are available to the league and then they do the schedule and they come back to us and they say you submitted Sunday at 6:00 p.m., we would like to make that game noon, because we may want to make that an NBC game. Now we have to make the decision, we know people will come at Sunday at noon, they're not real happy about it sometimes, but on the other hand it gives them an excuse to bring the kids, so they will come. Then there is a certain prestige with being on NBC on a regular basis. If you are not a good team and a good organization, they don't necessarily want to show you, so there is a certain amount of cache with that and we try to satisfy everybody, keep in mind the interests of the fans, keep in mind the fact that we do get a large amount of money from NBC, and balance that with all of the other interests. (personal communication, October 16, 1998)

NBC is the exclusive over-the-air broadcast partner for the NBA, and Turner Networks, both TNT and TBS, are the NBA's national cable networks. The NBA is part of the entire inventory of NBC and Turner programming, including not only sports, but prime-time entertainment, movies, or news. For the 2000-01 season, NBC televises the NBA (selection) every Sunday from the middle of January until the end of the regular season (frequency) in either the noon, 3:30 p.m., or 5:30 p.m. time slot (placement) depending on the location of the game and its other programming for that particular day, such as a golf tournament. Often two games are televised each Sunday and coverage expands to Saturday and weeknight prime-time broadcasts during the playoffs (amount of time/space devoted to a topic). Turner broadcasts the NBA on TNT on both Wednesday and Thursday nights and on TBS on Tuesday night, and coverage also expands to doubleheaders every night during the early rounds of the playoffs.

In formulating the NBA schedule overall, and the television schedule in particular, the broadcast partners are always involved. NBC and Turner have input into the initial drafts of the schedule of games that will be on their networks and the time that the games will be played. Mike Pearl, Senior Vice President and Executive Producer for Turner Sports, describes the process. The programming department from Turner submits a best wish list of games and the NBA makes its scheduling decisions with the input from its broadcast partners being considered. Pearl explains that the broadcast schedule for the playoffs is largely determined by the NBA with input from its broadcast partners. This negotiation of the program schedule is where the strength of the partnership between the NBA and the networks can be easily recognized. There is a mutual understanding that the national television broadcasts are the best opportunity to showcase the league from the NBA perspective, and the networks simply want the best teams, players, and matchups that will attract the most viewers. Commissioner Stern explains that "we used to be much more insistent that every team be represented a certain amount and frankly we have been more open to the network's strategic view, which is the way to grow the sport is to focus on those teams that people want to see and use the ancillary programming to promote those other teams to get them sort of ready for prime-time" (personal communication, April 14, 1999). Ed Desser describes the scheduling of the NBA in terms of the preference that is given to its broadcast partners. He explains in detail:

> It starts with a basic framework that is negotiated as part of the television agreement. We don't know what the games will be, but there are basic parameters of how many regular season, how many Sunday afternoon, how many Sunday prime-time. Then the next wave is actually putting together the schedule for the particular year and that is put together based upon accumulating building availability dates, and NBC and Turner scheduling availability dates. There are a bunch of place holders on their schedule for the NBA on NBC and it's a particular pattern. Generally speaking, most Sundays are now formatted in a triple-header format. There are a fair number of deviations, so there are some single headers during the NCAA Tournament and there are some split doubleheaders, but basically we occupy most of the 5:30 to 8:00 slots in the first quarter and usually at least one other, either 12:30 or 1:00 to 3:30, or 3:30 to 6:00 pretty much across the board. So you get that information then there are just certain things you know. For a 1:00 game on a Sunday afternoon you know you are basically limited to the east coast and central time zones. So you look to see what buildings are available on that particular Sunday. Is the Garden available? Is Miami available? Is Chicago available? Is Detroit available? And the flip side of what buildings are available, is what teams are available to travel. If a team isn't available, it doesn't have a building available to play a home game, then by definition they are available to play a road game. Even if they have the building they still could potentially play a road game, but that's the basic pattern. Then it becomes assembling this mosaic—last year in the playoffs the Knicks and Miami were a great matchup, there's a rivalry there, we got this slot from 1:00 to 3:30 and we got Miami arena. Are the Knicks available to play in Miami that day? Yes they are,

boom, done. And it's a series of things like that, trying to come up with good compelling matchups and assembling the network schedule is the first part of the process. Because after that, let's say the Knicks are in Miami Sunday afternoon, then you kind of create the road trip around it. So Orlando is free on Friday night, we'll have them play in Orlando Friday, and Miami on Sunday and maybe Monday night, since it's not the next day per se, they could play in Atlanta so there's a nice little road trip, boom, done, next. (personal communication, August 26, 1998)

The scenario of the television schedule helping to dictate the entire NBA schedule as described by Desser can be applied using the 2000-01 NBA schedule, most notably with the 1999-2000 defending NBA Champion Los Angeles Lakers. On three separate occasions the Los Angeles Lakers road schedule is strongly coordinated with the NBA on national television (see Table 3.3 and Appendix).

Table 3.3. Los Angeles Lakers 2000-01 Television Coordinated Road Schedule.

Day	Date	Opponent	National Network
Sun	1/28	New York Knicks	NBC
Tue	1/30	Cleveland	
Wed	1/31	Minnesota	TNT
Tue	2/13	New Jersey	
Wed	2/14	Philadelphia	TNT
Fri	2/16	Charlotte	
Sun	2/18	Indiana	NBC
Wed	2/21	San Antonio	TNT
Thur	3/15	Detroit	
Fri	3/16	Washington	
Sun	3/18	Orlando	NBC
Mon	3/19	Atlanta	
Wed	3/21	Milwaukee	TNT

(Source: NBA)

Through this scenario the networks are receiving the best of the NBA product in terms of the quality of teams and players that are involved in the games on these broadcasts.

Problems could arise between franchises as certain teams are obviously on national television more than others. Teams such as New York, Los Angeles, and Chicago might receive frequent national exposure. In the 2001-01 NBA season, the Los Angeles Lakers will appear on national television 25 times, 11 on NBC and 14 on Turner. National television money is, however, shared, and the rights fees from the leagues' broadcast partners represent the single largest source of shared revenue among the 29 NBA franchises. These franchises, in essence, have agreed not to compete with one another in the area of broadcasting. In a free open market in which each team has permission to negotiate its own national television contract, strong franchises from large media markets, such as the New York Knicks or Los Angeles Lakers, would easily earn more money than franchises in smaller markets, such as the Sacramento Kings or the Vancouver Grizzlies. The greater revenue could easily alter the scales of competitive balance among all the teams, with large market teams being able to sign more high-priced talent. Through the NBA broadcast agreements, each team receives the same amount of revenue. As Dave Checketts explains the situation:

> We don't forget about the fact that we get a major share of the national revenue, but you have to understand that we get 1/29th of the national revenue and our marketplace probably accounts for 1/7th of the watching audience, so if we were to really argue that case we would say we deserve much more than 1/29th and so you shouldn't put the Knicks on national television any more than you do anyone else. And the truth is they put the Knicks on a lot, as many times as they possibly can, because we do have such interest in New York. (personal communication, October 16, 1998)

The argument might be made that exposure should be equal, giving all teams an opportunity to be on national television and promote their players and help market their team. Two former NBA head coaches, however, view an equitable distribution of national television time as impractical. P.J. Carlesimo, who coached Seton Hall University to the NCAA Championship Game in 1989 before coaching at the professional level with the Portland Trail Blazers and the Golden State Warriors, claims it is not realistic for all teams to appear on NBC, stating, "we want the league to be successful, we want the contract to be lucrative so if that means the Knicks versus the Lakers, so be it" (personal communication, December 9, 1998).

Chuck Daly, who coached the Detroit Pistons to the NBA Championship in the 1988-89 and 1989-90 seasons, led the Olympic Men's Basketball team to the Gold Medal in 1992, and was elected to the Hall-of-Fame in 1994, agrees with Carlesimo, claiming that the networks operate in conjunction with the league in order to sell the product of the league. Daly explains that television contracts sell advertising and the network should show the best teams and the best stars. Daly simply states, "equity is not a fact of life" (personal communication, January 7, 1999). Carlesimo also contends that if your team's desire is to be on NBC, "get good enough." He points out that when he was the coach of the Portland Trail Blazers they were on NBC more often than when he was coaching Golden State.

More importantly, the disparity in exposure among teams does not impact the competitive balance of the NBA. Carlesimo explains that exposure is not as pivotal in professional basketball as in college, where being on television is imperative for recruiting, with college athletes hoping for the proper exposure to better position themselves for when they enter the NBA Draft. Television exposure having an impact on free agency at the professional level is described as a stretch by Carlesimo. He believes that a free agent player does not make a decision about which team to sign his next contract with based on the number of times that team will be on network television.

EXPOSURE: ADVERTISING AND PROMOTION

The proper exposure and positioning in the program schedule and offering the best product to viewers in the form of teams, players, and matchups are essential to achieve the best television rating, and subsequently to earn the greatest advertising revenue, which would initially benefit the network—and eventually the NBA—when negotiating its next broadcast rights contract. The proper positioning enhances the advertisers' opportunities to reach their desired target audience. In 1996, advertisers spent $4.7 billion on national sports. The National Football League attracted $1.3 billion, the Summer Olympics in Atlanta generated $740.7 million, the NBA produced $495 million, and major league baseball produced $400 million (e.g., McClellan & Jessel, 1997).

There are advertising advantages distinct to the NBA, especially the timing of the NBA Playoffs. While in the autumn the NFL is the major vehicle for sponsors, advertising is a year-round endeavor and in the spring the companies that were attempting to reach the target audience who watch sports programming turn to the NBA as the best option to reach that demographic. The NBA broadcast partners and advertisers also benefit from the timing of the NBA playoffs because competing networks are often only televising repeats of their prime-time programming, whereas the NBA is contesting its conference finals and overall championship in prime time. Commissioner Stern calls the second advertising quarter of the year, "our time to howl" (personal communication, April 14, 1999). Commissioner Stern explains the multiple advantages of televising and advertising with the NBA. He states:

> The beneficial characteristics of being associated with the NBA probably fall into three categories: One, our game is great fun to watch, easy to understand, and shows well on a rectangular screen. It is a great television sport, no long sleeve uniforms, no pants, just shorts, no helmets and the television camera replicates a court side seat and a court side seat in the NBA is the best seat in sports because of the attributes of the players and our game. Second of all, it demonstrates to our fans the best athletes in the world. It is inspirational in the context of an arena experience, a sense of community and it is additional fun and enjoyable for that reason of pitting well-known teams with significant followings, easily recognizable, and certainly building a sense of the community. Finally, because of all of the above it delivers to sponsors a demographic, young male demographic that is very hard to get anyplace else. (personal communication, April 14, 1999)

Tom Fox is the Vice President of Sports and Event Marketing for Gatorade. His primary responsibility includes coordination of all Gatorade's league, team, and athlete associations. When Fox talks about the temporal advantages for Gatorade of being an official sponsor of the NBA, he points out that Gatorade has a distinct selling season—warm weather. The temporal characteristics of Gatorade's selling cycle strongly matches the NBA Playoffs, which are contested from April through June.

There are natural connections between sports television as programming content, sports-related products, advertisers for these companies, and consumers. For example, the advertising related to sports is an incredible opportunity for sneaker or sports drink companies to attract consumers. As viewers enjoy the real-life drama of sports, the advantage for the sponsor companies is that the viewers not only see the product and the athletes sponsoring the product in commercials, they also see that athlete wearing or using the product in a real-life situation, the actual game. This opportunity is not available for many other types of companies. Jerry Seinfeld can advertise for American Express, or William Shatner can do commercials for Priceline.com, but the viewer does not see Seinfeld use his American Express card or Shatner this Internet service in their respective television programs, let alone any other real-life situations. However, when Nike or Gatorade sponsors Michael Jordan, the viewer not only sees Jordan in Nike or Gatorade commercials, but then when the game resumes Jordan is playing in his Nike sneakers or drinking Gatorade during a timeout. These products actually help these athletes perform their jobs. Tom Fox describes the real-life situation in which consumers can see Gatorade products being used as a great advantage for the company. Another great example of real-life advertising is when a viewer sees a commercial of a notable golfer endorsing a certain style of club and then sees the golfer actually playing with those clubs in a tournament. Trusdell (1997) describes one survey that found that over 70% of NASCAR fans purchase the products of NASCAR sponsors.

Sneaker companies get other distinct advantages from being associated with basketball, notably the NBA Playoffs, which attracts a larger audience of casual basketball fans. This has allowed networks to sign exclusive contracts with a sneaker company, as NBC has done in the past with Nike. Sneaker companies also have a built-in minor league system for their products and potential future endorsement personalities due to the popularity of college basketball. Many shoe companies have exclusive contracts with a university in which that school's athletes only wear that particular company's uniforms, sneakers, and other apparel. Nike is associated with prominent schools such as Michigan, Penn State, and North Carolina, and its logo is featured prominently on their uniforms. The sneaker companies then recruit prominent collegiate players entering the NBA, possibly having the inside track if the player comes from a school represented by their company. Many rookie players entering the NBA will sign a contract with a sneaker company before they sign a contract with their NBA team.

The NBA on NBC is a tremendous vehicle for promotion of all NBC programming. Stephen Ulrich is the Director of Talent and Promotion for NBC Sports. His primary responsibility is to produce the tune-in and image promotions for all NBC Sports, including the NBA. Tune-in and image promotions are commercials or announcer voice-overs for upcoming NBC sports broadcasts. This responsibility includes setting up a schedule of when promotions will air during sports telecasts, and where sports telecasts can be promoted in other NBC programming. The promotion of other NBC programs within sports includes not only other upcoming sports telecasts, but any upcoming NBC programming.

The promotions within the sports broadcasts could include a short video clip, or what NBC simply refers to as "green sheets," that is, when the announcer in the middle of the game, during a brief stoppage in the action, such as a player going to the free throw line, reads prepared copy that might state, "next Sunday at 5:30 on NBC see a matchup of first-place teams when the Knicks travel to the Staples Center to meet Shaquille O'Neal, Kobe Bryant, and the Lakers." In addition to the announcement, a visual image of the date, time, and one or more of the personalities involved in the upcoming event appears on the screen. This quick promotion not only gives important exposure information, but also begins to set up the story-line and introduce the personalities for the game (concepts whose importance will be explained in Chapter Four). This promotion then offers the viewer the opportunity to see these personalities and the drama of the storyline played out for them on live television.

The "green sheets" promotions are also used for other NBC programming. The announcer might, for example, state, "coming up tonight on NBC," or "on Thursday, don't miss a very special *Friends*." This promotion within the sports telecast takes tremendous advantage of the characteristic that is inherent in sports, but not indigenous to any other type of programming. The overall goal of these types of within-game or event promotions is to set up the importance of the next game or the next show. Ulrich, however, cautions that "in terms of the game you have to walk a pretty fine line to make sure that the promotion is appropriate and does not interfere with the game at hand. Sure, we want to get that point across as to what is coming up on NBC, but we never want to get into a situation where it is detracting from the game" (personal communication, October 21, 1998).

Determining the amount of NBC Sports promotion that will occur during prime-time programming and the amount of prime-time programming promotion that will occur during a sports telecast is a continuous negotiation among the different divisions of NBC as to which promotions and where in the programming schedule they will appear. The promotion of future sports programming within a current sporting event is at the full jurisdiction of Ulrich and the sports division; however, it is a lobbying effort on the part of Ulrich with the prime-time or news divisions to ensure adequate promotion of NBC Sports broadcasts during other NBC programming. For special sports events, Ulrich will try to get extra promotional time on a top NBC show such as *ER* or *Friends*. Ulrich also has to evaluate the requests from the prime-time and news divisions who are attempting to receive promotional time during NBC Sports programming.

After negotiation of the time devoted to the sports department in general, whether for the sports telecast itself or any other NBC programming, the more difficult decisions center on where to position the promotions for certain programs. Ulrich describes the approach and the objective: through its promotions the network is attempting to find the audience members whose interest might be piqued by a promotion about a game or an event for which they had no or only limited knowledge. Ulrich explains his philosophy:

> In general, while we do support the type of sport you are watching, we are promoting other sports within a sport. The philosophy behind that is the audience is watching, most of them are fans of that sport so you are sort of preaching to the choir. There is no use running a minute of Notre Dame spots in Notre Dame. A person who is going to tune into college football is usually going to know what the schedule is going to be. Sure, we build a reminder and a lot of times that is where the announcer copy comes in, but if I got that air time I am going to try to use it as best as possible knowing that the audience watching that show, how that mixes with our future programming. I am not going to load up a college football game with a lot of figure skating. Those audiences don't mix too well. I will put a figure skating spot in there because you don't want to neglect that show, but you try to match up the audience that is watching as to what they probably will watch in the future. My role is always trying to find that swing audience. You have got to figure there is a core audience that is going to watch no matter what. My job is to try to find those people who might watch if they knew and if they were compelled to watch and that is pretty hard to do. (personal communication, October 21, 1998)

The leadership of NBC Sports is very committed to promotion efforts. Don Ohlmeyer is the former Executive Producer of Sports and Ulrich says that Ohlmeyer had a pillow in his office that stated, "promotion is our life-blood." Ulrich states that he is in continuous contact with NBC Sports President Dick Ebersol, who believes that promotion is a key factor to success for NBC Sports programs. Ulrich calls promotion, "one of the most important parts of television that probably doesn't get the justice it is due" (personal communication, October 21, 1998).

The NBA and NBC are partners in their endeavors to secure advertisers and promotion. Interaction with the NBA regarding advertising and sponsorship possibilities was one of the reasons that NBC was awarded the broadcast contract from CBS. The broadcasting contracts with NBC and TNT require both of these networks to advertise NBA telecasts during other programming. In the original contract that awarded NBC the broadcast rights to the NBA, NBC agreed to provide $40 million of on-air commercials for NBA games over the 4-year length of the contract. Sixty percent of these advertisements had to be broadcast in prime time. The NBA and NBC agreed to split the profits from advertising sales. After NBC sells enough commercial time to guarantee a small profit, all money from advertising sales is equally split between both organizations. The NBA also agreed to assist NBC in selling its advertising space.

Ed Desser claims that there is a very close working relationship between the media and sponsorship groups of the NBA and the sales and marketing divisions of its broadcast partners at NBC and Turner. Desser explains that in the early to mid-1980s the networks sold their advertising time without any assistance from the NBA, as the network thought that the NBA was not qualified to help in the area of sponsorship and promotion. That philosophy, however, shifted with the switch to NBC as the exclusive over-the-air broadcast partner. Desser states, "in our NBC arrangement, NBC had an appreciation for what we could bring to the table in terms of our sponsor relationships and how marrying the process of supplying promotional rights, sponsorship rights, and media rights together, whether it's in a single package or simply a result of greater coordination, that was a much more powerful opportunity for sponsors" (personal communication, August 26, 1998).

Tom Fox explains that as the NBA was trying to emerge, one of the strategies regarding potential sponsorship of the NBA was that sponsor companies also had to purchase advertising time for games televised by the NBA's broadcast partners. For example, if Gatorade wanted to be the official sports drink of the NBA and have players drinking out of green cups with the Gatorade logo on them, Gatorade also had to buy commercial time on NBA television broadcasts. Fox credits NBA Commissioner David Stern for this strategy and the building of NBA and advertiser partnerships. Stern understood early on, according to Fox, that for the league to grow it was critical for the NBA to have advertisers lined up for the game telecasts. Fox claims this strategy was a tremendous advantage for the NBA broadcast partners as it would alleviate some of their pressure to sell commercial time.

From an advertiser perspective, Fox claims this arrangement was a little more risky because of the magnitude of the commitment that sponsors had to make to a league that had been struggling. Fox claims sponsors were "taking a chance" and as a straight media buy (commercials only), "it didn't make sense" (personal communication, May 25, 1999). Fox, however, points out that there was a confidence that sponsors had in David Stern and the potential growth of the NBA. There were also the advantages of being associated with the NBA, including the seasonal timing, the real-life elements, and most importantly, the demographic that the NBA could potentially reach.

Stephen Ulrich describes the NBA as a great promotional partner that will do whatever the network needs in terms of video or anything else to help promote the upcoming game. Ulrich provides an example:

> Charles Barkley was playing Michael (Jordan) on Christmas and we wanted Charles to say just some quick pickup lines, Hey Michael, Santa is not coming to your house, but I am. The NBA worked on Charles and he was hurting and limping around the court and he wasn't in a good mood, but they worked on him and worked on him and we had to be ready to go and it's not like you've got 10 takes with the guy or an hour. You had five minutes and you had to be ready to roll, but we got the go ahead and sent a crew and Charles was great. He'll give you a few jives, but he was great. Not only once we got him in there, he enjoyed it, did a great job, but they do a great job working with their players so they can work with TV. Their personality comes through, they know how to work with people, they even know—not they know how to direct, but they even know what's right. They will sit there and say this shirt doesn't look right, bring me a warm-up or they will say I need something in my hands, give me a ball. They will know that if they just sit there and [say] watch the game Sunday at two, that stinks, but they know if they are sitting there saying—I'm ready for you Michael—they know that is what makes the NBA different than any other sport. The players show a genuine interest in playing these games and having people enjoy watching them play. (personal communication, October 21, 1998)

The NBA was the first league to get its broadcast partners to cross-promote the league games for each other. NBC would actually have its announcers say, "tonight at 9:30 game two of the Western Conference playoffs as Phoenix plays Seattle on TNT." NBC also cross-promotes a continuation of its NBA Finals postgame coverage on its cable outlet CNBC. The difficulty of the cross-promotion idea is that NBC is in essence telling viewers not to watch its own network, but another. The cross-promotion is problematic for NBC's affiliates who might be losing viewers. Jim Waterbury, President and General Manager of KWWL (TV) Cedar Rapids, Iowa, and past chairman of the NBC affiliates board, states, "if you're inviting people to go to one of NBC's other channels, you are also inviting them to leave the affiliate that they're watching—and that doesn't play well to affiliates." Waterbury adds that "it's like owning a restaurant with a partner and your partner keeps inviting his family to eat free every night" (cited in Brown, 1996, p. 15). This cross-promotion provides a sense that watching the NBA is more important than watching what might be on NBC. The network, however, is providing a valuable service to the fans of the NBA. In helping its affiliates, NBC will receive free promotion from the Turner networks for its upcoming NBA telecasts. From the NBA standpoint, it is a clear victory as its product is continuously being promoted.

Stephen Ulrich's description of the NBA as the most promotionally savvy league goes from Commissioner David Stern down to the individual teams. Tom Fox explains that in addition to a national sponsorship deal with NBA Properties, sponsors can reinforce their national appeal through contracts with individual teams. Gatorade can be an official sponsor of the NBA and also be an official sponsor of the Chicago Bulls, New York Knicks, Los Angeles Lakers, or whichever other team and market it chooses to support its national NBA campaign. Fox explains the difference: As a NBA sponsor, Gatorade could not run a Bulls-only promotion. However, if it strikes an individual deal with the Bulls, it can offer a Bulls promotion within the Chicago area. Through this national and local arrangement, Fox explains, each NBA team creates 29 marketing offices to support any national marketing that is done by Gatorade with the NBA.

Howie Singer is the Coordinating Producer for both the New York Knicks and the New Jersey Nets as both the Madison Square Garden Network and Fox Sports New York are properties of Cablevision. In addition to overseeing both productions, he is the the game producer for half of the Knicks games and director for the other half, and has been involved with the Knick broadcasts for over 18 years. Singer describes some of the elements of a NBA broadcast that are sellable commodities to advertisers, but also cautions that it is important not to overload the viewer and to be sure that the sponsored elements are relevant to the game and the fan.

Singer claims that many sponsored elements, such as the Budweiser Dunk of the Game, are determined at the beginning of the season in coordination with the Madison Square Garden advertising sales and marketing departments. Singer explains the overall philosophy, stating, "we try to do things that we are going to show anyway and give it a sponsor as opposed to force things on the viewer. I'm going to show the leading scorer, so stick a label on it, going to show the highlights, so put a sponsor on it. The Delta upcoming schedule, we want to show the next few games, put a sponsor on it" (personal communication, August 26, 1998).

Joe Gangone is the Executive Vice President of Advertising Sales for Madison Square Garden. His responsibility includes overseeing the advertising sales department whose objective is generating revenue for every Madison Square Garden property, including arena signage and radio and television broadcast commercials. Gangone, however, points out that the approach of his department is more than sales oriented—it is to build relationships between Madison Square Garden and its sponsors. Gangone describes the advertising sales personnel as partnership brokers who "prospect advertisers who have needs and apply the resources [of Madison Square Garden] to meet those needs" (personal communication, May 10, 1999).

The major problem for these advertisers is simply that they might not be able to effectively reach a certain demographic through any other type of medium or programming. The solution is to receive exposure on television for their product or service to try to reach this difficult target audience. Gangone explains that "sports brings a hard to reach viewer to the set" and he also claims the sports viewers are "people who are dedicated viewers and consumers" (personal communication, May 10, 1999).

Gangone further explains that in brokering an advertising partnership for the sports broadcasts on the Madison Square Garden Network, he often points out that sports television does not feature any gratuitous sex or violence that a sponsor might be leery of being associated with. Gangone claims that there is "no place else on television without a comfortable view of what people are going to hear and see. Sports is the last bastion of pure programming" (personal communication, May 10, 1999). He points out that sponsorship not only includes commercials, but also offers sponsors a place to go and attend games.

Dave Checketts explains that Madison Square Garden hosts a sponsor day when representatives from companies who advertise with Madison Square Garden and the Knicks are invited to watch a portion of the Knicks' practice, then have lunch and an autograph session with the players. Madison Square Garden also hosts a sponsor luncheon for its other building tenant, the New York Rangers of the NHL. At the sponsor luncheon one player or coach is seated at every table with advertising representatives from the various sponsor companies. Gangone explains the sponsor luncheon is a service of Madison Square Garden granted to sponsors that enhances their partnerships. Gangone describes the sponsor luncheon as a "chance for sponsors to touch and feel" and it is the "final extension of what we [Madison Square Garden] have to offer" (personal communication, May 10, 1999).

The selling of sponsorship is enhanced by the inclusion of players in promotional spots. Gangone, however, points out the transient nature of sports and player movement as he cautions sponsors and carefully manages expectations regarding players' involvement with the sponsor. He tries to emphasize the positive opportunities of being associated with the franchises (Knicks and Rangers) and Madison Square Garden, whose tradition and name recognition endure long after a player retires or is traded.

In addition to sponsorship, the team must make efforts to properly promote itself to make its local television contracts more attractive and to increase attendance; the two major sources of basketball-related income on the local level. For example, Dave Coskey, Philadelphia 76ers' Vice President of Marketing and Communications, explains that the 76ers were the first franchise to have a beanie-baby give away night, a promotion that consistently increased ticket sales to that particular game in many sports. Coskey explains his primary responsibility is not basketball, but to help the 76ers develop team relations with sponsors. He states, "there is great amount of promotional inventory in addition to television time, teams must sell program advertising and court side signage" (personal communication, February 1, 1999). Coskey defines the goals of his department as facilitating the 76ers' consistent presence throughout the media and keeping the community involved.

The New Jersey Nets compete in the New York-New Jersey metropolitan area, which has nine professional teams from football, baseball, basketball, and hockey. The Nets are especially competitive with the Knicks, who play only minutes away across the Hudson River. To try to better market the franchise and increase attendance, the Nets annual marketing, promotions, and in-game entertainment budget has substantially increased (see Table 3.4).

The Nets created a mission statement entitled "Community, Character and Championship," with the philosophy that community involvement, likeable players, and winning basketball will create a product worthy of having people spend their money. Michael Rowe, former Nets President, stated, "community, character and championship is part of every decision we make. Everything we do to package ourselves, to market ourselves, to build our brand is informed by that idea. It is sort of like a three-legged stool. If any of the three sides don't work, if any of them come up short, the stool falls over" (cited in Parks, February 7, 1999). Not only have the Nets made

Table 3.4. New Jersey Nets Marketing Spending.

Season	Marketing & Promotion	In-game Entertainment	Avg. Atten	Record
1995-96	$250,000	$225,000	15,685	30-52
1996-97	$250,000	$225,000	16,357	26-56
1997-98	$700,000	$700,000	17,524	43-39
1998-99	$1,000,000	$780,000	16,614*	16-34*

*Note. NBA Lockout Season.
(Source: New Jersey Nets, NBA, Parks, February 7, 1999)

some progress on the basketball court, by making the playoffs in 1998 for the first time since 1994, but with winning basketball and a new logo, in-arena merchandise sales jumped from $360,000 in 1996-97 to $780,000 in the 1997-98 season (Parks, 1999).

Another emerging form of sponsorship revenue for a team, in all sports, is the naming rights to the stadium or arena (see Table 3.5).

The players of the NBA have been the beneficiaries of the success of the NBA promotion and advertising ventures. Although the economic advantages are obvious, the sponsor also benefits. According to Tom Fox, a spokesperson, "puts a face and a personality on your brand" (personal communication, May 25, 1999). It is a spokesperson who can help a consumer with product name recall and an increased chance of a purchase. Fox, however, cautions that this association could be positive or negative depending on whether the athlete performs well and stays away from scandal. Fox points out that Gatorade has been fortunate in that its only NBA spokesperson, Michael Jordan, is extremely successful.

On the Forbes list of athletes' earnings, which calculates both salary and endorsement contracts, in 1993 only four NBA players were on the list of 40. Michael Jordan was first with $36 million, $32 million of which came from endorsement contracts. The other three NBA players were Shaquille O'Neal, who was sixth, David Robinson, who was eighteenth, and Charles Barkley in spot 34. In 1997, the number of NBA players grew more than any other sport as 11 players made the Forbes list of 40. Jordan remained first with a total of $78.3 million, $47 million of which came from endorsements. O'Neal also remained in the top 10 at seventh, and Grant Hill finished at the

Table 3.5. NBA 2000-01 Teams and Arena Sponsorship.

Team	Arena Name
Atlanta Hawks	Philips Arena
Boston Celtics	Fleet Center
Charlotte Hornets	Charlotte Coliseum
Chicago Bulls	United Center
Cleveland Cavaliers	Gund Arena
Dallas Mavericks	Reunion Arena
Denver Nuggets	Pepsi Arena
Detroit Pistons	The Palace of Auburn Hills
Golden State Warriors	Arena in Oakland
Houston Rockets	Compaq Center
Indiana Pacers	Conseco Fieldhouse
Los Angeles Clippers	Staples Center
Los Angeles Lakers	Staples Center
Miami Heat	American Airlines Arena
Milwaukee Bucks	Bradley Center
Minnesota Timberwolves	Target Center
New Jersey Nets	Continental Airlines Arena
New York Knicks	Madison Square Garden
Orlando Magic	TD Waterhouse Center
Philadelphia 76ers	First Union Center
Phoenix Suns	America West Arena
Portland Trail Blazers	Rose Garden
Sacramento Kings	Arco Arena
San Antonio Spurs	Alamodome
Seattle SuperSonics	Key Arena
Toronto Raptors	Air Canada Center
Utah Jazz	Delta Center
Vancouver Grizzlies	General Motors Place
Washington Wizards	MCI Center

(Source: NBA)

tenth spot. The other eight NBA players all finished in the top 30 of the Forbes list. Horace Grant was 13, David Robinson 18, Alonzo Mourning 20, Juwan Howard 23, Gary Payton 24, Hakeem Olajuwon 26, Dennis Rodman 27, and Reggie Miller 30 (see Table 3.6).

Table 3.6. Forbes Top 40 Athletes Earnings List by Sport

Sport	1993	1997	Change
NBA	4	11	**+7**
baseball	8	7	-1
boxing	5	7	+2
golf	3	4	+1
tennis	8	3	-5
auto racing	6	3	-3
hockey	1	3	+2
NFL	5	2	-3

(Lane & Midgett, 1993; Spiegel, 1997)

Note. In place of the Top 40 Athletes, Forbes now publishes a celebrity 100 list that has athletes, actors, and artists merged into one. It utilizes a criteria of headlines, cover stories, Internet eyeballs, and salary to rank its members. In the list published on March 20, 2000, of the 25 sports personalities who made the list, six are or were NBA players: Michael Jordan (rank #5), Shaquille O'Neal (rank # 28), Grant Hill (rank # 33), Karl Malone (rank # 43), Patrick Ewing (rank #46), and Kevin Garnett (rank #55) (Newcomb, 2000).

AUDIENCE MEASURES

The success of the changes in exposure framing methods implemented through the NBA and television relationship is measured by the NBA through the behavior of the audience in essentially three categories: television ratings, game attendance, and purchasing of NBA-licensed merchandise. These three audience behavior measures have direct implications on the financial success of the NBA. Television ratings are clearly the most important audience behavior measure for a television network as they do not receive the direct benefits from game attendance or merchandise sales. For the NBA, however, television ratings are also the most important measure because television is the greatest revenue source for the league and the vehicle of its greatest exposure as more fans watch than attend games.

The television ratings for the NBA Finals increased from 1994 to 1998 with game six of the 1998 Finals between the Bulls and the Jazz being the highest rated NBA game of all time. It had a 32.3 rating and a 38% share. The ratings for the NBA Finals from 1996 to 1998 were double the ratings in 1980 and nearly triple the ratings for the 1981 Finals, which were largely tape-delayed broadcasts.

Although the overall average rating decreased for the 1999 and 2000 NBA Finals, all but one of the NBA Finals games in those two years were the highest rated television programs in their respective time slots and nights (game three in 2000 with the Los Angeles Lakers holding a 2-0 series advantage over the Indiana Pacers was beaten by "Who Wants to be a Millionaire"), and all games finished in the top-10 television programs for the week (see Table 3.7).

The ratings for the 17 years that the NBA Finals were on CBS produced a mean of 12.0 (SD = 2.8) and the share produced a mean of 28.8 (SD = 3.1). The ratings for the 10 years that the NBA Finals have been on NBC produced a mean of 14.9 (SD = 2.6) and the share produced a mean of 27.6 (SD = 4.8).

The NBA All-Star Game is another major showcase and promotional tool. The NBA All-Star Game is now much more than one single game on a Sunday afternoon as it had been prior to 1984. The All-Star Game in 1984 mushroomed into All-Star Weekend with the debut of the Slam Dunk Contest and the Legends Classic Game, which was replaced by the Rookie Game in 1994 but once again added in 2000. In 1986, the 3-point contest was added to All-Star Weekend and a promotional event named 2-Ball debuted in 1998. This event featured a NBA player and a Womens' National Basketball Association (WNBA) player from the same city on the same team in a shooting contest. For example, Allan Houston from the Knicks and Rebecca Lobo from the Liberty were the inaugural representatives from their New York franchises. More importantly, each of the on-court events had promotional sponsors, so it was not simply the NBA Rookie Game, but the Schick NBA Rookie Game, Sony 2-Ball, AT&T Shootout, and NBA.COM Dunk Contest. All-Star Weekend includes the NBA's All-Star Jam Session, a NBA-oriented theme park that features a weekend of interactive basketball events, all of which are sponsored.

The All-Star Game has given the NBA an event that consistently earns a higher television rating than the average regular season or playoff game. The ratings for the 17 years that the NBA All-Star game was on CBS produced a mean of 9.85 (SD = 1.1) and the share produced a mean of 22.8 (SD = 3.9). The ratings for the nine games (there was no game in 1999 due to the NBA lockout) that have been on NBC produced a mean of 10.6 (SD = 2.3) and the share produced a mean of 18.7 (SD = 4.2) (see Table 3.8).

The ratings for the last four regular seasons for the NBA on CBS (1986-87 to 1989- 90) produced a mean of 5.4 (SD = .41). The regular season ratings for the 10 years that the NBA has been on NBC produced a mean of 4.5 (SD = .51). The ratings for the playoffs for the NBA on CBS from 1986-87 to 1989-90 produced a mean of

Table 3.7. Average Ratings for NBA Finals.

Year	# of Telecasts	U.S. Households		Teams (winner listed first)	Network
		Rating	Share		
1974	7	13.5	32	Boston/Milwaukee	CBS
1975	4	10.1	28	Golden St./Washington	CBS
1976	6	11.5	29	Boston/Phoenix	CBS
1977	6	12.7	33	Portland/Philadelphia	CBS
1978	7	9.9	25	Washington/Seattle	CBS
1979	5	7.2	24	Seattle/Washington	CBS
1980	6	8.0	29	L.A. Lakers/Philadelphia	CBS
1981	6	6.7	27	Boston/Houston	CBS
1982	6	13.0	28	L.A. Lakers/Philadelphia	CBS
1983	4	12.3	26	Philadelphia/L.A. Lakers	CBS
1984	7	12.1	26	Boston/L.A. Lakers	CBS
1985	6	13.5	30	L.A. Lakers/Boston	CBS
1986	6	14.1	31	Boston/Houston	CBS
1987	6	16.7	35	L.A. Lakers/Boston	CBS
1988	7	15.4	31	L.A. Lakers/Detroit	CBS
1989	4	15.1	30	Detroit/L.A. Lakers	CBS
1990	5	12.3	25	Detroit/Portland	CBS
1991	5	15.8	32	Chicago/L.A. Lakers	NBC
1992	6	14.2	27	Chicago/Portland	NBC
1993	6	17.9	33	Chicago/Phoenix	NBC
1994	7	12.4	23	Houston/New York	NBC
1995	4	13.9	25	Houston/Orlando	NBC
1996	6	16.7	31	Chicago/Seattle	NBC
1997	6	16.8	30	Chicago/Utah	NBC
1998	6	18.7	33	Chicago/Utah	NBC
1999	5	11.3	21	San Antonio/New York	NBC
2000	6	11.6	21	L.A. Lakers/Indiana	NBC

(Source: Nielsen Media Research)

7.28 (SD = .17). The playoff ratings for the 10 years that the NBA has been on NBC produced a mean of 7.27 (SD = .79) (see Table 3.9).

The overall rating for a playoff series can be skewed if the series only goes four or five games, as it is the series-determining sixth and seventh games that draw a higher audience. Although there is not always a dramatic increase in the ratings, the more impressive characteristic of the NBA's performance on television is the relative consistency of the ratings. The consistency of ratings is not only a valuable factor for the NBA, but for most sports television

Table 3.8. NBA All-Star Game Ratings.

Day	Year	Network	Location	Rating	Share
Tues	1973	ABC	Chicago	12.6	19
Tues	1974	CBS	Seattle	11.2	20
Tues	1975	CBS	Phoenix	12.1	24
Tues	1976	CBS	Philadelphia	9.3	17
Sun	1977	CBS	Milwaukee	8.6	24
Sun	1978	CBS	Atlanta	10.1	28
Sun	1979	CBS	Detroit	7.8	22
Sun	1980	CBS	Landover	9.9	27
Sun	1981	CBS	Cleveland	9.2	23
Sun	1982	CBS	New Jersey	8.9	22
Sun	1983	CBS	Los Angeles	9.2	21
Sun	1984	CBS	Denver	9.0	21
Sun	1985	CBS	Indianapolis	10.9	26
Sun	1986	CBS	Dallas	10.9	26
Sun	1987	CBS	Seattle	10.3	24
Sun	1988	CBS	Chicago	10.5	26
Sun	1989	CBS	Houston	10.0	24
Sun	1990	CBS	Miami	9.5	12
Sun	1991	NBC	Charlotte	7.8	21
Sun	1992	NBC	Orlando	12.8	26
Sun	1993	NBC	Salt Lake City	14.3	22
Sun	1994	NBC	Minneapolis	9.1	14
Sun	1995	NBC	Phoenix	10.7	17
Sun	1996	NBC	San Antonio	11.7	20
Sun	1997	NBC	Cleveland	11.2	19
Sun	1998	NBC	New York	10.6	17
Sun	1999	*No Game Lockout*			
Sun	2000	NBC	Oakland	6.9	12

(Source: Nielsen Media Research)

programming. Ed Desser comments on the value of consistent ratings for a network that makes sports television appealing to broadcasters. He states:

> Their [NBC] purchase of multi-year broadcasting rights is a smart investment because there's a predictability for them. You put a show on the air, very rarely do you buy multiple years. You may just buy six episodes then wait and see, very rarely do you

Table 3.9. Average Network Television NBA Ratings: Regular Season and Playoffs.

Year	Network	Regular Season	Playoffs
86-87	CBS	5.9	7.5
87-88	CBS	5.4	7.2
88-89	CBS	5.4	7.1
89-90	CBS	4.9	7.3
90-91	NBC	4.5	6.7
91-92	NBC	4.5	7.2
92-93	NBC	4.5	8.2
93-94	NBC	4.4	7.2
94-95	NBC	5.0	8.1
95-96	NBC	5.0	8.0
96-97	NBC	4.7	7.4
97-98	NBC	4.8	7.7
98-99	NBC	4.3	6.5
99-00	NBC	3.3	5.7

(Source: Nielsen Media Research)

make a four-year commitment to a television show, it's very rare. The Olympics, sports, and *ER* [NBC's prime-time drama about an Emergency Room], and even *ER* was only three years. So it's kind of a unique element of the sports business that there's a certain predictability and that's an important element in terms of what NBC is about and what NBC is selling to sponsors, a pretty narrow range of expectation for what is going to be delivered audience wise. Sports programs are far more predictable than entertainment shows in terms of what the rating is going to be. Does it vary, sure. Does it go up and down, yes. But, the range—you launch a new entertainment show the range could be number one, it could number 151 and there a lot of other points in between. We pretty much know within 20-25% what the Finals is going to do. (personal communication, August 26, 1998)

The comment by Desser is supported through the low standard deviation figures for the regular season and the playoffs. The ratings for the NBA Finals on NBC have only differed by 19% in the years without Michael Jordan in the Finals (1994, 1995, 1999, and 2000) and by only 24% for the years with Michael Jordan in the Finals (1991-93 and 1996-98—the impact of Michael Jordan on television ratings is discussed in more detail in Chapter Five).

For a NBA-oriented program such as *NBA Showtime*, ratings are for the most part the only audience feedback measure available. Ricky Diamond explains the value of *NBA Showtime*, stating:

> It doesn't do the same rating as the game, it does maybe half the rating of the game in some cases, or 60% of the game rating, but we think it helps promote the game. It helps people want to watch the games more, and informs them about the league. What its value has been is obviously impossible to quantify. We hope it is serving in some way to promote the league, to promote the NBA and there is no way of telling that other than that the ratings have generally been reasonably solid. (personal communication, October 21, 1998)

Another source of feedback that measures audience behavior toward the NBA is the attendance at league games. The trend of increasing NBA attendance for both the regular season and the playoffs demonstrates the public has responded and participated in the growth of the league (see Table 3.10).

The NBA, or any other sports league, however, does not survive on fan attendance alone, either from a popularity or, more importantly, a revenue standpoint. The fans cannot rely on attending games as their sole means of staying fully informed and educated about the game because only half are played at home, and even if one attends every road game there are other teams about which one cannot receive information without some input from a media source. This is where media dependency theory makes its best argument on an individual level. This type of media dependency reverts to the initial agenda-setting study of how people need the media to get information.

The final audience behavior measure that directly equates to revenue for the NBA is the purchasing of NBA-licensed merchandise. Recognizing the marketing possibilities, in 1982 the NBA created a department of the league called NBA Properties. This is the marketing and licensing division for the league, and it oversees the global marketing of the NBA through numerous consumer products, events, media sponsorships, and promotions. The objective of NBA Properties is to generate revenue and create awareness for the NBA and its 29 teams.

One of the divisions within NBA Properties is the marketing and media group, which sells NBA promotion and advertising rights to leading United States and international corporations and helps direct corporate sponsors to purchase advertising packages from the

Table 3.10. NBA Attendance.

Regular Season

Year	# of Teams	Attendance	# of Games	Average
68-69	14	3,721,532	574	6,484
69-70	14	4,341,028	574	7,563
70-71	17	5,330,393	697	7,648
71-72	17	5,618,497	697	8,061
72-73	17	5,852,081	697	8,396
73-74	17	5,910,023	697	8,479
74-75	18	6,892,378	738	9,339
75-76	18	7,512,249	738	10,179
76-77	22	9,898,521	902	10,974
77-78	22	9,874,155	902	10,974
78-79	22	9,761,377	902	10,822
79-80	22	9,937,575	902	11,017
80-81	23	9,449,340	943	10,021
81-82	23	9,964,919	943	10,567
82-83	23	9,637,614	943	10,220
83-84	23	10,014,543	943	10,620
84-85	23	10,506,355	943	11,141
85-86	23	11,214,888	943	11,893
86-87	23	12,065,351	943	12,795
87-88	23	12,654.374	943	13,419
88-89	25	15,464,994	1,025	15,088
89-90	27	17,368,659	1,107	15,690
90-91	27	16,876,125	1,107	15,245
91-92	27	17,367,240	1,107	15,689
92-93	27	17,778,295	1,107	16,060
93-94	27	17,984,014	1,107	16,246
94-95	27	18,516,484	1,107	16,727
95-96	29	20,513,218	1,189	17,252
96-97	29	20,304,629	1,189	17,077
97-98	29	20,373,079	1,189	17,135
98-99	29	12,134,906	725	16,738
99-00	29	20,058,513	1,189	16,870

Playoffs

Year	# of Teams	Attendance	# of Games	Average
68-69	14	505,765	39	12,968
69-70	14	555,830	40	13,896
70-71	17	489,213	40	12,230
71-72	17	525,128	37	14,193
72-73	17	607,571	41	14,819
73-74	17	593,345	41	14,472

Table 3.10. NBA Attendance (cont'd.).

Playoffs

Year	# of Teams	Attendance	# of Games	Average
74-75	18	685,291	47	14,581
75-76	18	698,100	51	13,688
76-77	22	806,994	53	15,226
77-78	22	797,758	51	15,642
78-79	22	903,563	53	17,048
79-80	22	739,916	48	15,415
80-81	23	765,216	53	14,438
81-82	23	726,894	47	15,466
82-83	23	606,470	43	14,104
83-84	23	1,095,940	79	13,873
84-85	23	984,589	68	14,479
85-86	23	978,597	68	14,391
86-87	23	1,090,877	71	15,364
87-88	23	1,397,447	80	17,469
88-89	25	1,076,567	62	17,364
89-90	27	1,202,710	72	16,704
90-91	27	1,109,012	68	16,309
91-92	27	1,227,670	73	16,817
92-93	27	1,338,868	76	17,617
93-94	27	1,349,163	77	17,522
94-95	27	1,347,367	73	18,457
95-96	29	1,283,704	68	18,882
96-97	29	1,351,719	72	18,774
97-98	29	1,409,458	71	19,851
98-99	29	1,315,119	66	19,926
99-00	29	1,426,506	75	19,020

(Source: NBA)

NBA's broadcast partners. Tom Fox explains that what a company such as Gatorade receives when sponsoring through NBA Properties is the right to collectively use all 29 NBA team logos, and the right to game footage, provided it is not focused on an individual player and promotional spots are national.

The NBA's global sponsors include Coca-Cola, IBM, McDonald's, and the Miller Brewing Company. NBC's NBA advertisers include Chrysler, Coca-Cola, General Motors, Honda, McDonald's, Prudential Insurance, and Toyota (Stroud, 1998). McDonald's is also the sponsor of the McDonald's Open basketball tournament, an annual international tournament in Europe in which one NBA team competes against teams from around the world. The McDonald's Open has been broadcast on NBC, but more recently on TNT, and it usually takes place right before the beginning of the NBA season.

The NBA experienced an approximately 20% increase in its United States merchandise sales from 1993 to 1997. The 1998 figure for NBA sales dropped approximately 38%, largely due to the NBA lockout; however, between 1994 and 1998, the NBA ranked second in total United States merchandise retail sales by a sports league, trailing only the NFL (see Table 3.11).

The success of NBA Properties and the volume of NBA retail sales led to the opening of the NBA Store on Fifth Avenue in New York City. According to The Sporting Goods Manufacturers Association, 80% of the survey sample believe a product featuring a NBA logo has a higher perceived value than one without it, and 98% are willing to pay more for a product with a brand identification. On August 27, 1999, the NBA opened its first restaurant, NBA City in Orlando, Florida, through a joint venture with the Hard Rock Cafe. The restaurant features NBA video archives, a NBA playground, a NBA City Club, an upscale lounge where fans can watch NBA games live or select a classic NBA game, and a NBA City Shop that offers merchandise previously only available at the NBA Store in New York. The Orlando restaurant is the first of at least 10 worldwide locations to be created by the NBA and the Hard Rock Cafe over the next few years.

Table 3.11. U. S. Sports Licensed Products Retail Sales: Major Sports Leagues/Collegiate (sales in billions).

	1992	1993	1994	1995	1996	1997	1998	94-98 Total
MLB	2.4	2.5	2.1	1.5	1.8	1.9	2.2	95.0
NBA	1.4	2.1	2.5	2.6	2.6	2.6	1.6	119.0
NFL	2.0	2.6	3.0	3.2	3.3	3.6	3.6	166.5
NHL	.6	.8	1.0	1.0	1.0	1.2	1.2	54.0
Coll.	1.8	1.9	2.0	2.1	2.1	2.0	2.0	102.0
Total	8.2	10.0	10.6	10.4	10.8	11.3	10.6	536.5

(Source: Sporting Goods Manufacturers Association [SGMA]).

Source Note. The Sporting Goods Manufacturers Association is the trade association of North American manufacturers, producers, and distributors of sports apparel, athletic footwear, and fitness and sporting goods equipment. The American Sports Data's Superstudy of sports participation monitors 103 sports and fitness activities. Data for the 1999 report are based on a nationally representative sample of 14,891 adults and children aged six and older (see SGMA, www.sportlink.com).

There are also survey data that provide trends on the behavior of NBA fans with regard to watching NBA games. The significance of this data is that the percentage of people who plan to watch NBA games on television has consistently increased. This increase is an indication of audience uses and gratifications in which the NBA fans are planning to watch, to use the media to satisfy their needs (see Table 3.12).

The data reveal that in 1998 over half (55.8%) of the United States population were fans of the NBA. These NBA fans also watched an average of two games per week (1.96 games). Sponsors were receiving continuous exposure and being seen consistently. The 88.9% who watched a NBA game within the last year also gave sponsors a high level of product exposure, even if the fans only watched one game.

The NBA has not only become a more successful league and a more successful business, the game of basketball has also grown with people playing the game more often. Between 1987 and 1999, the number of people who play basketball, the number of days they play each year, and those who view basketball as their favorite sport increased by over 10% for the 12-year period (see Table 3.13).

In 1999, basketball ranked as the most popular participation team sport in the United States (see Table 3.14).

Table 3.12. Trends of NBA Fans.

Percent of U.S. Population who:	1995	1996	1997	1998
are NBA Fans	57.1%	60.8%	58.9%	55.8%
are avid NBA Fans	19.0%	21.0%	20.0%	18.6%
chose the NBA as their favorite spectator sport	10.8%	11.1%	12.3%	11.7%
Of NBA Fans	1995	1996	1997	1998
Mean games watched in past week	2.21	1.90	1.77	1.96
Percent who watched a NBA game on TV within a year	88.6%	84.7%	89.5%	88.9%
Percent who plan to watch NBA games on TV	52.9%	53.2%	56.1%	58.0%

(Source: ESPN Chilton Sports Poll)

Source Note. The ESPN Poll provides intelligence to the sports industry with clients including major leagues, sponsorship companies, sporting goods manufacturers, and the media.

Table 3.13. Basketball Participation in the United States (participation in millions).

	1987	1990	1996	1997	1998	1999	Change 87-99
Players age 6+	35.7	39.8	45.6	45.1	42.4	39.4	+10%
Play 52 or more times	6.5	7.7	10.0	10.5	9.7	8.8	+35%
Basketball—favorite sport	6.5	6.8	10.0	9.1	11.2	9.6	+48%
First time players	6.4	6.5	6.6	6.6	6.6	6.0	-6%
Avg. days played	36	38	42	44	40	42	+17%

(Source: SGMA/American Sports Data, Inc.)

Table 3.14. Most Popular Participation Sports in the United States.

Sport	# of Participants (millions)
1. Basketball	39.4
2. Volleyball	24.2
3. Softball	19.8
4. Football	18.7
5. Soccer	17.6
6. Baseball	12.1
7. Cheerleading	3.0
8. Ice Hockey	2.4
9. Field Hockey	1.0
10. Lacrosse	0.8

Note. U. S. population: six years or older; participated at least once in 1999.
(Source: SGMA).

The overall increase in basketball participation between 1987 and 1999 occurred for both males and females, with 50% of the surveyed boys and 41% of the girls ages 12 to 17, and 45% of the boys and 26% of the girls between the ages of 6 and 11, participating in basketball in 1999 (see Table 3.15).

Table 3.15. Basketball Participation by Gender.

	1987	1990	1997	1998	1999	Change 87-99	Avg. Days 87/99
Males	24.7	27.2	31.4	29.5	26.7	+8%	39/46
Females	11.0	12.6	13.7	12.9	12.7	+15%	28/33
Total	35.7	39.8	45.1	42.4	39.4	+10%	36/42

Note. Participation in millions; six years and older.
(Source: SGMA/American Sports Data, Inc.)

The overall increase in the critical economic audience behavior measures of television ratings, game attendance, and purchasing of NBA-licensed merchandise represents an acceptance of the NBA. It would, however, be short-sighted to believe that all this success is simply the result of NBA games being exposed to the audience at a better location in the television program schedule. This would ignore the potential effects that could be produced through proper portrayal-framing strategies (Level Two of agenda-setting).

4

THE NBA PORTRAYAL STRATEGY

Once the proper exposure framing methods in terms of placement in the program schedule and content selection have been determined, the network has to make the content the most attractive to viewers and demonstrate the quality of the product of NBA basketball. Portrayal framing methods had to be implemented in conjunction with exposure broadcast strategies to give the NBA its best opportunity to attract and engage an audience and advertisers. An explanation of the portrayal broadcast strategies is important because the NBA had a poor perception and placing a product with a poor perception in a different location does not alone create a positive change. Several portrayal methods have been implemented, both network and NBA originated, to enhance the NBA and portray it as a marquee sports league.

PERCEPTION OF THE NBA AND THE EDUCATION STRATEGY

The concerns regarding exposure were not the only reasons for the NBA's initial lack of success. The NBA was suffering from several negative perceptions throughout the late 1970s and early 1980s. The negative perceptions of the NBA included players not giving any effort and rampant drug use within the league (the negative perceptions of the NBA were reiterated in several interviews, most notably in discussions with Bob Ryan, Mike Burks, and Ted Shaker). Another perception of the NBA was that the league featured too many African-American players. These perceptions created disinterest in the NBA as evidenced by the low attendance and low television ratings. Regarding the racial perception, the reality is that there are more African-Americans playing the majority of minutes today (based on the top five players from each team in terms of minutes played for the entire season) and there are more African-American head coaches today than when this negative perception first existed (see Table 4.1).

The fact that there are more African-Americans playing the majority of minutes and more head coaches demonstrates a larger overall African-American presence in the NBA. However, the increases in fan attendance, television ratings, and merchandising sales indicate that race is not a problematic issue. The negative racial perception as a means of explanation for the failure of the NBA was not based on the entertainment that the NBA can provide viewers, but was more an indictment of the league's inability to properly communicate the quality characteristics of the NBA to its audience.

There were also negative perceptions of the NBA brand of basketball. These criticisms were that the game was not competitive until the final two minutes and that it lacked any strategy—it was a bunch of players just freelancing and throwing up shots without any passing or other team concepts. Bob Ryan, a NBA columnist for the *Boston Globe* who has been covering the NBA since the 1969-70 season, called the perception of NBA games not being decided until the last two minutes one of the greatest myths as any NBA game could be decided at any point. In summarizing the problem Ryan simply comments, "the game was poorly and improperly framed" (personal communication, December 2, 1998). It was these perceptions that in essence created an exposure problem for the NBA. Ted Shaker describes the situation:

> I remember going in my first year to the All-Star Game in Los Angeles [1983] and at that time it was just the All-Star Game on Sunday and the players didn't want to do it—it was all negative and so one of the things I asked them to do is if I could talk to coaches and let them know what we're going to try to do and to see if we could get into some places we hadn't been before. Because it was the mid-point of the season all the coaches would go and they would have the coaches' association meeting. I remember going to that and being introduced in that and just getting tattooed. The coaches thought that what was being put on the air was such crap. You guys don't show the strategy, you don't show the game. (personal communication, October 9, 1998)

Table 4.1. NBA Racial Profile; 1979-80, 1989-90, and 1999-2000.

		1979-80	1989-90	1999-2000
	# of Teams	22	27	29
# of Players[a]	Black	84	108	126
	White	26	27	19
	% Black	76	80	87
# of Head Coaches[b]	Black	2	6	8
	White	24	24	27
	% Black	8	20	23

[a]Based on the top five players from each team in terms of minutes played for the entire season.
[b]Includes head coaches hired during the season.

The plan of the NBA was to utilize television as a key resource in changing the perception of the league and creating a new message; and this new message of what NBA basketball could provide as entertainment would then be the agenda that would hopefully be transferred to the public. Exposure was only one key element. In addition to proper positioning in the program schedule and showing the right content in the form of the best teams, the third key component was to better produce and frame the games and the league. The objective was to create and implement new strategies that would enhance the league and demonstrate to the audience the best of what NBA basketball had to offer to a potential viewer. The challenge for the league and its broadcast partner, CBS, was to take what they all knew to be a good game with a horrendous public perception and change the image by educating the viewers. Commissioner Stern comments that "the number one strategy was put out the fires, determine what the product was, and then to grow it by focusing on the players, their talents on the court, their talents off the court, their sense of personality" (personal communication, April 14, 1999).

Mike Burks was the Coordinating Producer and the Lead Game Producer for the NBA Finals on CBS from 1980 until 1990. As Coordinating Producer, Burks was the main daily interface with the NBA and was responsible for ensuring that each CBS broadcast, particularly the playoffs when there are a variety of broadcast crews, had the same tools in terms of graphics, music, and animation. Burks is also a Game Producer for the NBA on TNT. He describes the role of Game Producer as an orchestra leader with a talented group of musicians—the producer simply waves the wand. Burks describes the challenge to CBS during the early 1980s as "how do we make a viewing audience understand the game, care about the people, and want to watch. The broadcast was customized to change the perceptions of the American public. It was customized to entertain and educate, to teach while entertaining" (personal communication, December 1, 1998).

One of the key points of education that Burks stresses is that people did not know about the professional game and its differences from the college game. Bob Ryan says that at the time, the NBA had allowed people to think the NCAA was better without overly challenging this notion. Ryan believes that if any of 50 to 100 NBA games were chosen, no matter which teams were playing, and placed into a college atmosphere such as Phog Allan Field House at the University of Kansas or Cameron Indoor Stadium at Duke University, with the proximity to the court and the bands, people would say it was the greatest game they had ever seen because the quality and skill level of the play would be that much better. Ryan (1985), in a column in the *Boston Globe*, wrote about "the fact that the sporting public does not have the proper appreciation for the magnificent spectacle that is the National Basketball Association" (p. 63). Ryan commented:

> From time to time during the winter, someone connected with college basketball will in the course of comparing his game with professionals rather cavalierly make reference to the supposed "fact" that the collegians routinely play harder than the players do in the NBA. When that someone is a layman, I will merely laugh. When that someone is a coach, I have the urge to vomit. There are many nice things that can be said about college basketball, but I have watched too much NBA basketball not to recognize (1) the sizable difference in talent between the collegians and the professionals, and (2) the astonishing effort often put forth by the latter. (1985, p. 63)

In the same article Ryan claimed, "someday I'm going to figure out why the NBA has become the most unfairly maligned social institution in America" (p. 63).

Even in Boston, where the Celtics had already won 11 NBA championships prior to 1970, Ryan still felt the public needed to be educated about NBA basketball. The Celtics were part of the New England culture, but they were still second to the NHL's Bruins in terms of popularity. The public was mainly there for the playoffs, with only a few die-hards attending the games in January.

In terms of educating the public about the NBA, Mike Burks claims it is important to take advantage of the people with whom you are working: overall there is a great combination of talent with announcers who have knowledge of the game and television personnel who have the skill to translate visually this basketball knowledge. The people with expert knowledge of NBA basketball are the former coaches and players who perform the analyst role for NBA games. Providing strategic details to the basketball game is one of the major functions of the analyst during a NBA broadcast.

Hubie Brown coached in the NBA for 10 seasons with the Atlanta Hawks and the New York Knicks, winning Coach of the Year honors with the Hawks for the 1977-78 season. Brown also coached the Kentucky Colonels to the ABA Championship in 1975. Brown is the top NBA analyst for Turner Sports, a position he also held at CBS when that network lost the NBA broadcast contract. Brown claims the NBA used to be presented as "ten guys who just met at one o'clock and are now playing at 1:30" (personal communication, January 27, 1999). He sees the analyst as the teacher who must "explain the nuances that make professional basketball different than junior high, high school, or the college game" (personal communication, January 27, 1999). He claims that the untrained eye is only watching four people during a NBA game, and the true test of an outstanding coach is to see all 10 players. Brown states, "you cannot expect a fan to see all 10, so you teach the fan about the continuity of action away from the ball—that is what professional basketball is all about" (personal communication, January 27, 1999).

Brown claims the NBA is now being showcased to explain the differences of the NBA game, and the game is being presented for what it is: "a game that is played one foot above the rim with players who have size, as guards are now 6' 8" and centers 7' 2", speed, body fat of under ten percent, and can be described as 'acrobats in ballet'" (personal communication, January 27, 1999). He also describes himself as being pro-coach and he considers it an "incredible insult to people who coach if you say they [the coaches] just roll the ball out" (personal communication, January 27, 1999). Brown claims that he is attempting to advance the education of the game by explaining to the viewer that the NBA game is one of negotiating space, timing, and continuity in trying to score within the parameters of a 24-second shot clock. One of the challenges that Brown cites for the NBA analyst is the small amount of time allowed to explain the action in comparison to a NFL analyst, who has 30 seconds between each play. Brown states, "I have five to eight seconds when the basket is made to when the ball is over half court to tell the viewer why and how" (personal communication, January 27, 1999).

John Andariese, analyst for the New York Knicks on the Madison Square Garden Network, describes his role as trying to explain to the viewer why certain events are transpiring on the court. Andariese explains:

I think the job of the analyst is to help the viewer or the listener see things that are in front of him [or her], but because of their level of sophistication they're not seeing it for their enjoyment. You want people to enjoy the parts of the game that make the athletes so special when they display their various skills and that's my challenge game in and game out and that's expressed in defensive matchups. Why does one player have trouble offensively against another player who might be perceived as a lesser impact player than perhaps a better known player? Logic doesn't prevail in sports in matchups. There are reasons for that and they are not available to the naked eye a lot, you can't see it, you've got to talk to experts, you've got to feel out why, why is the question all the time. Why do teams seem to win consistently when they don't seem to have the skill level of another team when you look at their reputations and backgrounds? So I think the job of the analyst is to have a constant thirst for the whys. What I'm always trying to think of is the answer to the whys of everybody. (personal communication, August 3, 1998)

Kelly Tripucka played in the NBA for 10 seasons with the Detroit Pistons, Utah Jazz, and Charlotte Hornets, was selected to two All-Star games, and finished third in scoring in the 1982-83 season, averaging 26.5 points per game. Tripucka is also an analyst for the Pistons, announcing on WKBD in Detroit. As a former player, Tripucka still does not consider himself a member of the media, but describes his objectives when announcing as an analyst:

I want to relate my experiences, that is the number one thing. I was a player, I know this game, I've been in the locker room, I know what goes on, I've been there in the huddle listening to coaches, I've been there for the last 10 seconds of the game with the game on the line, I've been to the foul line with a chance to win it, I've been there when you missed a shot and you lost a game. So that is all there to translate to the person sitting in his chair and if I am that person sitting in that chair, if I had not played, that would be the most believable guy from my perspective to want to listen to, to really pay attention to what goes on. He [or she] has a certain trust and I try to lend that trust to the viewer, I think that is my responsibility so he [or she] can sit there and say, you know what I believe him because he has been there, he knows what it is like. (personal communication, December 4, 1998)

One of the essential personalities involved in the education of the NBA public as an analyst was Tommy Heinsohn, who was the top analyst during the early transformation of the NBA on CBS. Heinsohn is an analyst for the Celtics on WSBK in Boston and SportsChannel New England. Heinsohn was a player on eight, and head coach for two, of the Boston Celtics' 16 NBA Championships. Heinsohn was also the rookie of the year in 1957, selected to six All-Star games, and elected to the Hall of Fame in 1985. Before an education of the public about the NBA could occur, there had to be an education of the television personnel involved in the broadcast about the game of basketball.

Mike Burks emphasizes a willingness and an eagerness on the part of the personnel at CBS to learn about the NBA game of basketball and then figure out how to best translate it visually. Their education included a huge amount of time watching game film and going over mock game plans. In addition to his notable status as a player and a coach, it was Heinsohn who performed the role of educator for the CBS staff. Shaker describes the television-related qualities of Heinsohn that appealed to CBS:

> Tommy kind of had the every man quality that was attractive. He also was a coach and as a coach Tommy was far more interested in getting into the strategy of the game to show that there really is a plan here and this is a really complex game that takes a lot of athletic skill, but also you have to be really bright to excel and these are the best players in the world. So we played up the best athletes in the world, the incredible complexity of the game, the physicalness of the game. Heinsohn was so much a critical part of bringing back the NBA, I think, because he was willing to take the chalkboard play and to diagram it and you hear it now all the time, his phrases like the go-to-guy, my go-to-guy, that was Tommy Heinsohn who started that and now it is everywhere, everybody in every sport has got a go-to-guy. It was Tommy Heinsohn on the NBA on CBS where that began. So I would say that Tommy was critical. (personal communication, October 9, 1998)

Brian McIntyre agrees with Shaker's assessment of Heinsohn stating that,

> Tommy Heinsohn doesn't get the credit I think he deserves in terms of educating their broadcasters to knowing what is important, what to look for. He taught them [their cameramen] to anticipate, when the Bulls are coming down they are going to

play like this, or when the Celtics come down . . . here is what is
going to happen. His role has been very underappreciated. (personal communication, December 16, 1998)

Heinsohn explains that basketball coverage had a very pre-
determined formula in which a player would score and then there
would be a camera cut to a "hero shot," a closeup of the player who
scored, and the viewer would be missing action while the other
team brought up the ball—whether it was the defensive team
putting on a full court press or the offensive team taking the ball
out of the basket to start a fast break. This was a critical education
point because at the time the two prominent teams, the Boston
Celtics and the Los Angeles Lakers, employed a fast break style of
play: If the rebound was secured or if the other team scored, these
teams would quickly outlet the basketball and attack the defense.
Heinsohn stressed a break from this formula by pointing out to
CBS personnel what to look for and then utilizing his own knowledge and ability to describe and enhance the action. According to
Heinsohn, the role of an analyst is to explain why a certain situation is occurring, to explain the strategy of the game in a way that
will compel the audience, and to get people to understand how great
the skills of the athletes are.

Heinsohn compares watching a NBA game to that of watching a magician, explaining that whereas the magician shows you one
hand similar to the way the viewers see the ball, the analyst should
"let the audience peer into the other hand, to explain what the magician is doing in the hand you aren't watching" (personal communication, November 10, 1998). This type of analysis includes what is happening away from the basketball to help develop the concept of the
NBA as a team game and, more importantly, dispel the perception of
the NBA as just a one-on-one game.

In addition to the explanation provided by the analyst, the
video content must also help educate the viewer. One of the major
framing methods for describing the NBA as a team game and the complex strategy that is being displayed on the court is the use of replays.
Heinsohn was again instrumental in the early education of the proper
replays to utilize. He emphasized that there cannot be a coach's film
approach to broadcasting a game. One of the early ideas of how to utilize replays was to take each replay five seconds back from the moment
of interest to demonstrate how that play developed, with the analysis
coming from Heinsohn explaining what was occurring on the court.
Hubie Brown comments that when analyzing a replay he never simply
offers an explanation of what happened, but why and how a certain

play occurred, often guiding viewers to look to the left or right of the screen and to pay attention to the action away from the basketball.

Tommy Roy, co-Executive Producer of the NBA on NBC, emphasizes that one of the major objectives, or framing methods, of NBC's broadcasting of the NBA is to demonstrate it as a team game. Roy says that it is preferable to show a replay that demonstrates the team concepts, "pass, pass, dunk is more preferable [as a replay] than a dunk only" (personal communication, October 21, 1998). According to Roy, in terms of replays, the placement of cameras at a NBA game provides an advantageous characteristic that is inherent in the broadcasting of the NBA as opposed to any other sport. In covering basketball, the court is more accessible as cameras can be placed only feet away from the playing area, while they are further away in football, hockey, or baseball.

The league reinforces the importance of the positioning of cameras. Before a team is granted permission to move into a new basketball arena to play its home games it must meet the facilities requirements that are provided by the NBA. There are a series of items that must be approved by the league. The facilities requirement is designed to make the entire NBA arena experience more enjoyable for all fans. The facilities requirement also has stipulations regarding camera placements and where the media will sit for the game. McIntyre explains the rationale of the NBA stating,

> we have sacrificed seats in arenas to put cameras because we realize that 99% of the people who are watching the game are watching it through television. They either don't live close to a city, can't get access to a ticket, that is every sport—only way they have access to it, so it is imperative. We have done a lot of things in working with our broadcasters and our arenas to get better positions and more cameras to cover it. (personal communication, December 16, 1998)

The proximity of the cameras allows better replays in terms of game strategy, which has been identified as a critical objective of a broadcast. The proximity also allows the emotion of the game to be identified. In the NBA you can see the players' faces, there are no helmets as in football or hockey—even in baseball players wear a cap or batting helmet. Brian McIntyre believes that seeing the players' faces and emotion is key, and even other sports are trying to follow the model of the NBA. The NFL now encourages its players, when they get to the sideline, to take off their helmet and put on a team cap so their faces can be seen. This concept is helpful for advertising as the audience sees

a face they now recognize in a commercial. Moreover, because the player takes off a helmet, the NFL now has a way to market new caps.

The chief instrument for portrayal of the NBA on television is
obviously the camera. In not overstating the obvious, the visual component is what creates the dependency on television from both an organizational and an individual perspective. If the visuals did not matter,
radio could be the major economic and exposure source. The overall
objective of the portrayal framing methods of the NBA is to visually
enhance the game and the broadcast. What the viewer actually sees is
going to be the single greatest determining factor in the presentation.

In addition to game action, tight face shots and reaction shots
are an objective of many camera operators. According to Tommy Roy,
the objective of the camera positioning is to obtain the type of shots
that capture the strategy and emotion involved in a NBA Finals
matchup. For a NBA Finals telecast, NBC utilizes 18 cameras (see
Figure 4.1 and Table 4.2).

The first camera is designed to follow the live game action.
This camera is located at mid-court and maintains a wide enough
angle to allow all 10 players to be seen. Even with all the exposure

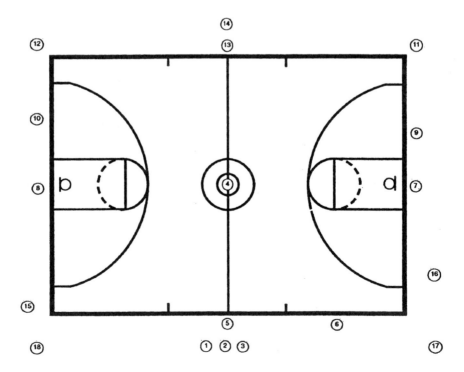

Figure 4.1. NBC camera placement for the NBA finals

Table 4.2. Camera Objectives for the NBA Finals on NBC.

1. Play-by-play: Follows game action live
2. Isolation on Player #1
3. Isolation on Player #2
4. Overhead
5. Super slow-motion: Follows tight action
6. Super Slow-motion: Follows tight action
7. Mini action: Baseline cameras
8. Mini action: Baseline cameras
9. Behind backboard glass: Follows action only (slam cam)
10. Behind backboard glass: Follows action only (slam cam)
11. Bench, reactions
12. Bench, reactions
13. Coaches
14. Reverse angle
15. Tunnel: Fixed camera getting shots of teams walking on and off the court
16. Tunnel: Fixed camera getting shots of teams walking on and off the court
17. Fast breaks: High angle
18. Helicopter: Scene set

and portrayal framing methods designed to enhance the broadcast, the game and its outcome is the prime event that the audience is tuning in to see. While the actual game is being played, the majority of what the viewer sees comes from only one of the 18 cameras, the mid-court camera. All the other cameras are utilized for cut-away shots during breaks in the action or replays. Cut-away shots normally occur when there is a dead ball situation—after a foul, or when the ball is out of bounds. Cut-away shots include close-up shots of players or coaches.

Isolations on key players who are involved in the game help visually enhance storylines. These cameras profile every movement of the players whom the audience most wants to see. For example, during the telecast of the Chicago Bulls NBA Finals games, these two isolation cameras might have been on Michael Jordan and Scottie Pippen, respectively. The overhead camera is designed to provide replays. This camera angle might be employed when an announcer uses a telestrator to explain a play. It might also be utilized for the opening jump ball.

The two super-slow motion cameras follow the game action, but the camera is in tighter focus on the ball than the mid-court play-by-play camera. The two mini-action baseline cameras are designed to cover action on the low post. This is where the game of basketball is the most physical as centers and power forwards are constantly battling for position. The two cameras behind each backboard are used for replays of a slam dunk or a rebound when players elevate above the rim. Bench cameras are designed to depict reactions of players on the bench. This camera might also focus on a key player who is not in the game. A camera on the head coach is designed to feature one of the stars of the game. Storylines can involve a coach as much as any player on the court, as when a head coach competes against his former team.

The reverse angle camera is designed for replays of the action that occur on the side of the court that is the furthest from the main play-by-play camera. The tunnel cameras are mounted on a wall near both teams' locker rooms and are used to get the reactions of players as they walk to and from the basketball court. The high-angle-fast break camera offers a visual angle to help explain the strategy because the team concepts of passing and the full court aspects of the game can be demonstrated. This camera might also be utilized with an announcer explanation and a telestrator. The helicopter camera is outside the arena and functions as the scene set. The camera shows the arena and the surrounding city and is used before the game or when coming back from commercial to transition to the broadcast.

The challenge of producing and directing a NBA game, or any other sports events, is the coordination between all camera operators and having them understand their objective and the types of shots they are trying to obtain. The producer and the director have to understand which camera is capable of obtaining their desired shot, and they must have an ability to anticipate. Howie Singer explains that there needs to be communication between the production truck and the camera people. He offers an example: "If Ewing [former New York Knicks center Patrick Ewing] and Olajuwon [Houston Rockets center Hakeem Olajuwon] are doing a lot of banging I'll tell him [or her, camera operator] let's iso [isolate] on Ewing and Olajuwon for awhile and try to get good replays that way" (personal communication, August 26, 1998).

Singer also describes the objective of reaction shots: To show the emotion and intensity of the players which adds to the broadcast. He states:

You live for that stuff [reaction shots]. I do that with Starks [former New York Knicks guard John Starks]. Starks is on the bench, he gets fired up. There are times when I've isod [isolated] on him and he gets so into it if the Knicks get on a run. If the Knicks are down, let's say they are down eight, and they just got six points in a row. The other team misses and the Knicks have the ball. I'll send a camera right to Starks because I know he's going to blow up. I know if the Knicks score the other team is going to call timeout and he's going to run out and chest bump people and we get that a lot. (personal communication, August 26, 1998)

This example demonstrates the importance of the ability to anticipate and the knowledge of the producer of the sport and the personnel involved in the broadcast and what they can contribute from strictly an enhancement and television entertainment perspective.

PORTRAYAL: PERSONALIZING PLAYERS

Whether strategic or emotional replays, these shots are critical in developing two key framing methods for covering the NBA: personalizing the players and developing a storyline for the game. In addition to showing the NBA as a team game, Tommy Roy states that a second major strategic objective, or framing method, of NBC's coverage of the NBA is to personalize or humanize the players. Kevin Smollon is a NBC Game Producer for NBA broadcasts and is responsible for the content of the show, including developing "interesting stories about the players' childhood, or anything we could bring out to personalize the player." The objective is to "create a persona rather than a number. You create an interest of why you [the viewer] should be interested in this guy [the player]" (personal communication, September 23, 1998).

Mike Breen is a play-by-play announcer for NBC and for the Knicks on the MSG Network. In terms of personalizing players, Breen believes it is important to tell viewers a little something about the players and not just provide basketball stories, but off-the-court stories that humanize the players and show things the average fan is not aware of. Breen claims that this humanizing approach can enhance the league and the image of the players. Breen, however, cautions that there is a time in the game for personalizing players, but also other moments in which the outcome of the game has got to be the major focus of the broadcast. Breen believes that personalizing players should be done early in the game:

I think as the game takes and you have a good game going that
stuff goes out the window, you just focus on the game. That is
what people want to know, they don't want to hear about [a player's] charity work with two minutes left to go in the fourth quarter. They just want to hear, he is going to the free throw line,
what is he shooting from the line this season in clutch situations.
(personal communication, November 4, 1998)

Ricky Diamond is the Coordinating Producer of the NBA on
NBC studio shows, including the pregame program, *NBA Showtime.*
He explains that the need to personalize the players is to "make you
as a viewer somewhat invested in the players, in the success or lack
of success in the players. To create interesting stories, to tell interesting stories" (personal communication, October 21, 1998). The personalizing of a player can be from an on-the-court performance standpoint, but often the attempts to personalize a player involve their off-
the-court lives in order to influence the viewers to root for a player.
Diamond states:

Sometimes the reality behind a story is that a guy sort of
deserves the wrath of the fans or of the viewers or the people
watching the game and sometimes they are heroes. And you
want, however the portrayal is, to give people some sort of a rooting interest, some reason to latch on to this. I think when you see
a story of an athlete that comes to the arena and they have a
heavy heart and their mom is dying of cancer and they are playing, that is one example of the sort of thing we are talking about.
We want to deal with sometimes the real-life things that are
going on off the court. And sometimes it's simply a guy is having
a terrible year and here in the playoffs is his redemption. Just
the human dramas that are unfolding that we think we can capture the best. (personal communication, October 21, 1998)

The NBA as an agenda-setter itself is very aware of the value
of trying to personalize their players and how television can capitalize on this aspect. Brian McIntyre explains that it is great for fans to
know NBA players as tremendous athletes and the personalizing of
players is an objective of the NBA Communications Department. He
feels that the personalizing of NBA players is, however, better
achieved through the work of the league's broadcast partners.
McIntyre states that personalizing players is "what we try to do,
what our network partners have more time to do, is to take the person off the court and show the other side, show the human side. If

you can humanize anybody, you have gone a long way toward acceptance. You can marvel at those exploits [on the court], but just like anyone there is more than what you see physically" (personal communication, December 16, 1998).

Ed Desser comments that the personalizing efforts of the NBA and its broadcast partners are enhanced in combination with initiatives of camera placement. "Personalizing the players is taking advantage of the intimacy of the game. Unlike any of the other major sports, these guys are running around wearing very little. You see their facial expressions, you're seeing them sweat, it's a much more kind of in your face intimate program. Maybe not from the regular play-by-play angle, but the tight shots are widely used and an important part of the game" (personal communication, August 26, 1998).

Chris Brienza, former NBA Director of Sports Media Relations, also points out that personalizing players is a major objective in helping the fans' perception of the NBA players, particularly as they often only have knowledge of the players' very high salaries. Brienza states:

> These are human beings and I think people should understand that. They shouldn't look at them as nameless faces with dollar signs next to them. I think it is incredibly unfair. I think people should know that these are real human beings who are in many instances not unlike us. There are a lot of similarities except in the fact that they are exceptionally good at playing basketball. They are real people and unfortunately, for a variety of reasons, I don't think very often they are portrayed that way. (personal communication, August 12, 1998)

Personalizing the players was a philosophy for the NBA on CBS. The NBA tried to create not only sport stars, but in many aspects, television stars. Burks states that, in terms of recognizing players, the game has always been star driven. He comments that "great stars get people to see movies, great stars get people to see games" (personal communication, December 1, 1998). Burks believes there is more loyalty toward individual players than toward teams in sports today. By creating stars the audience almost has a reason to watch the game regardless of how the competing teams may be performing that season. For example, Tommy Roy says that people will watch the NBA superstars such as Patrick Ewing because people will want to watch Ewing play even if the Seattle SuperSonics are not playing well. Mike Pearl describes the NBA as entertainment, adding that "players are entertainers and our job is to translate and show them as great athletes" (personal communication, February 25, 1999).

In creating stars, NBC is actually paying broadcast fees for the rights to broadcast Michael Jordan, Shaquille O' Neal, or any other NBA star as much as they are paying to broadcast the game of basketball. NBC is the network of not only Jerry Seinfeld and Kelsey Grammar, but also Michael Jordan. The rights fees are not different than the network buying a situation comedy or drama series because the show has a known star in the series. For example, NBC chooses to air *Just Shoot Me* because the show features David Spade, a person that is recognizable to the audience and who has already had comedy success with *Saturday Night Live*. For much of NBC's television contract they have had the luxury of broadcasting Michael Jordan and the Chicago Bulls. Former Bulls coach Phil Jackson commented, "the Bulls have personalities and right now, televised NBA games are about that. We've become sitcom personalities" (cited in D'Alessandro, June 12, 1998).

Broadcasting NBA stars as television stars is another unique characteristic inherent in the NBA. In basketball the stars that people came to the arena to see, or turned on the television to watch, are playing for the majority of the game. There is no difference if the team is on offense or defense, the player remains on the court. The camera is able to see all 10 players almost all of the time. In a 48-minute NBA game, most stars will play over 40 minutes, providing the game is competitive. In the 1997 and 1998 Finals, the four major stars playing, Michael Jordan and Scottie Pippen for the Bulls and Karl Malone and John Stockton for the Jazz, were all on the court for the majority of the action (see Table 4.3).

The fans who were tuning into the NBA Finals to see Michael Jordan perform were able to do just that. Other than tennis, boxing, or golf, where a television network can follow a star such as Tiger Woods for the entire tournament, or at the end of a tournament focus on the leaders, few sports have the advantage that the NBA possesses. The amount of playing time is an advantage in contrast to football, in which the stars are only on the field when their team is on offense or defense. In Super Bowl XXXIII between the Denver Broncos and the Atlanta Falcons, the two biggest stars of the game were Bronco's future Hall-of-Fame Quarterback John Elway and the NFL's Most Valuable Player for the 1998 season Terrell Davis, who became only the fourth running back in the history of the NFL to rush for over 2,000 yards in one season. With the offensive and defensive specialization of football, in the Broncos 34 to 19 win over the Falcons, both of those stars could only be on the field for the maximum of 31 minutes and 23 seconds that the Broncos were on offense in the 60-minute game.

Table 4.3. NBA Finals Minutes Played.

1998								
	Game	1	2	3	4	5	6	AVG.
Bulls	Jordan	46	40	32	43	45	44	41.7
	Pippen	44	41	35	46	45	26	39.5
Jazz	Malone	43	39	31	43	44	43	40.5
	Stockton	35	31	26	31	38	33	32.3
1997								
	Game	1	2	3	4	5	6	AVG.
Bulls	Jordan	41	45	40	42	44	44	42.7
	Pippen	43	39	24	47	45	43	40.2
Jazz	Malone	41	41	42	43	34	44	40.8
	Stockton	38	39	37	38	36	37	37.5

Note. In 1998, the average would have probably increased had game three had a closer score—the Bulls won by 42 points, 96-54. The Bulls had established a 49-31 lead at the half, and the lead expanded to 27 points, 72-45, by the end of the third quarter.

(Source: NBA)

Baseball is also a game that, because of its structure, cannot feature its stars constantly. Even when watching a pitcher, that player is only on the field for about half the game. When a viewer is anxious to see a hitting star such as Mark McGwire, that player only bats four or five times a game. That could translate to once every 40 or 45 minutes when the viewer is actually seeing the major attraction that might have caused her or him to tune into the game in the first place. In the 1998 World Series between the New York Yankees and the San Diego Padres, one of the feature players was Padre hitting star Tony Gwynn. Among Gwynn's accomplishments are 3,000 hits, 15 All-Star Games, and a record-tying eight National League batting titles (tied with Honus Wagner). He will probably be a first ballot Hall-of-Famer. It was only Gwynn's second World Series in his career and his first since the 1984 season (a series the Padres lost four games to one to the Detroit Tigers). However, if fans wanted to see Gwynn perform on the game's grandest stage, they only saw him for 16 of the 283 official at bats (which do not record walks, sacrifice bunts, or run scoring fly balls) during the Yankees' four-game sweep of San Diego (Gwynn did have 8 hits in his 16 at bats in the 1998 World Series).

The NBA, in developing the star concept, also has a valuable tool in the popularity of NCAA college basketball. The NBA is receiving players through its draft with whom the audience is already very familiar. (This opportunity is diminishing with the increasing trend of collegiate players leaving school early and several players jumping from high school to the NBA.) Instead of looking at the NCAA as a form of competition for the basketball audience, David Stern saw this as a great opportunity to help further the NBA. With the college season ending early in April, there are still two months of NBA basketball remaining. The NCAA Tournament allows people to simply get excited about the game of basketball, just in time for the NBA playoffs. Shaker describes the feeling of CBS regarding the correlation between the broadcasting of NCAA and NBA basketball: The NBA was not going to compete with college basketball, but rather utilize the name recognition and status that several collegiate players were developing prior to joining the NBA. Shaker explains the situation:

> CBS also did the college tournament and a fair amount of college basketball and he [David Stern] never was this has got to be the NBA network and nobody [else]. He [Stern] saw the value of Patrick Ewing being on dozens of times as the center at Georgetown or Michael Jordan at North Carolina. Patrick Ewing came in as a bonafide, big-time player to the NBA and that was part of our experience in saying it was okay to play up the college guys, that's great. (personal communication, October 9, 1998)

Although CBS was not broadcasting many games, it often telecast the first professional game in the career of a potential new star, including Magic Johnson, Ralph Sampson, Hakeem Olajuwon, and Patrick Ewing.

Bob Ryan also attributes a large part of the NBA growth in popularity to the popularity of college basketball. Ryan claims that the role of ESPN and Dick Vitale as "valuable silent conspirators" who "created stars before they were drafted" cannot be underestimated (personal communication, December 2, 1998). Ryan credits Vitale's role for creating the stars almost by himself with his energy, enthusiasm, and knowledge while broadcasting college basketball, and his well-known sayings which describe athletes such as a PTP'er (prime time player) or Diaper Dandy (an outstanding freshman). Fans already knew that Tim Duncan and Vince Carter were going to be "scintillating and sensational" thanks to the efforts of Dick Vitale. Mike Burks also stresses that satellite technology and ESPN's *SportsCenter* are valuable in showing highlights of games to the entire country. He states, "players that were seen only as type [previously] now had a face" (personal communication, December 1, 1998).

NBA ACCESS TO PLAYERS AND COACHES

The major concepts of getting the NBA message across of this being a great and enjoyable game and personalizing players depends on providing media personnel access and information to the game's players and coaches. The media can then provide this information to the fans. The NBA rules for access to players and coaches are provided as a league-wide standard timing format. On game day locker rooms are open 90 minutes before and then closed 45 minutes prior to the start of a game. With most NBA games starting at a local time of 7:30 p.m., locker rooms are open from 6:00 to 6:45. The locker rooms reopen 10 minutes after the conclusion of the game. On off-days, teams also have to make the players and coaches available for 30 minutes. (These rules were reiterated in several interviews, most notably in discussions with Fred Kerber, Brian McIntyre, Chris Brienza, and John Mertz.)

Dave Checketts explains:

> You end up working very, very hard to get coverage. It is a crowded marketplace, not just in New York, but nationally. You strive to make your sport relevant. You want it to be number one in the hearts and minds of people from November to June and you do everything in your power to do that, that means giving them [the media] access, that means getting them into the locker room 45 minutes before the game for interviews, and certainly opening the locker room 15 minutes after the game for interviews, as well as you supply footage, you give the broadcasters talent tickets, you treat their families good, and you build a relationship then when anything happens with the franchise or with the team, you break your back to be available to them to comment on the latest signing, or the latest trade, or the latest controversy, or the latest disciplinary action, or why you fired the coach, or why you hired the coach, it goes on and on and on. It is one of the biggest things we do and we employ a whole staff of people to service these people. (personal communication, October 16, 1998)

It is the media members themselves who go into the locker room on a daily basis and who must also balance the interests of the fan and those of the players and coaches whom they cover. Wenner (1989) points out that the sports journalists who cover the game can influence its portrayal. The ethics of the sports journalist is also a factor. He states:

> The sports journalist is servant to many. Professional ethics call on the sports journalist to report the news accurately and fairly to the audience. At the same time, the sports journalist often reports for a media organization that may make stylistic or substantive demands on that reporting. And finally, the sports journalist must remain on good terms with sports organizations, their teams, players, coaches, and other personnel, for without access to these sources, there is no access to the "inside story" that is so valued by the mediated sports audience. (p. 38)

Bob Ryan says that in the universal utopian concept the obligation of the reporter is to serve the reader as the reporter has the ability to "gain access to circumstances the fan does not have," providing the audience with "information that is filtered through your perspective" (personal communication, December 2, 1998).

The difficulty for the NBA is in trying to provide a balance among the interests of its players and coaches, the media members, and the public who ultimately receives this information. Brian McIntyre describes the situation:

> What a lot of players and coaches forget, or conveniently forget, is that the media represent the fans. In an ideal perfect world, they are the eyes and the ears so if you are not talking to the media, you are not going to get the word out to your fans. There are some media who abuse that, some who have no idea what it means to them. But you have to, and this is where our role is, walk right down the middle. We work for the NBA and for our teams, therefore our players, at the same time we are trying to get the word out to the media so they can get it out to the fans. That is why it is very important for us to try to foster the relationships between the players and the media so the fans can get the ultimate word. (personal communication, December 16, 1998)

McIntyre explains that the league recognizes the timing difficulty of the access schedule, but also the importance of the interactions between the media and the NBA players. He states:

We have worked with our teams, our coaches, our broadcasters, and print reporters to try to come up with things that make sense for everybody. It [being an athlete] is the only job in the world where the employees after their shift have to come out and talk to people while they are changing their clothes. It is rather strange on the surface. Is it the best way? I am not so sure. You could protect an athlete or a coach by having a little longer period to cool off, also allow them a little dignity to be able to dress before reporters come in scrambling all over the place, but on the other hand we are trying to get emotion. You want the real emotion. (personal communication, December 16, 1998)

Kelly Tripucka describes the difficulty of playing a game for 48 minutes at an extremely high level of intensity that few occupations experience, then having to talk to the media and answer reporters' questions:

I know when I played, it is hard to get over a certain game quickly enough. You carry that with you and they are in there 10 minutes after the game and you might have just thrown the ball away or missed a shot, and you are just in knots and that is when they want to come in. You are already edgy, and then they got to stick the microphone or camera in [front of] you and that is when bad things [could occur]. You really got to do your homework as a player. I know they [the NBA] try to send people to teach the players, take a perspective, calm down, look, think before you talk because that only gets you in trouble. So it really takes some doing, not only learn to speak well in front of a camera and know what to say, but how to control your emotions in the heat of battle, because they are in there right after the game and that's when it's probably the most difficult to get a perspective, to make it seem like you are not angry, and sometimes that could be very difficult, particularly in a loss. Obviously you never really see a problem when you win, but that is part of the emotions of the game because of the fact that things happen so quickly. (personal communication, December 4, 1998)

Tripucka does, however, understand the value and the necessity of the media and the simple recognition of them having a job to do. Tripucka claims that he always tried to be very accessible to the media providing the reporter was fair. Regarding the media, Tripucka states, "they are covering what people don't get a chance to see. They are trying to get the inside scoop of what goes on during the day-to-day operation, not just during games, but what we are thinking before the game or after the game or during practice, what leads up to the game and what have you. So in that regard, I never had a problem if somebody wanted to talk to me" (personal communication, December 4, 1998).

Tripucka offers some insight as to where problems can begin to occur from a player's perspective:

> I think where the rift starts is when they [the media] throw their two cents in, their opinions and start making things personal and I think that is the big thing players don't like about the media. It is not so much talking to them. It is when you play this game, or a game all your life, and all of a sudden this guy who covers it, he thinks that he knows as much about the game as you do or the coach does and that is where oil and water don't mix. I had my share of problems, not many, but when guys give their opinion that you should hang it up or you should have done this or should have done that. They can cover the game, that is fine, cover the inside stuff, that is fine, obviously you are going to be criticized, but when it gets to take a personal sort of characteristic, then I think that is a little crossing the line and I think that is where all of your problems start. (personal communication, December 4, 1998)

Players might not always be interviewed after each game, but the head coach and his strategic decisions are always an angle for reporters when working a game. Chuck Daly describes his philosophy for dealing with the media, particularly after a game. It begins with the approach from day one that as a head coach he is not going to be adversarial to the media. The second technique for a postgame press game conference that Daly utilizes is to have statistics from the game available. Daly speaks with either an assistant coach or a team public relations representative and obtains some of the game's key statistics. Daly states that such data provide a foundation and an "explanation of why a team lost might be found in statistics" (personal communication, January 7, 1999). The final suggestion that Daly offers regarding the postgame press conference is to always have something to drink, in case a question is asked and some time is needed to compose the proper response. The importance of this philosophy, according to Daly, is that the coach is always in a lose-lose situation and cannot go head-to-head with the press because the press always has the last word.

Hubie Brown echoes these sentiments. Regarding the head coach's response to questions, he comments that "for the 30 seconds [where you do lose your composure] the press will make you pay everyday you coach in that city" (personal communication, January 27, 1999). Brown explains that a head coach in the NBA is on a roller coaster of emotions: Each coach is coaching by his God-given personality and a certain personality is not necessarily a better coach. He describes the postgame press conference where there are many media people and each person has an agenda. Brown claims as the head coach that you try to be "cooperative, professional and it is difficult on many nights. Many [members of the media] have not played and they are critiquing you on your philosophy of offense and defense in the game and how you maneuvered the players. Hopefully at the end you are calm, but there are nights where individuals attack and do not accept your explanations" (personal communication, January 27, 1999).

Game announcers must also balance the interests of the players whom they cover and those of the fans to whom they are providing the information. The balance between these interests and how it is handled is even more critical for announcers because more people will see the game telecast than read any one particular newspaper column about the game. John Andariese, Knicks announcer, describes announcers as extensions of the players and the sport—people will approach an announcer and ask for an autograph or talk about the game because announcers are more accessible for the fans who do not get the opportunity to speak with the players or coaches. He claims players are aware and care about negative commentary by an announcer. Andariese explains:

> Every player is very, very sensitive, and they get reports from their loved ones, and their fans and friends who have access to them on the negatives. They expect the positives. If a player ever walks up to an announcer in sports and says to that announcer, that was very nice what you said about me the other day, that will be the first time. But, if there was something he didn't like about what was being said, that might get voiced, or most athletes being young guys would kind of suppress it and develop this I don't like that guy face on them every time he sees them, but that is part of the business and you have to accept that. (personal communication, August 3, 1998)

As previously stated, the play-by-play announcer for the game also has to balance the interests of the fans and the players. Mike Breen says that the basic approach of the play-by-play announcer is to "detail the action, what's going on, who's doing what, with hopefully an entertaining way of doing it, whether it be with some humor or even basketball knowledge" (personal communication, November 4, 1998). Breen believes that the play-by-play announcer should also take on an analytical role during the broadcast. This is where the interests of the fan who might be trying to understand a certain play and the player who might have made an errant play can come into conflict. Breen offers his philosophy:

> You have to state it like it is, but you also have to be fair. I believe there is a way to criticize without being vicious, without being mean. There are two ways to say everything. You could say, a player is horrible tonight or you could say, well a player is really struggling with his shot tonight. There are two ways to do it and I think to be fair to the players, who are putting their effort out there, I think there is an easier way to say it without just hammering a guy. Off the field stuff they do, that is a different story, but for performances you have got to treat the player fair. One way that I always go by is I won't say anything on the air about a player that I wouldn't say to his face. I'll tell a guy, hey I said you were struggling tonight, you didn't play well tonight. If you can't say to a player's face what you are saying on the air, you shouldn't be saying it on the air, that is kind of a guide that I go by. (personal communication, November 4, 1998)

Breen, however, explains the difference between criticism of a player's on-court behavior and his personal effort in the game:

> I think it is important to show the different sides of these players. In many cases good, because there are more [good] stories than bad. I also think it is important to show negative sides, or to criticize the negative sides. I'm very, very old fashioned in terms of on court conduct. I hate this taunting and this in your face trash talking and no care if they get technicals or get in fights and get thrown out of the game. I am very critical of players who get technicals, I'm very critical of players who taunt and I'm not afraid to say that and I think that is important for an announcer to do that because the kids see it and the kids mimic what they see on TV. (M. Breen, personal communication, November 4, 1998)

Ian Eagle, New Jersey Nets announcer, adds another dimension to the responsibility of the announcer—responsibility to the employer. Eagle stresses that his employer, Cablevision, which owns Madison Square Garden and therefore the MSG Network, and also the other major New York sports cable channel, Fox Sports New York, which covers many of the New York area games including the Mets, Islanders, Nets, and Devils, wants honesty above all other elements in his broadcasts. Eagle would agree with Breen in the importance of being fair and honest to fans and players, especially as fans of the NBA have advanced knowledge of the game in terms of when a team is playing well or poorly because there are so many outlets for fans to gain knowledge and formulate an opinion. Eagle states:

> In my mind it is impossible to pull the wool over the eyes of any fan, they know what is up, but you need to walk that line of being journalistically sound and also being honest. So my responsibility is rather simple, the journalism end of it—report what is happening, the entertainment end—stay enthusiastic and provide the fans with a detailed play-by-play, and to the team—be fair, that is the bottom line, be fair. I think as long as I can walk into that locker room or walk into the coach's office and not be ashamed of anything I said. They might not agree with it, but as long as there could be dialog afterwards and that my point of view is at least a fair one, than that is fine, I feel comfortable with that. (personal communication, November 18, 1998)

Eagle also states:

> I'm certainly not going to go out of my way to sugarcoat anything, because I'm not going to put my reputation on the line, and your credibility at the end of the day is all you have. If you lose that then it is hard to really gain the trust of the viewer and I think if a viewer catches you on something where you are being a shill or you are overly promoting something and you know that it really isn't the right thing, it is tough to then go back six months later, a year later, five years later, fans remember things. (personal communication, November 18, 1998)

John Andariese describes a hypothetical solution that would get players to further understand the relationship between players, coaches, and announcers. Andariese states:

> I feel like going into the locker room before the season and making a statement to that effect, which I haven't done because it seems to be inappropriate, and say look guys here's my story, I'm here to do the games, I hope you go 82 and 0, but if you get criti-

cism or people telling you I'm criticizing you it is only because I have to be objective like the coaches so don't take it personally. I'm rooting for you, I want you to know that. You want it to all be a happy story. When the Knicks are doing great I'm on easy street, people want tickets, it helps my business life, people on the street are saying nice things to you, it's happy time. I really want that. (personal communication, August 3, 1998)

The primary job of the announcer is not merely that of a critic, but more of a journalist who provides information to the fans that will enhance the telecast. Much of the information provided involves extensive preparation in terms of knowing the players, gathering individual and team statistics, and talking to players and coaches about strategy, matchups, and injuries. Hubie Brown says that his preparation for a telecast on Turner will include attending the team shoot-around on the morning of a game, talking to the coach, and getting to the arena 2 hours before the game to try to talk with some of the players while they warm-up. In between the shoot-around and the game, Brown claims he spends approximately 2 1/2 hours on the day of a game compiling all his personal notes, as he keeps a file on each team. Brown explains that if it is a great game he might use one-third of his prepared material and if it is a bad game he might use 80% to 90%. In providing this information Brown states, "my job is to keep you from flicking your clicker and changing your dial, to convince you to stay" (personal communication, January 27, 1999).

John Andariese explains that the timing of the NBA schedule—with many games within one week—makes acquiring all the potential information regarding the game's matchup a very difficult challenge for the analyst. Andariese claims that good preparation for a NBA game will allow the analyst to use 20% of the available information, but it is still important to have the other 80% available in the event that a game necessitates more announcer input. Andariese cautions that the announcer has to be careful about overloading and wearing out the fan with statistics and information. He states:

You always have to remember that the game is the thing, people are viewing the game, they are tuning in not to necessarily hear you, to watch the game and I'm always very sensitive to over talking. So you don't want to tell everybody all that you know because they don't care. They are watching the game and what you know as it fits with the game as it evolves and it works that's terrific to use, but you go off into left field with facts and show people how much you know, you cease becoming an asset to the performance. (personal communication, August 3, 1998)

As play-by-play announcers, Mike Breen and Ian Eagle both have charts that include basic information such as the players' height, weight, college, draft position, how they were acquired, their vital playing statistics such as field goal percentage, free throw percentage, and multiple bullet points (for example, an announcer might comment, "Shaquille O'Neal has scored 30 points in eight consecutive games") at their finger tips that they could use immediately. The announcers gain a tremendous amount of knowledge about the team they are covering because they announce almost all their 82 games; there is not an overwhelming need to review their broadcast team, so they can focus on the opponent. One tool that both Breen and Eagle deem extremely valuable is talking with the opposing team announcers, who see their respective team 82 games a year.

Preparation is dependent on the game and who their broadcast team is playing. Mike Breen describes the difference in his role as the Knicks announcer when New York plays a rival such as the Chicago Bulls, the Miami Heat, or any team with which the Knicks have a history. There is more of a familiarity on the part of the announcers about the players and the strategy in comparison to when New York plays a western conference opponent they only see twice a year. Breen explains that if the Knicks are playing the Golden State Warriors or the Sacramento Kings he will do more reading of newspaper clips, media guides, and game notes. Breen will also try to watch upcoming Knick opponents' games.

The teams involved in the game not only affect the preparation aspects for the telecast, but require an understanding on the part of the announcer as to who the audience might be for that particular game. Ian Eagle explains:

Circumstances will change game to game. If it's Nets-Grizzlies, you know it's the die-hards, you know it going in. Nets-Bulls, with Michael Jordan of course involved in the equation, you realize that you are going to start getting some of the ancillary fans. You are going to start getting some of those casual basketball fans that just either happened to stumble upon you or they know Jordan is on and they want to hear what is happening. So I will be cognizant of that going into a game. Someone might say you treat every game the same, I don't think so. I realized early on that you don't get a lot of feedback from those Nets-Raptors games and you better be aware that when it is Nets-Bulls, Nets-Knicks, Nets-Jazz, high profile teams, you know your viewership is going up. You also know that people are listening a little more intently as opposed to just a game being on in the background so you might be a little more scrutinized than on your average run of the mill Wednesday night game in the middle of January. (personal communication, November 18, 1998)

Both Breen and Eagle also announce national broadcasts that are not only seen in the broadcast team home market. Breen announces the NBA on NBC, while Eagle does NCAA Tournament basketball and NFL telecasts for CBS. Whereas there is an emphasis on the home broadcast team on a local telecast, both announcers point out the difference to a national broadcast. There now has to be more balance between the two teams in terms of personalizing players, storytelling, and statistical information. Breen explains the difference:

> There is a big difference between doing a network game and doing a game for a local team. Obviously when you do a game for the Knicks, you gear the broadcast for the Knick fans. Yes, you give some talk about the opponent, anecdotes about the opponent, statistics about the opponent, and you want to give them [the fans] some information so they know the opponent better, but you still gear the broadcast toward the Knicks. You know the team much, much better because you are around them more. You know more about players' tendencies, what they are going through at this point. So you gear the broadcast toward that. You don't totally cover the Knicks, but you emphasize the home team, and that is the way it should be. Whereas on a network you really have to balance it. When I do a Knicks game for the network I really have to watch to make sure that I don't go too much in terms of the Knicks. If I'm doing a Knicks game on MSG and we are going to a commercial break and the Knicks are trailing the Pistons by four, I'll say, 6:35 remaining Knicks down by four. But on a network game, if it's the same game I'm saying, 6:35 remaining Pistons with a four point lead. It is kind of a subtle, very small example, but it is kind of the way you have to do it and I find myself when I am doing a Knicks game on network that I almost lean more toward the opponent. I'm exaggerating just so I'm not putting too much emphasis on the team I know better. (personal communication, November 4, 1998)

MEDIA RELATIONS

The people responsible for coordinating the interaction between the players, coaches, and the media are the individual team public relations directors. In addition to his role as Vice President of Marketing and Communications with the Philadelphia 76ers, Dave Coskey is the former Public Relations Director for the Sixers. Coskey explains that the first responsibility of the public relations personnel for the team is the game operation and to service the media who attend games. John Mertz is the Director of Public Relations for the New Jersey Nets and has been with the team for over 14 years. He describes his primary responsibilities in media relations for the Nets as being a "conduit not only with the daily sports sections that cover the team for basketball purposes, but also a proactive PR service promoting what we do off the court, community business, marketing—kind of cover the whole gamut of the organization's role in the community and the business Meadowlands area and nationwide" (personal communication, July 31, 1998).

From a strictly media standpoint, Mertz and his office are the primary day-to-day contact with the media, particularly the print media and the six daily newspapers that cover the Nets on a regular basis, whether traveling or at home. He explains that these contacts include "keeping them supplied with whatever statistical or biographical background information they may need to get their job done, dealing with the sports editors for special requests for maybe special sections or features they may be working on, working with the photo departments, credentialing, or any special features they are working on" (personal communication, July 31, 1998).

It is the individual team public relations offices who will field the requests from the various media outlets, whether the request is from *Sports Illustrated*, a local newspaper or television outlet, or a broadcast partner. After the first contact is made, the public relations personnel then notifies the player or coach and offers their advice regarding the media request. Mertz explains, "we will sit down with the player and say a request has come in and we'll make a recommendation or if it's something that isn't beneficial to the player or the club we will let them know that this is going on and they may or may not want to do it—even without our recommendation, but normally they trust us with the requests we bring to them" (personal communication, July 31, 1998).

Mertz describes the media request procedure:

In that regard we work closely, when we are on the road or even when we are at home somebody comes up to a player and says could we schedule this or that—they are going to point over and say just go through their office. They know our role—what we are there for and they use us as shelter or protection as they want to turn down or schedule. Some of them [the media] will go to guys for something separate, but usually the players are good at telling us they are doing it or after the media outlet has gone to the player and asked, they will come back to us and say we spoke to Jayson [former New Jersey Nets center Jayson Williams] and he said he will do this for us. There is nobody out there who feels the need to circumvent our PR department because we turn them down consistently. (personal communication, July 31, 1998)

Dave Coskey, who was the 76ers' Public Relations Director when Philadelphia had superstars Julius Erving, Moses Malone, and Charles Barkley, provides his philosophy: "It is not your job to limit, but to exploit and create as much access as you can." Coskey adds that "the tone you take on requests sets the perception. You cannot fulfill every request, but the goal is to fill as many as possible and to get the others [media organizations] to understand" (personal communication, February 1, 1999). One suggestion that Coskey offers is to rotate the media organizations whose requests are granted.

One of the limits for filling all of the media requests is the hectic NBA schedule. Mertz explains:

We try to be as helpful as possible in keeping guys' schedules where they have time for family, where we are not tying them up full time day and night and just assuming they are going to do every last thing that comes down the pike. We are cognizant of the fact that we just came off a six day road trip and we have one day off before we play at home the next night—we are not going to look at the schedule three weeks in advance and say okay when we come home that day we know it is going to be an off day, but we are scheduling an interview. (personal communication, July 31, 1998)

Public relations directors also have the role of providing information to the game announcers so they can be more prepared for the broadcast. Mertz describes the service the New Jersey Nets public relations office provides for visiting team announcers, stating

we put together a packet with information including the game notes for that night, recent press clippings, whatever information they need available, and we send that to the hotel, so that the TV and radio guys for the visiting team can read up for the game that night, the visiting writers have recent press clippings. You are providing them with enough information so that they could do a good job on the club that night. (personal communication, July 31, 1998)

The NBA league office offers much support in helping the individual media and the teams' public relations directors do their job. As the former Director of NBA Sports Media Relations, Chris Brienza explains this department "oversees the daily relations between the NBA and its teams, with all North American print, radio, TV, and online media who cover us on a regular basis" (personal communication, August 12, 1998). He claims the services that the NBA Sports Media Relations Department provide have two overall objectives per the league's proactive approach to getting information out to try to serve media constituents and hence the fans all over the world: to make the NBA the easiest sport in the world to cover and to help grow the sport of basketball. Brienza explains:

It is both a service role and an active [role], helping present our players and our teams and our coaches in the most positive light possible. From a service standpoint we've become a 24-hour operation. A couple of years ago we got into fax on demand. Anyone covering the NBA from anywhere in the world would be able to access game notes, box scores, statistics, all of that 24 hours a day just by having a fax machine. We really took it a step further with NBA.COM which is now like one-stop shopping, if you are a media member. It has game notes, box scores, stats, shot charts now. It is an archive now as well, which is something we didn't have before. You can go get a box score from two years ago. (personal communication, August 12, 1998)

Information service also entails proactively providing the media with stories, or at least being sure to provide the media with the NBA perspective on a story. Brienza explains, for example, that the NBA utilizes video news releases in which the NBA, "will buy the satellite time, produce video, and send it up on the satellite for any television station in the country to pull down to help them tell their story better" (personal communication, August 12, 1998). One instance offered by Brienza was when the NBA used a video news release during the NBA lockout in which Russell Granik, NBA Deputy Commissioner, explained the policy of how the NBA would reimburse fans who had tickets to cancelled games. The NBA uses a similar strategy in catering to radio news organizations. Brienza explains, "we have a radio hotline number where if there is a breaking story we'll take audio, place it in a specific mailbox so radio stations know if they can't get a live interview because it's a huge story, you call this number, go to mailbox [#] and there will always be a NBA official with two or three sound-bites of a story" (personal communication, August 12, 1998). The importance of these strategies that provide the NBA perspective are that the NBA itself is now being a proactive advocate in providing a story or assisting in the framing of a story rather than operating at the mercy of the various mass media organizations' interpretation of events.

Brienza explains the role of the NBA Media Relations Department as "an active [role], helping present our players and our teams and our coaches in the most positive light possible" and "being able to explain issues, being able to set up interview requests, being able to help people who cover the game—help them understand things where they might have a viewpoint for certain reasons, because they don't understand everything that is going on behind that story" (personal communication, August 12, 1998). Because of these extensive duties, Brienza must be continuously accessible to the media and is on 24-hour call. The home phone numbers of the media relations department personnel are included in the NBA Media Directory (called the Blue Book) that is provided to any media member who covers the NBA.

Chris Brienza describes the relationship between the league media relations office and the individual team public relations directors as one in which the individual teams act as 29 branch offices of the NBA. He points out that "the teams' PR directors are the people who deal with the players on a day-to-day basis and a lot of times communication is easier and more effective if you work with the PR director because they have a daily relationship with that player" (personal communication, August 12, 1998).

PORTRAYAL: STORYLINE

Providing information is a major initiative that helps in developing the framing methods of personalizing a player and developing a storyline. The storyline is the theme of the game that will be expressed before the game and remain in focus throughout the telecast. Mike Pearl, Senior Vice President and Executive Producer for Turner Sports, is primarily responsible for overseeing the on-air game and the studio operation of Turners' NBA broadcasts. Pearl claims that a major objective of Turners' NBA broadcasts is storytelling. He states, "storylines make people watch. If San Antonio is playing Seattle, you have to give people in New York a reason to watch" (personal communication, February 25, 1999). He describes that each broadcast for Turner is more than a game because there is a national perspective. Pearl explains that Turner is getting the hard-core NBA fan who will watch games with teams other than the one in his or her own area, but there must be the proper promotion and storytelling to engage the viewer.

Ed Desser explains how every game has the luxury of having a storyline associated with it to help viewers be more involved in the telecast. He describes the storyline possibilities involving team trends of winning, losing, or a rivalry, or a player or coach storyline angle. Desser claims that "there are tons of stuff [storyline possibilities] and television has gotten much better at telling a lot of different stories, weaving them into a telecast and it's really just part of making the product better" (personal communication, August 26, 1998). Desser further explains the importance of having these storylines explicitly pointed out to fans throughout the production of the game. He states,

the television environment is more competitive than ever, there are more alternatives than ever, you've got to captivate the audience and keep them watching. Two-and-a-half-hours is a long time to commit to doing something in today's world where you've got people who have time constraints. There are huge pressures on people's discretionary time and to get them to the set and then to keep them there requires great creativity. (personal communication, August 26, 1998)

Knicks producer Howie Singer also explains the importance of creating a storyline:

It's not necessarily important in a Knicks-Heat game, you know what it is, but if the Knicks are playing the Clippers you got to give people a little bit of a hook. Why should I watch this game? Maybe they don't know that when the Knicks play the Clippers almost every single time the game goes into overtime, that they are always close games. You've got to come up with some reason for them to want to watch. Maybe they don't know who's the star of the Clippers or Vancouver. Maybe they don't know about Abdur-Rahim [Vancouver Grizzlies forward, Shareef Abdur-Rahim], so you show a few plays and you show what his numbers are and where he ranks in scoring, all of a sudden, hey this guy is good I've never seen him play. So it's more of a hook. (personal communication, August 26, 1998)

The storyline will be illustrated to the viewer continuously during the telecast through the use of replays, many of which will be the product of isolation cameras that are only following the featured storyline players of the game. Storyline updates for the viewer are provided through the use of graphics—actual words formatted onto the screen that provide statistics or other background information. The storyline is also referred to throughout the game in the analysis of the announcers and in the analysis of studio personnel at halftime or postgame.

The original storyline ideas are the creation of producers, directors, and announcers, and the quality of the broadcast is strongly related to having these people understand the storyline that will be focused on during the game. The coordination of all personnel involved in the broadcast is achieved during production meetings that occur either the day before or the day of the game. New Jersey Nets play-by-play announcer Ian Eagle describes a production meeting:

> It [the production meeting] is between play-by-play guy, analyst, pre- and postgame host, producer, director and if you put enough heads together I think more often than not you will really come up with some items that maybe one guy would not have come up with on his own. I realized that there is no way you can rely solely on the producer to come up with everything, that is just not fair. And vice-versa, the producer can't just rely on the play-by-play guy to carry a broadcast. So it really is a dependent relationship where you travel with these guys the whole year. They are kind of your family away from home and you develop tight relationships and I think that can transcribe itself on to the air. (personal communication, November 18, 1998)

In terms of the actual game production, the element that best introduces the storyline is the game's opening tease, which is a produced segment that is the first element seen by the viewers as the game broadcast begins. Kevin Smollon, NBA on NBC Game Producer, points out that "generally you start out with a tease and then you follow that tease thought throughout, you try, and late in the game go back to what you talked about in your tease and opening on-camera, kind of tie it all into a story. A lot of times the game is different from what you had in mind originally and you have to adjust on the fly" (personal communication, September 23, 1998).

The tease is normally followed by an on-camera with the announcers. The purpose of both of the opening tease and the

announcer on-camera production elements is to indicate to the viewers the storyline and the key personalities involved in the game. To
complete the storyline, prior to the start of the game strategy, NBC
uses its multiple cameras to obtain tight face shots of all the essential personalities and storyline players of the game as they are walking onto the court for the opening tip.

Mike Breen describes the importance of these techniques in
broadcasting the NBA. He states:

> All games have game opens where you come on and discuss what
> is going on and there are certain things that you look for in that
> game. Whether it is a team storyline, this team has lost six in a
> row, they are struggling and they need something. A particular
> player storyline, so and so is having an MVP type season, he has
> just been unstoppable. A matchup storyline, two of the best cen-
> ters, it is the Knicks and the Rockets, two of the best centers
> Olajuwon and Ewing. You discuss those beforehand and as the
> game goes through you follow those points and try to stay up-to-
> date throughout. You will constantly be saying Ewing and
> Olajuwon, right now the matchup and you will show the numbers
> what each has, points, rebounds. Things like that you just stick
> with through the course of the game. (personal communication,
> November 4, 1998)

Breen, however, cautions:

> Storylines develop on their own and you can't be stubborn enough
> to say we have to keep harping on this. If something else develops
> you have to go with it and that is what I believe. There are so
> many things going on in one particular NBA game that if you get
> caught up with trying to stay with one storyline that you did in
> the pregame show it is not good for the fan. You have some stuff
> in the beginning to go with, but you really have to let the game
> develop. (personal communication, November 4, 1998)

In updating the viewers about the storyline, communication
between the on-air announcers and the production truck is pivotal in
providing viewers the most valuable and accurate information. This
communication is a primary responsibility of the game producer.
Whereas the director is responsible for obtaining the shots that com-
pliment the storyline, the producer is responsible for coming up with
the selection of replays and speaking to the announcers during the

game to indicate what the viewers are about to see and to update them as to storyline items. Singer claims the most important skill of the producer during a telecast is to listen. He comments:

> Making sure you are listening to everything the announcers are saying and making sure everything they are saying is backed up or if you want to show something that they [the announcers] know what it is before it comes up [on the screen]. Make sure they are prepared, make them look good. I communicate with the graphics coordinator. He [or she] is trying to sell me different graphics or I'm asking him [or her] if I noticed the Knicks have made like five in a row, I'll ask the graphics coordinator how many have the Knicks made in a row—Knicks have made five their last five field goals—get it up there. I'll make sure the announcers know before we see it so everyone looks like geniuses. Also communicate with the director. If I notice that they [the announcers] are talking about something and he [or she] is not showing it, I ask to make sure the director shows that. (personal communication, August 26, 1998)

Hubie Brown describes the analyst as part of a team—who is only as good as the play-by-play announcer, producer, and director—and that there must be tremendous coordination between all in the communication of the game to the audience. He states that "if all are not in sync the telecast will be a flop" (personal communication, January 27, 1999). From a play-by-play announcer perspective, Mike Breen describes the difficulty and the importance of the communication between the announcer and the production truck.

> It is always set up where you have a talk back and they have a button where they can talk to us at the same time, another they talk to us one at a time. That takes some getting used to because sometimes they are talking to you while you are actually doing the play-by-play and you have to get used to being able to talk while they are in your head and kind of realize what they are saying. For a producer, he has got to be able to talk concisely, some producers are very wordy and it can be very distracting. But others know how to say something in the smallest amount of time and the smallest amount of words. You have such a team atmosphere on the TV end because you have to work so closely with the producer and director. I think it is harder for the producer and the director because they are following you, you are still the guy on the air talking, in most cases they are following you

and they have to get a feel for what you like to talk about, which kind of things you like to follow. You have to have confidence and trust in them. I think that is enormous. You have to have confidence that they know the sport, that they know what they are talking about and I think that is vital. If you are going to a replay and the producer or director tells you we are going here you have to have confidence you are going to see what he is telling you so you don't lead into it and sound silly. (M. Breen, personal communication, November 4, 1998)

Breen also contends that it is important for the announcer to be proactive in informing the producer and director as to where the critical action is occurring on the court so that the producer can instruct the camera operators to capture it. He explains:

A certain play will happen and maybe there will be a great move to the basket on one side of the court, but at the other side the way a guy came off of a screen is really perfect, you want to be able to talk to the producer and director and say when you show the replay don't show the shot, iso [isolate] on the screen and roll and stuff like that enhances the telecast because the producer and director they are not out there, they see what they have on the cameras, but they are not out there and I think it is important for announcers to talk to producers and directors to tell them, look for this or look for that. I'll frequently say if the ball is coming down and two guys are really going at it, I'll say to Howie Singer [Knicks producer], watch Oakley [former Knick forward Charles Oakley] and Kevin Willis [NBA veteran forward] they are really going at it, keep an eye on those guys closely. Or if a coach is going crazy, get a shot of Van Gundy [Knick Head Coach Jeff Van Gundy], he is really losing it right now. So you really need a lot of communication. (personal communication, November 4, 1998)

The storyline will also be advanced and referred to during the halftime segment. The utilization of halftime has been an area of improvement in the broadcasting of the NBA. On a local level, Brian McIntyre says that when he started working for the Chicago Bulls in 1978, halftime was simply the color commentator interviewing whomever he could grab at the game, a scout, or as the Bulls Director of Public Relations, he was often interviewed. McIntyre claims this practice did nothing to advance the NBA and overall was incredibly dull television. When the rights were held by ABC, network halftime features included one-on-one contests between star players. CBS had a halftime feature called "Red on Roundball" in which Boston Celtics legendary Head Coach Arnold "Red" Auerbach, who coached the Celtics to nine NBA Championships, would explain a fundamental basketball skill.

Ted Shaker, NBA on CBS Executive Producer, was brought into the position of overseeing the NBA on CBS because of his ability to develop studio programming, including the extremely successful *NFL Today*, to support the game's telecast using the ideas of personalizing players and creating or advancing a game storyline. He explains the overall philosophy:

> I had more experience with trying to put faces on players. The studio operation is one where we did a lot of feature stories and there was a lot of time spent in trying to create auras around these players and make them stars and so the feeling was that maybe I could bring some of that. Part of the show was to take halftime and turn it into a show within a show and [we] asked a guy named Pat O'Brien who at the time was a reporter at CBS Sports to host it and he had never done anything quite like that before. But he had a great flair for interviewing people, he is a terrific writer, and has a terrific sense of humor. And so we tried to make it kind of a hip halftime show, created a name, "At the Half" it became a show onto itself and people would talk about what happened at halftime. So [the strategy] played into my strengths a little bit from the past and Pat was sensational, loved the NBA, players loved him because he was a smart guy coming in and asking good questions. (personal communication, October 9, 1998)

In addition to personalizing players, updating the game storyline, and analyzing first half action, halftime is used to promote the next game. For example, if NBC was showing a doubleheader of NBA games and the second game featured the Lakers, halftime for the first game might be an interview with Laker stars Shaquille O'Neal or Kobe Bryant.

In reality, the storyline and the attempt to personalize the players has already been introduced to viewers prior to the telecasting of the actual game through previous promotions and the pregame show on the day of the game. On a local level, Singer describes the production of the pregame show:

> The pregame show is a big chunk of work because the game is a ball game and if you don't have any elements in the game there is

still something to show. The pregame you have to start from scratch so there is a lot more creativity involved in trying to get a pregame show on the air. So we try to balance it between giving updates on injuries, roster changes, highlights of the last game, whatever controversial things that might be going on. Then we will do a feature on one of the players on the Knicks or other team coming in or something topical. (personal communication, August 26, 1998)

Ricky Diamond is the Coordinating Producer for the studio shows at NBC, including *NBA Showtime*, the first regular weekly network pregame show for the NBA, which began when the broadcast rights contract shifted to NBC. Diamond describes the two major objectives of *NBA Showtime*: (a) to get the audience prepared for the game they are going to watch and peek people's interest in the game and (b) to follow what is going on in the league as a whole. Diamond explains that piquing the interest of the audience is a "generic sort of credo that goes for every pregame whether it is in football, baseball, whatever pregame show I've ever worked on. It's to sort of make the viewing of the game enhanced by introducing some of the stories or strategy, however it is you want to arrive at doing that, that is sort of the mentality" (personal communication, October 21, 1998).

In following the league, *NBA Showtime* updates stories about teams that are involved in the upcoming game and focuses on stories that may be occurring league-wide. Diamond explains the philosophy:

I especially mean that during the regular season because during the playoffs it is obvious we are more singly focused on teams in the playoffs and what is happening in the playoffs. Again, not just the game you are about to watch, but if we come on in early in the playoffs when there are still 16 teams around and we are coming on before a Knicks-Pacers playoff game, then we are certainly going to do our share on the Knicks and the Pacers, but we obviously do some on the Hawks and the Bulls and the Heat and the Western Conference teams as well. We are more there to cover the playoffs and not just the game. There are 29 teams, and there aren't 29 teams that appear on NBC on a regular basis, that is for sure. There are a lot of these teams such as the Vancouver Grizzlies and the L.A. Clippers that we don't cover much if at all, but we want to make sure there are good stories so our focus during regular season is much more league wide and that focus narrows during the playoffs. (personal communication, October 21, 1998)

In addition to personalizing a player or developing a storyline for the game, *NBA Showtime* is very much a news and information program in providing an update of league happenings. Diamond continues:

> We're looking to again give people as much information, it is not just to tell human interest stories, sometimes it is just dispensing cold, hard facts. That we are a half-hour before the game and so and so has shown up for the arena and he has got the worst flu bug you could ever imagine. We don't want the game to start and all of a sudden the guy is playing terribly and nobody has explained why. So we want to make sure all of the information that we could possibly gather is being dispensed to viewers and also to tell human interest stories and give people a reason for rooting one way or the other and to personalize the players, to humanize the players, to just make you realize that these guys are dealing with some of the same life situations that the viewer is and so there is sort of a bonding there between the viewer and the player on some level. (personal communication, October 21, 1998)

The method NBC uses to develop the human interest aspects of the *NBA Showtime* program is careful and meticulously produced feature segments about players or coaches. Vincent Costello's primary responsibility in working on *NBA Showtime* and NBC's halftime is to produce features about players, coaches, or perhaps an issue of relevance that needs coverage, such as free agency. Costello states that NBC Showtime does not go after average basketball stories, but will go into more family oriented or personal angles with the "hope it makes people care more about the player, care more about the team, feel more and know more about the player. It just brings more of a personal end of that player" (personal communication, September 23, 1998). Costello explains that NBC will do player profiles just to introduce the player a little bit more or get a viewer to know him better, and will do the stars because "people want to see them and what is going on with them in their lives" (personal communication, September 23, 1998). The first decision in producing a feature is to determine which athlete will be chosen to be profiled. This is often done in accordance with a key storyline for the upcoming game. Once the athlete is selected, according to Costello the process of putting together a feature is really broken down into four parts: research, on site-interview, gathering other footage and production elements, and eventually the editing process.

Costello explains that the purpose of the research is to go beyond what is happening in the game because the audience might already have a decent knowledge about the player's performance for the season. By obtaining a story about a player's background, whether the story involves an event in the past or present, the public gets to learn more about the individual than as simply a basketball player.

The on-site interview involves asking the athlete the proper questions regarding the story that have emerged through the diligent research of the feature producer, and making the interview visually appealing. Costello explains the creation and combination of compelling spoken and video content, stating:

> You have to set up a background for what it is when you sit them down, sometimes you get put into crappy rooms or sometimes you get put in a locker room, but the locker room is kind of plain, it all has to look right for TV so you're setting up a backdrop so it looks nice visually and you work with your camera crew on that. There is a lot of lighting involved and a lot of moving around, getting props, that all takes a couple of hours to set up something that looks good. Sometimes we do the interview ourselves, it's one-on-one and it would be one camera where we are not worried about my questions or anything it's just getting the player's answers, but we would go out and do that. Other times we would go with talent, someone that is on our air and they would go down and ask questions. (personal communication, September 23, 1998)

After the interview is completed, Costello claims the real work begins as the next step is to screen the videotapes of the interview and determine which sound-bites are the most interesting and best fit into the story. Extra footage that was obtained also has to be screened. This footage will include game highlights or video shot by NBC at practice that will be used as background video (b-roll) when the player is speaking to provide a change from seeing only a tight shot of the athlete or coach's face. Additional interviews and personal items such as photographs might be obtained from the athlete, teammates, or family members to enhance the feature.

All the interviews, footage, and any other items now have to be edited within the timeframe that the feature has been allotted for broadcast within *NBA Showtime* or halftime. The editing process also includes a selection of background music, complementary graphics, and various production elements such as fades, which transition from one video shot to another. In terms of the amount of work necessary to produce a feature, Costello explains,

> the more involved the piece, the more high profile, if it is for a NBA Finals, a Super Bowl, the more you are putting into it. You actually have to cut corners for the regular season because if you did that every week you wouldn't sleep, you wouldn't see your family, so obviously the bigger the occasion and the more rating it is going to get, you are going to do more and it is going to be more involved, but it is week by week and it is feature by feature. (personal communication, September 23, 1998)

Often the production of a feature serves as a three or four minute promotion for the upcoming game. Costello explains:

> If we have the Utah Jazz versus the Chicago Bulls we want people to not just care about that game or the final score, but maybe care about the players that are involved. So we will do an interview with somebody from Utah, or somebody from Chicago. We hear from the player, you get to know the player and then we can come out and say today this player is going to go up against this guy and now we can talk about the game. Obviously we do features for a lot of different reasons, but a lot of times we structure it towards what our game is going to be. (personal communication, September 23, 1998)

All these portrayal broadcasting strategies operate in conjunction with and are supportive of the exposure strategy. The portrayal strategies are vital in enhancing the NBA and the communication of the quality of its game product.

5

THE NBA MANAGEMENT OF ITS PRODUCT

The NBA, itself, does not have much control over the actual on-the-court game product, which is more a result of the talent of the players and coaches. Fortunately, the quality of the NBA product is the pinnacle of what basketball can offer in that the best players want to compete in the NBA. Therefore, the lack of control over the talent quality is not a critical loss to the NBA. What the NBA can control, or at the very least strongly manage, is enhancing its product—the games and merchandise. Regarding the game, the NBA does implement measures to assist in managing the competitive nature of its product. The league's greatest management is over the perception of the product. The perception not only includes the game itself, but the perception of the players, coaches, and teams that is reflected in the behavior of the audience. The communication strategies are essential in creating a positive perception. The overall goal is thus simple: A quality basketball product and quality communication strategies that work in synchronicity to create the best possible image perception of the NBA. The combination of a quality product and quality communication strategies is the optimal scenario for any company or organization trying to attract consumers and transfer an agenda.

Both independently and in coordination with its broadcast partners, the NBA is continuously trying to grow its industry from a basketball and marketing perspective. These synchronous goals are prominent in the league's mission statement:

the NBA's mission is to be the most respected and successful sports league and sports marketing organization in the world. It strives to make basketball the most popular global sport while maintaining the NBA's position as the best in basketball, and to create and maximize business opportunities and relationships arising from basketball. Success in these efforts enhances the economic value of its member teams. (NBA.com)

SUPPORT PROGRAMMING

NBA Showtime on NBC is just one of the support programs whose design is to enhance the NBA through the efforts of personalizing players and creating storylines. In this endeavor of support programming the NBA demonstrates an understanding of the value of television vehicles in helping to project the agenda the NBA wants to perpetuate.

The creation of NBA Entertainment in 1982 was a strategic initiative by the NBA to provide television programming to support NBA games through telling stories and personalizing players. In the 1980-81 season, the NBA instituted a videotape retrieval system for obtaining and preserving game footage. NBA Entertainment is the exclusive licenser for all NBA and WNBA footage. NBA Entertainment facilities are located in Secaucus, New Jersey, and contain a 6,000 square-foot sound studio, a full range of editing facilities, and an extensive basketball video and photographic archive. NBA Entertainment also "supports the NBA's mission to grow the sport through extensive video production and services, by fulfilling photographic needs of clients and by overseeing the league's global broadcasting relationships" (NBA.com). NBA Entertainment produces four weekly television programs: *NBA Inside Stuff* on NBC, *NBA Matchup* on ESPN, *NBA Action* on Fox Sports Net, and *NBA Jam*, which is distributed internationally. Commissioner Stern explains the philosophy of NBA support programming, stating:

> Most of it [the NBA communication strategy] flows from the recognition that we really do have a product that will be effective by different delivery systems and that can flow to our consumers in a variety of ways and is not limited to games. So, NBA games are preceded by *NBA Showtime*, *NBA Inside Stuff* is on Saturday mornings, *NBA Action* is on cable, *NBA Today* is on ESPN, *NBA Tonight* is on ESPN 2, *Rock and Jock* is on MTV, things are on Nickelodeon. The whole notion was kind of a shoulder and ancil-

lary program that reinforced a variety of images that we attempted to portray for the NBA and that was very important. And
then, although we came to realize and not necessarily direct it
that much, although we thought it would be fan friendly, that our
players reinforced the NBA through their own appearances in
commercials, our players reinforced the NBA by being on
Seinfeld, or *ER*, or *Friends*, or *Murphy Brown*, going on
Letterman, or Leno, or Arsenio Hall, or Conan O'Brien. There is a
self-perpetuating machine here that is extraordinary. (personal
communication, April 14, 1999)

The creation of *NBA Showtime* and NBA Entertainment to
produce programming, particularly *NBA Inside Stuff* which airs on
NBC every Saturday morning, was a critical development in the
shifting of the broadcast rights contract from CBS to NBC. Ed Desser
explains the feeling of the league during the shifting of the network
contract:

At the time the negotiations took place CBS was doing a pretty
good job of presenting the games, largely because of Ted Shaker
and the changes that he brought. In terms of the games themselves, they were doing the job. But, what they weren't doing was
Showtime, what they weren't doing was *Inside Stuff*, what they
weren't doing was providing us with promotional air time outside
of sports programming. And those were the things together with
being prepared to step up additional regular season coverage that
NBC was ready to do and it made the NBC proposal very entic-
ing. That coupled with the fact that the other key element of it
was they [NBC] recognized that CBS's pricing was well below
market potential and as a result they took a fresh look and they
said you know what, we can re-price this because it's a premium
product, it's not a second rate product, and therefore we believe
we could pay substantially more than CBS has been willing to
pay historically. And so it was the combination of their willingness to substantially up what they would pay, and probably could
pay, together with their being willing to put on more games and
more additional programming and promotional support. Those
were the key elements in the original NBC deal. (personal communication, August 26, 1998)

Adam Silver, President and Chief Operating Officer for NBA
Entertainment, states that the overall goal of this organization is to
"market and distribute programming throughout the world to NBA

fans" (personal communication, December 16, 1998). He further explains that "the largest revenue source [for the NBA] is network television money. All [the work of NBA Entertainment] is geared to develop the value of NBA game programming" (personal communication, December 16, 1998). Silver emphasizes that the overall objectives of NBA Entertainment are to sell programming for network television, to promote the game telecast, to make this NBA element the most attractive, and, most importantly, to get people to watch NBA games on television. Gregg Winik, Vice President Programming and Broadcasting and Executive Producer, adds that the programming produced by NBA Entertainment is "designed to make the NBA pull through all of its different shows to reach a different target audience" (personal communication, December 16, 1998). Winik is responsible for the content produced in three different programs: *NBA Inside Stuff*, *NBA Action*, and *NBA Jam*, each program with a distinctly different target audience. Commissioner Stern comments that

> because there are so many niches, defined by networks themselves, the programming really goes to the niche. So Lifetime, for example, is a great network and it is directed at women and the WNBA is terrific there. ESPN is purely male, tends to be, and they like to see more action and that is *NBA Today*. *NBA Tonight* on ESPN 2 are the fanatics about the playoffs, they can't get enough. NBC is more general and *Inside Stuff* is a magazine show. (personal communication, April 14, 1999)

NBA Inside Stuff is one of the longest running shows on television and serves as a tremendous outlet to personalize players. Chris Brienza describes how the league personalizes players through *NBA Inside Stuff*:

> It is more presenting players in the best possible light. We might know things about our players that most people don't know. We might know that Mugsy Bogues went back to finish up his degree, so that is a great story, let's find the best outlet to promote this. One of the great vehicles we have now is *Inside Stuff* which is a weekly half-hour show on NBC then rebroadcast on ESPN. You've got a lot of hours and a lot of air time to fill and I think we are committed to doing that—to showing players in ways that you are not used to seeing them. The off the court side, some of the interesting or some of the off beat things that players are involved in. (personal communication, August 12, 1998)

In addition to the weekly NBA programs, NBA Entertainment is responsible for being proactive in creating national NBA advertising campaigns such as the "I Love This Game" or the "NBA Action is Fantastic" commercials. Home videos are another major aspect of NBA Entertainment's properties, whether they are year-end perspectives on the championship team or videos featuring one player such as Michael Jordan. NBA Entertainment also develops video games through contracts with Electronic Arts Sports and Sony Playstation, and there is a creative services department within NBA Entertainment that acts as a clearinghouse and approves any marketing-related changes teams might make to their logo, uniform, or home court designs.

NBA Entertainment contains a licensing department that controls and distributes photos and video footage which are officially licensed by the NBA, and the league receives a fee for their external use. Silver explains that the NBA is the exclusive licensee of all its footage, and networks that broadcast the NBA only have the rights to the live broadcast of the games. There is, however, a 72-hour news window in which any network can use the footage for highlights. So if ESPN SportsCenter or NBC News (or any other sports or news report) wants to use NBA game footage for a feature on its evening news, it has 72 hours to use the footage without being in violation of the NBA official licensing agreement and having to pay the NBA a fee for its use. Winik explains that for every NBA game, NBA Entertainment has two recordings of the game, one of them recorded by a play-by-play game camera and the other a low-angle camera which provides footage often used in player features. The two recordings are then sent via Federal Express back to NBA Entertainment for the next morning. Additionally, NBA Entertainment covers approximately 200 NBA games with its own video crews. As part of the overall rights contract with their broadcast partners, NBC and the Turner Networks do have privileges to acquire and utilize footage in their broadcasts without having to pay additional fees to the NBA. Tom Fox of Gatorade explains that sponsors also have the right to utilize NBA footage.

Utilizing communication technology as part of the overall strategic priority of getting people to watch NBA games, the league—without a connection to any other broadcast network—has established a Direct Broadcast Satellite (DBS) Package for its games. The NBA offers a DBS package called NBA League Pass which delivers approximately 1,000 games a year to anyone with a satellite dish for less than $160 per season, or less than 20 cents per game. Ed Desser describes what the league accomplishes with the inclusion of League Pass into its television lineup:

> You look at it kind of closing the loop, you now have 52 games on
> NBC, and 80 games on the Turner Networks, about 1,050 games
> on the dish, leaves only about 50 games that aren't televised
> somewhere. So we've basically taken all of the product and we
> now got it in some sort of distribution window available and kind
> of the art of this is taking 1,189 regular season games and poten-
> tially 89 playoff games and figuring out how to best slice and dice
> that product to generate maximum exposure, maximum revenue.
> (personal communication, August 26, 1998)

Winik explains that every local telecast is also now a national telecast through the League Pass DBS Package. For League Pass, the
video feed is often, but not always, the telecast of the visiting team
because it is easier to utilize with the broadcast signal already on the
satellite.

The broadcast initiatives of the NBA, from the television programs it has created, to the home videos that are produced by the
league, and the League Pass Package, demonstrate that the NBA
itself is proactive in setting its own agenda. These diverse initiatives,
although all broadcast oriented, indicate that the NBA understands
that its audience is not monolithic and there are multiple ranges of
support needed to reach the NBA's entire fan base. In addition to the
game exposure the league receives from its broadcast partners and
the various cable and over-the-air stations that provide games, the
NBA has created support programming vehicles to reach a certain
target audience. This diverse support programming, which tries to
reach a certain target audience, increases the potential for different
types of advertisers who might be interested in reaching a particular
audience. It leaves the NBA with at least some form of its product
geared for almost every audience demographic—no group is left out.

There are NBA fans who are only interested in viewing
games. These fans have their local stations, Turner networks, and
the marquee matchups on NBC every week. There are fans who are
interested in the players and want to learn about the people who play
basketball by watching programs such as *NBA Showtime* and *NBA
Inside Stuff*. Then for the die hard NBA fanatics who have to see the
Philadelphia versus Sacramento game that has playoff implications
for their favorite team, or for a Celtic fan not living in the Boston
area, the NBA provides its League Pass Package.

Adam Silver characterizes the WNBA as yet another venture
that is designed to attract another segment of the audience, trying to
get women interested in basketball and make them fans of not only
the WNBA, but also the NBA. Silver explains that the WNBA was

created as a television project along with NBC because "there were ratings points to be made" (personal communication, December 16, 1998). The WNBA plays a 32-game schedule that begins in late May, and its championship series is played in early September.

The WNBA began in 1997 with eight franchises. The league has expanded every season, largely due to the folding of the American Basketball League, a rival women's league that ended mainly due to its failure to secure wide-scale national television revenue and exposure. Sixteen WNBA franchises competed in the 2000 season, and all WNBA franchises are located in NBA cities (see Table 5.1).

The information and promotional services that the league supplies and utilizes for the NBA are applied to the coverage of the WNBA. The WNBA has three networks broadcasting its games: NBC, ESPN, and Lifetime. The promotion and the coverage of the WNBA includes having film crews from the league present at all of the games. These film crews must feed video highlights of the game back to the NBA offices by a certain time so that the league can then feed the highlights to ESPN, CNN, and Fox in time for their late evening sports report programs.

The WNBA benefits from the temporal context of its league as only major league baseball competes during the summer months of the WNBA. For the 1998 and 1999 season the WNBA had an average attendance of over 10,000. In 1999, there were 99 games in which attendance reached over 10,000, up from 73 games in 1998 and 41 games in the inaugural season of 1997. The WNBA also has a tremendous promotional vehicle as the NBA Finals precede the WNBA season. Campaigns are produced to promote the WNBA such

Table 5.1. The WNBA 2000 Season.

East	West
Charlotte Sting*	Houston Comets*
Cleveland Rockers*	Los Angeles Sparks*
Detroit Shock	Minnesota Lynx
Indiana Fever	Phoenix Mercury*
Miami Sol	Portland Fire
New York Liberty*	Sacramento Monarchs*
Orlando Miracle	Seattle Storm
Washington Mystics	Utah Starzz*

*Original WNBA Franchise
(Source: WNBA)

as "Everybody Join In," which center around personalities like Lisa Leslie, Chamique Holdsclaw, Rebecca Lobo, Sheryl Swoopes, and Nikki McRae, all of whom gained notoriety through college basketball and participation in the Olympics.

NBA INITIATIVES OF PORTRAYAL SUPPORT

Because of the value that is gained from its television broadcasts and the realization that television is the vehicle in which its product is most often seen, the league has developed seminars to educate its key television constituency groups of broadcasters and players. The NBA annually coordinates the league broadcasters' meeting where producers, directors, and announcers from every team get together to discuss different methods and techniques to improve the telecasts with the objective of producing the best possible presentation of NBA games. Adam Silver describes the broadcasters' meetings as a valuable clearinghouse: The league has created a system and a process to share television production information. Silver emphasizes there is "no need to reinvent the wheel," and production personnel can learn what techniques other people in the industry are practicing (personal communication, December 16, 1998). Gregg Winik simply refers to the broadcasters' meetings as a valuable research tool for people involved with televising the NBA.

Due to his experience working on New York Knicks broadcasts, Howie Singer is often asked to do a presentation at the meetings. Singer describes what occurs at the broadcasters' meeting:

> David Stern addresses the whole place, they have a lot of executives from the league to show how the league is growing. It is kind of a talk on here's where we are, things are great, everything is unbelievable. Then we break up into smaller groups and talk about ways to improve our productions. Different producers bring in tapes and show how they can better their broadcasts, which is great. It's good for the league for everybody to have a good broadcast because it reflects well on the league. The league wants all of the teams to do top-notch productions. They know a small station in San Antonio can't afford an eight-camera show, but in the meetings maybe their producer who will be a younger guy and might not have the experience of the person in L.A. can get some ideas and improve their broadcast. The rules, it's the most underrated thing in the world to me that announcers and producers don't know the rules. They stress that and every year

they bring in a Hubie Brown or somebody to go over rule changes or Rod Thorn [former NBA Senior Vice President, Basketball Operations] will go over rule changes, it's great. They have discussions on things they want to improve, things as small as head shots, different ways to do head shots, instead of a still face, a moving background, having a guy throw the ball up in the air. (personal communication, August 26, 1998)

Winik and Silver both emphasize that the objective and often the result of the meetings is giving a sense to the broadcasters that everyone involved in the production of NBA games is working together to make the coverage better.

In addition to assisting broadcasters, the NBA is equally as proactive in educating players, obviously the most critical public in the NBA's efforts to put on the best presentation. One of the methods the NBA utilizes to educate its players is offering a seminar during the Rookie Transition Program, which is mandatory for any player entering the NBA, that is devoted solely to media relations. During this seminar several veteran players offer their advice and experience regarding media relations. Chris Brienza explains some other training ideas that the NBA provides its players during this seminar, including a 12-minute videotape that is produced by the NBA and given to every rookie player (and which is also available to any other player). Brienza comments that the videotape instructs players, "how to deal with the media, explaining why a beat reporter is different than a columnist, and why a local TV guy is different from a broadcast partner, why they might be asking for different things, and why that is what they are looking for" (personal communication, August 12, 1998).

Brian McIntyre explains that the league provides additional training for players if necessary, stating:

If they don't understand it, you explain it. I have had sit-downs with a number of players over the years to explain, usually in anticipation of something that might have happened the prior year with another player. You learn something and you explain the whys. Explain, anticipate, and if you work closely with the team PR Directors you can usually get what you need. We tell the players every time we do media training with them, every time you go to talk, what message are you trying to say, whenever you go into an interview have a message you want to get across. Number two, keep it simple—if you want to say we worked together well as a team, that is your theme, stay with it. (personal communication, December 16, 1998)

McIntyre comments on the increased importance of media relations due to the growth of the media as evidenced by the fact that the sheer amount of media personnel has become a factor. He explains that when he began working for the Chicago Bulls there might only be 10 reporters at a NBA game, aside from New York, and now there might be 100 reporters, or maybe 200 in New York or Chicago for a regular season game. There are also different techniques that media organizations are utilizing, including the local cable network which broadcasts the games and conducts postgame interviews live from the locker room. While taped interviews from the locker room are common on the late local or next evening's six o'clock news, there is an opportunity to edit the videotape. McIntyre offers his view of live locker room interviews on television:

> TV likes the locker room because it gives you a setting that the average person never gets into. A lot of teams now are doing postgame segments live from the locker room, there are a lot of possibilities about what could go wrong there, but to date we haven't had any problems with it. As a viewer it is riveting because those of us in the industry, be it television or print, take it for granted. You go in the locker room it is no big deal, a matter of fact most people try to avoid going into locker rooms. For the guy or the woman sitting at home you don't get to go into locker rooms and it is riveting television, you are in the inner sanctum and so it makes good TV. (personal communication, December 16, 1998)

According to McIntyre, the playoffs are another time when the league makes an extra effort to ensure the players understand their media responsibilities and, more importantly, why these requirements are necessary in the overall effort of informing the fans and continuing to grow the NBA. He comments:

> For the Finals, the playoffs, our locker rooms are not meant for 2,000 people so you have to bring them out to separate interview areas. Satellites [ESPN News, CNNSI] may go live with this, so anticipate the numbers we are going to have and how to best serve everyone. You lower expectations in that [the media] are not going to have much access on a one-on-one basis. Obviously we work with our broadcast partners because they are being seen. If you take everyone [reporter] in the room, they are not going to reach as many people as the network. We go out of our way to help bring the players-coaches to our network partners.

Everyone gets access, but it is in our best interests to work with our people to present the best show we can. It is reinforced with every team before the Finals so they know what to expect—here are the bare minimums with what we need. Obviously Chicago we have worked with over the past number of years, they have a pretty good idea of what we are doing. The first year you work with someone, maybe, maybe not, but as you work with them again they understand what you are doing and we really make it easier for the players. We show them, regular season you might stay by your locker for a half-hour and answer a whole bunch of questions while you are getting dressed. But then if you come to us and give us your five minutes or ten minutes in a formal setting, you are at a table, an informal back and forth, you are clothed, you are sitting down, the media are sitting down, they are not all in your face, there are sound systems so you can hear every question, it is more civilized and it works better for the masses. You don't get that one-on-one feeling and players love it. (personal communication, December 16, 1998)

All these initiatives are to encourage the audience to watch the games. Because the viewing of games is the most important audience behavior—for the obvious reasons of the revenue paid to the league through rights fees and the exposure provided—the NBA does demonstrate a degree of preference to its broadcast partners. It is easier for a broadcast partner to receive access to a one-on-one interview with a player or coach than a newspaper reporter. In addition to the unmatched revenue, television provides unmatched exposure. Brian McIntyre points out that the NBA can reach as many people in one broadcast as it can in numerous newspapers or local newscasts. He characterizes a game broadcast, whether it is local or national, as nothing more than a 2 1/2 hour infomercial for the product. McIntyre explains the advantage:

What is different with our broadcast partners—local NBC has three to four minutes a night on their local news, multiply that times seven and it is 21 to 28 minutes a week—one broadcast gives us 2 1/2 to 3 hours, depending on if you have a pregame and a postgame. Our broadcast partners, we are going right to your target audience, the Finals and the All-Star Game you are going to a bigger audience, bringing the casual fans with you gives you a tremendous platform to be able to focus in on various players, or teams, or issues. (personal communication, December 16, 1998)

Preference has previously been explained in terms of scheduling and access to players, but other areas of preference are provided in terms of the service provided to the broadcast partners during the actual game. Each televised NBA game has a standard format for when timeouts are provided, if neither coach has called a timeout for the purposes of allowing the networks to go to commercial breaks. Mandatory television timeouts are explicitly stated in Section Seven, Rule C of the Official NBA Rules:

> There must be two timeouts per period. If neither team has taken a timeout prior to 6:59 in each of the four regulation periods, it shall be mandatory for the Official Scorer to take it at the first dead ball, and to charge it to the home team. If neither team has taken a second timeout prior to 2:59 in each of the four regulation periods, it shall be mandatory for the Official Scorer to take it at the first dead ball, and to charge it to the team not previously charged in that period. (*The Sporting News*, Official NBA Guide, 1997-98 edition, p. 669)

Kevin Smollon explains the process he undertakes as the producer of the game in dealing with timeouts:

> It's always the timeout under the seven minute mark, so in the next dead ball—if it's seven on the nose you can't go, but if it's 6:59 then you go. If we were approaching the seven minute mark the AD (associate director) will say to me Kevin next dead ball commercial and then I will tell my talent it is the next dead ball, so they know as soon as there is a whistle don't start a story because we are going to commercial and I usually give them a seven second count in their ear soon as the dead ball hits—seven. Unless a great play has happened I might do two or three replays to commercial and then we will try to be shorter on the other end coming out. If you do a lot of replays to commercial you don't want to take a lot of time on the other side so you kind of balance it out. You don't want to interfere with the game. You can fudge it a little bit, but you don't want to start being a factor in the outcome of the game with players sitting there for three or four minutes, that's crazy. (September 23, 1998)

It is important to understand that a head coach can call for a timeout at any other point during the game. Each team receives six full timeouts (100 seconds each) and two 20-second timeouts (one per half). Teams cannot utilize more than three timeouts in the fourth quarter, and no more than two in the last two minutes of regulation. In addition to the commercial breaks planned, the network has floater commercials that can air at any time during the game depending on a head coach calling a timeout. The network also obviously goes to commercial in-between quarters.

It is during timeouts that the NBA is very cooperative with the desires of NBC. The network may want to show additional replays or a short clip of an interview to enhance the telecast of the game. Smollon explains:

> If it is a long break they don't want you to extend it that much, but if it is a minute and a half break, they don't mind making it two minutes for you. And what we do generally to save time sometimes is start a talking head and stick it back into the corner and let them play so we kind of move the game along that way. There is a league representative at every game who is on the headset with our AD who is signaling to the referee when to stop the game. And the great part about the NBA is that it is such a partnership that we can actually say we want to do this talking head or this flashback—want to hold the game up 30 seconds and they will keep the timeout going an extra 30 seconds so we can and it serves both parties. It enhances their league image, promotes their league, and it helps our telecast, so it is a partnership. In a way it is [a responsibility to enhance] because it helps both parties, because the more interest we create the more people are going to watch and the more it is going to build up their league. In a sense more than any other sport we've ever had here, it's really a partnership. The NFL for example, if we were doing something and kickoff was scheduled for 1:01 and you're in a taped flashback or you're in a b-roll, they are kicking at 1:01, they are not holding anything. Same thing, the breaks are 1:50 in length from gun to play and if you're not back from commercial in 1:50, they are going. (personal communication, September 23, 1998)

Talking heads and flashbacks are production elements designed to enhance the viewer's enjoyment of the game. Talking heads are simply interviews with the essential personnel, players and coaches, involved in the game. The NBA and NBC coordinate so that the announcers and producers have the opportunity to sit down with both teams the day before the broadcast. The NBA has a representative at the meetings, acting as a buffer between the networks and the players, to help out and apply a little pressure if some player does not want to be interviewed by the network. Flashbacks are short video clips of a memorable NBA moment that has a connection to the game currently being played. It might be a clip of the last time the teams played, or a more historical moment. The flashback usually has a sponsor connected to it. The Miller Brewing Company has often sponsored this segment, creating "Miller Moments." Smollon describes the collection of these production elements and the coordination necessary with all members of the game broadcast staff, including announcers, during the three days leading up to the game telecast on NBC. He explains:

> Thursday is my homework day. I'll sit from morning to night and reads all the clips and all the press releases and watch the games. The great thing about the NBA is also the DSS, where they have all of the games on so all week I'm watching that teams' games to get ready for that as well. Friday we will travel to the sight, usually get there mid-afternoon, generally try to have dinner with the announcers to discuss stuff on Friday night. Saturday we will meet with the home team in the morning—generally after practice, watch practice, then meet with the team. Depending on the coach, sometimes the practice is closed, generally it's open and we will sit and watch practice. We will meet with the players, do talking heads on camera with them. Go down to the trucks in the afternoon to check on everything there. Generally the visiting team comes in about five or six o'clock Saturday night and we'll meet with them at their hotel and then we will have our own production meeting after that and go over what we will do. We have a VHS in the room so we will view all of the flashbacks, the tease items, the promos, discuss our *Showtime* on-camera. We will do a *NBA Showtime* pop, and we will discuss our game on-camera and anything else pertaining to the game. (personal communication, September 23, 1998)

Personnel from the NBA and NBC also meet on a weekly basis to discuss how coverage of the games could improve. The NBA is very accommodating to NBC's ideas for the broadcast. Tommy Roy explains that if "NBC proposes to do something, other leagues question why, the NBA says why not" (personal communication, October 21, 1998). One example that echoes Roy's comment occurred during the 1999-2000 season when NBC wanted to place a microphone on the head coaches during the broadcast and the NBA complied. Comments from the coaches would not be aired live, but screened before being played. Several coaches did not approve of the microphone arrangement and teams were fined $100,000 by the NBA if the head coach did not wear a microphone during a NBC telecast. Paul

Westphal, former head coach of the Sonics, and Butch Carter, former head coach of the Raptors, received fines on March 12, 2000, for violation of the policy. Due to the extensive coach backlash, the NBA later that week rescinded the fines and came to an agreement in which the coaches had the option of either a clip-on microphone or a boom microphone over the huddle during time outs.

From the league perspective on the relationship and cooperation with NBC, Brian McIntyre says:

> Our relationship with NBC, not that we don't have our disagreements with the way some things might be covered, or somebody might have said something, or the way we promote things, but we talk them out. We have weekly meetings within season with the production team at NBC and a number of people here. Sometimes tough words are said, sometimes tough love is given, but you work out your differences of opinion and you come together with some story ideas and how we could better do it because it is in everyone's best interests. The better we can get our players to work with them, the better we can help them with interviews, the better storylines there are, the better the broadcast is, the more compelling the story, the better the rating should be, the better the ratings, more interest in the NBA, more interest in the NBA, more money that comes into us for rights fees, more money they can charge for advertising. It all works together and the fan benefits because they are getting the best possible deal that these two entities have worked on. (personal communication, December 16, 1998)

Chris Brienza adds:

> There are certain things that come with spending an enormous amount of money to be our exclusive over-the-air partner. We do keep in regular contact with NBC, and meet with them once a week, basically trouble-shoot. My role there is if there is an upcoming game—the last time we broadcast a game involving team X we really had a hard time securing an interview with someone for whatever reason and we want to make sure that is not a problem any more. Hey NBC, if you have a game coming up in two weeks, here's a great story I think will make a great half-time feature. It's a good give and take and they have been an awesome partner for us, they have been great to work with. We have great relationships with the production people and the over-the-air guys, it's been a very good relationship for us. I have

absolutely no complaints and in fact nothing but praise for the way we have been able to deal with them and it's been an honest give and take too—Something we think is unfair, we tell them and if something they think is unfair they tell us too. But it's good, it's a healthy open dialogue. (personal communication, August 12, 1998)

Mike Pearl, Senior Vice President and Executive Producer of Turner Sports (which until 1998 also broadcast the NFL), describes the relationship between the NBA and its broadcast partners as the closest he has witnessed between a rights holder and a network. Pearl says that there is a great amount of dialogue on a daily basis between Turner and the NBA and that there is a great amount of "caring by the NBA about its product and how its product looks on the air." Pearl adds the NBA is "protective of its image" (personal communication, February 25, 1999).

Vincent Costello, NBC Feature Producer, provides an example of one of the ways that coverage might have been altered at the instruction of the NBA. He states:

It is a partnership and it's not so much instruction, but we are definitely kind of working together in this, not every step are we saying let's call up the league and see if they want us to do this. At the same time we will get feedback from them as to things they would like us to do. For example, during the NBA Finals we do a lot of two-ways which is having our announcers at the site doing an interview with somebody from another site by satellite. When you do that it is pretty much live, there is not much time to overly produce it where you can put so much footage and music into it. We would do that, we would bring on live guests and when it is live you don't know what he is going to say, you can't prepare for things, you can't do anything that is overly produced. The NBA likes our produced features where it is done before time and we come back and we edit it all down and we put music to it. They like those better, they said they prefer us to do that, that is what we did. We went away from the live interviews, they thought it put the NBA at a better look, the pieces were more attractive. (personal communication, September 23, 1998)

Ricky Diamond summarizes NBC's position and points out that NBC is still an organization independent of the league in many respects. Diamond cautions:

We can't become or we don't want to become an extension of the league because otherwise the league could do this themselves and that is not the way it works and thankfully when there are tough stories to tell, even if they are negative ones as far as the league is concerned, but they are true, we need to address those stories and we feel there is enough independence from them that we are not afraid to report what has to be reported. In this modern age of mass media we are quite aware that if we don't report it, a non-rights holder is going to report it, whenever it might be. So it behooves us to report the truth and the facts as we see them and as we've gathered them. (personal communication, October 21, 1998)

Diamond, however, points out that there is no doubt that NBC has an interest in promoting and enhancing the NBA through its coverage. He states:

I think that the game sells itself, but we benefit from the popularity of the league and if we can be part of growing the popularity of the league, we stand to benefit. So absolutely, without being altruistic about it or anything, just from a business standpoint it makes sense that we would [promote and enhance]. We and the NBA are partners, the NBC-NBA relationship is a very, very strong one and it has been so from the day it started, and we think that as the league's popularity grows then more people are going to watch it and if more people are watching it then we get higher ratings and we all know that ratings translate into profits in television. It is sort of that simple, so absolutely we have an interest in growing the league, but on the other hand we have to maintain our independence. (personal communication, October 21, 1998)

The preferential treatment toward the networks is not only a league service, but, if not overt preferential treatment, there is at the very least a strong awareness among players and coaches that the team is going to play on NBC, and they are apt to cooperate with whatever information the television people desire. The coaches' only major requirement in dealing with the media is speaking to the press 10 minutes after a game. P.J. Carlesimo, former NBA Head Coach, explains that you "want to cooperate, whether a league rule or just common sense. You want them [NBC, TNT, and local television broadcasters] to know as much as they can about the team as they can" (personal communication, December 9, 1998). Carlesimo contends there is a mutual benefit to both the network and the league for all entities to work together.

   Chuck Daly, Hall-of-Fame Head Coach, agrees with the ideas of Carlesimo that media and television people need help and information and that dealing with the media is "the basis for selling the game" (personal communication, January 7, 1999). Daly contends that basketball people are very conscious of their broadcast partners and players are very aware when their team's game is going to be on NBC. In some instances Daly claims that playing on national television makes his job as head coach a little easier: players have an extra edge and the game has a heightened intensity.
   From a player's perspective, Kelly Tripucka describes it as human nature to cater to the national network:

> The organization did and that kind of filtered down. You want to get as much exposure as possible and in order to get as much exposure as possible the best way to do it was through a national network. That is where more people are going to watch. They have a lot more resources to cover things instead of covering just the game. They do the inside stuff, whatever it may be in the locker room, or the personalities, or what you are like at home. (personal communication, December 4, 1998)

Tripucka also contends that most players are accommodating to whatever the network wants them to do and most networks are accommodating to whatever the players are willing to provide.
   Ted Shaker credits the NBA players with helping to change the perception of the league. He points out that "the players knew they had to go a little further to try to get the game up off the floor. Everyone was going to benefit if there were some positives that came out of what we were trying to do" (personal communication, October 9, 1998). Kevin Smollon would agree with Shaker. He explains that the receptivity of the NBA players toward working with the broadcast partners remains very strong. Smollon states:

> More than any other sport, they get it. They have been trained, the NBA talks to them, they see what Larry Bird and Magic Johnson did. They see how the league has built up from when it was on tape delay at that point to where it is now, and they know the reason is that they built the star concept, and they know the help of the media in the long-run is going to help them. In a sense with the players it is a partnership as well, a Charles Barkley or these guys [will provide] whatever you want. I mean there are exceptions of course to every rule, but most of them, 99% of the coaches are the greatest guys with cooperation and then for the

most part the players will do anything you want. (personal communication, September 23, 1998)

Overall, the underlying philosophy is that all entities stand to benefit from the NBA being well-presented on national network broadcasts. The education of players and the responsibilities that are required for both players and coaches strongly represents the concept that every person involved with the NBA, in whatever capacity, can all help grow the league and make a positive impression on a potential fan. To create and maintain an image, the "everyone working together for the better of the league" philosophy is also explicit in the league rules. In a section of the official rules entitled "Comments on the Rules," Section II speaks to basic principles, and subsection J deals with player/team conduct and dress. There are five provisions by which the players must abide: (a) each player when introduced, prior to the game, must be uniformly dressed, (b) players, coaches, and trainers are to stand and line up in a dignified posture along the sidelines or on the foul line during the playing of the National Anthem, (c) coaches and assistant coaches must wear a sport coat or suit coat, (d) while playing, players must keep their uniform shirts tucked into their pants, and no T-shirts are allowed, and (e) the only article bearing a commercial logo that can be worn by players is their shoes (*The Sporting News*, Official NBA Guide, 1997-98 edition).

NBA RULES: COMPETITIVE BALANCE

The NBA management of the quality of the game product noticeably exists in the rules it creates to help ensure competitive balance. The NBA has instituted several measures, from both a financial and player personnel standpoint, to facilitate, although not guarantee, competitive balance among its 29 franchises. The importance of competitive balance among all teams is that it helps maintain fan interest by giving them the hope that their favorite team can win a NBA Championship. Regarding competitive balance, Commissioner Stern states:

> You sell two things on the court. The first thing you sell is the athleticism and the extraordinary performance of our athletes. The other thing you sell is competition, not just for the particular contest, but from the point of view of continued support in a city of a team and it becomes important for a city and the fans in that

> city to have a sense that they can hold their ownership and man-
> agement accountable for not competing so long as we give them
> the tools to compete. And we thought that our last collective bar-
> gaining agreement [end of the 1999 lockout] which put a cap on
> individual players salaries and also lengthened the amount of
> time that a team would have rights to a player, enhanced compet-
> itiveness. (personal communication, April 14, 1999)

Commissioner Stern adds that "as long as the community gets a broader sense that this year is better than last and next year is likely to be better than this, it is a whole other situation" (personal communication, April 14, 1999).

The major NBA rule that embodies the "everyone working together" philosophy is one of the most prominent and distinctive concepts of the league—the salary cap—which the NBA was the first sport to adopt. It was instituted for the 1984-85 season. The salary cap set up a system in which a maximum and minimum rate of salaries being paid to players would provide some degree of cost awareness for the NBA owners. In 1983, the NBA owners and the players association agreed through collective bargaining that 53% of gate receipts and television revenues would be shared with the play-ers in the form of salaries. Brian McIntyre describes the general overall objective of the salary cap: "In essence it made both labor and management partners. It was then in everyone's best interests to grow the sport, the more we grew it, the more everyone made" (December 16, 1998). The original salary cap for the 1984-85 season was a maximum of $3.6 million for each team (see Table 5.2).

The salary structure, however, is a soft cap with multiple exceptions for teams to sign players, including the Larry Bird rule that allows teams to exceed the salary cap in order to resign their own players who are free agents, if that player played for the team for some or all of each of the prior three consecutive seasons. This provision has created the greatest escalation of salaries for NBA players.

In addition to the salary cap there is a system of revenue sharing for the owners of NBA franchises. Through agreements between the league and its 29 franchises, it is the NBA that has received from its teams the exclusive right to license and control the trademark and logos of the NBA and its franchises. This is controlled by NBA Properties, the marketing division for the NBA. Teams are also not allowed to individually produce and sell a home video involv-ing NBA basketball without the permission of the NBA. Revenues from national and international marketing contracts, as well as

Table 5.2. NBA Salary Cap.

Season	Salary Cap Figure
1984-85	$3.6 million
1985-86	$4.233 million
1986-87	$4.945 million
1987-88	$6.164 million
1988-89	$7.232 million
1989-90	$9.802 million
1990-91	$11.871 million
1991-92	$12.5 million
1992-93	$14.0 million
1993-94	$15.175 million
1994-95	$15.964 million
1995-96	$23.0 million
1996-97	$24.3 million
1997-98	$26.9 million
1998-99	$30.0 million*
1999-00	$34.0 million*

*The figures for the 1998-99 and 1999-2000 season are based on the 1999 lockout agreement.
(Source: NBA)

national television broadcast contracts, are distributed equally among the 29 franchises. The rationale for the revenue sharing in the NBA is commented on in *Chicago Professional Sports Limited Partnership and WGN Continental Broadcasting Company v. NBA*: "it is not disputed, and it is plain from the financial figures, that the prosperity of the league currently depends on the volume of the shared revenues generated by the league's economic activity on behalf of the teams and particularly on the revenues generated by the broadcast contracts with the national networks" (1991, p. 1340).

The NBA teams are, however, independent in three financial endeavors: (a) their local broadcasting contracts, both television and radio, in which teams receive 100% of the revenues produced in the contract, (b) ticket sales, as only a very small percentage of the revenues are shared from the live gate attending the game (Commissioner Stern comments that 6% of the gate goes to the league), and (c) local marketing. As stated in the WGN court case, "the most significant sign of their economic independence is the fact that all the teams calculate their own profits and that what they earn on their own and keep for themselves is more substantial than what they produce together" (*Chicago Professional Sports Limited Partnership and WGN Continental Broadcasting Company v. NBA*, 1991, p. 1341).

The Boston Celtics accounting balance sheet demonstrates how one franchise earns and spends its money. The Boston Celtics are utilized because they are a publicly traded company listed on the New York Stock Exchange and the Boston Stock Exchange and traded under the symbol "BOS." Their 1997 Consolidated Statements of Income reveal the origins of their revenues and expenses (see Table 5.3).

In offering an explanation of their basketball-related business operations, the Boston Celtics annual report (1997) states, "the Boston Celtics derive revenues principally from the sale of tickets to home games and the licensing of television, cable network and radio rights. A large portion of the Boston Celtics' annual revenues and operating expense is determinable at the commencement of each basketball season based on season ticket sales and the Boston Celtics' multi-year contracts with its players and broadcast organizations" (p. 18). The amount of ticket sales, local marketing, and the local broadcast revenue could create an economic and, therefore, competitive imbalance. Teams that are in larger markets receive higher broadcast and marketing revenues, somewhat regardless of team performance. Teams' ability to perform well should increase fan support and ticket sales.

Ed Desser comments on the league revenue sharing ideas and the importance of these objectives in the overall operation of the NBA:

> The fundamental premise under which we operate and I guess maybe underlying all of this, and it's I think an important additional point is, recognizing how the revenue aspects of this play into issues of competitive balance. There are a whole variety of systems that are designed to help maintain the integrity and quality of the product. It goes beyond just how it's televised or how it's presented, but the fact that Milwaukee and San Antonio get the same amount of network television revenue as the Knicks and the Lakers is about giving them the same number of chips or close to the same number of chips to play with as they compete for talent. The whole salary cap system is about trying to level the playing field and provide both continuity in terms of free agents and relative balance in the ability of teams to attract and keep players. (personal communication, August 26, 1998)

Table 5.3. Boston Celtics Consolidated Statements of Income—1997.

	For The Year Ended		
Revenues	*June 30, 1997*	*June 30, 1996*	*June 30, 1995*
Basketball regular season-			
Ticket sales	$31,813,019	$35,249,625	$22,036,880
Television and radio broadcast fees	$23,269,159	$22,071,992	$20,956,405
Other-principally promotional advertising	$7,915,626	$7,458,651	$7,418,487
Basketball playoffs			$1,913,481
Total	$62,997,804	$64,780,268	$52,325,253
Costs and expenses			
Basketball regular season-			
Team	$40,941,156	$27,891,264	$31,203,697
Game	$2,386,042	$2,606,218	$2,880,566
Basketball playoffs			$696,583
General and administrative	$13,913,893	$15,053,333	$14,085,982
Selling and promotional	$4,680,168	$2,973,488	$2,692,208
Depreciation	$189,702	$140,894	$86,347
Amortization of NBA franchise and other related assets	$164,702	$164,703	$164,703
Total	$62,275,285	$48,829,900	$51,810,086
Net Income of Revenues/Expenses	$722,519	$15,950,368	$515,167

Note. The 1997 financial report is utilized to depict revenue from the Celtics' appearance in the 1995 NBA playoffs. The Celtics generated $1,913,481 in their first round loss to the Orlando Magic which featured two home games in Boston.
(Source: Boston Celtics, 1997)

Desser adds that these measures of competitive balance are central to the creation and maintenance of the product. Moreover, these measures give NBC confidence that its purchase of multiyear broadcasting rights is a smart investment (personal communication, August 26, 1998).

In addition to the extensive revenue-sharing measures that the league employs, the issue of competitive balance and providing each franchise an opportunity to win and play for a championship is demonstrated through multiple player personnel initiatives. The NBA collegiate player draft is an initiative that is created by the league to achieve competitive balance by giving teams with poor records the previous season a greater opportunity to select the best players available from the college pool, including European players who have declared themselves eligible for the draft. The NBA Draft consists of two rounds in which each team has a selection to either utilize on an eligible player or trade to another team who in turn will use the pick.

An element of the draft that speaks to competitive balance, and provides an incentive for teams to continue to try to win despite a bad record, is the NBA Draft Lottery. From 1966 to 1984, the teams that finished with the worst records in each conference participated in a coin flip to determine the first selection in the draft. The remaining franchises would then pick in order depending on their record the previous season with the teams having the worst record getting the higher selection in the draft. In June 1984, the NBA Board of Governors created a lottery system to be implemented for the 1985 NBA Draft in which all teams who did not qualify for the playoffs became eligible for participation in the lottery. Originally the lottery gave each of the teams that had qualified an equal opportunity for the top selection as each of the seven non-playoff teams had one envelope placed in a tumbler. It was the first lottery in 1985 that gave the New York Knicks the top selection and Patrick Ewing.

The lottery has not been a perfect system: Only twice has the team that finished with the worst record been awarded the top selection. In 1993 the Orlando Magic, although finishing the season with a 41-41 record, and only missing the playoffs due to losing a tiebreaker with the Indiana Pacers, won the lottery and selected Chris Webber, whom they traded to the Golden State Warriors for Anfernee "Penny" Hardaway. The Magic parlayed their lottery success in obtaining Hardaway with their 1992 success of winning the lottery and drafting Shaquille O'Neal into an appearance in the 1995 NBA Finals (a four games to none loss to the Houston Rockets). In 1986 a change was implemented in which the lottery would essentially only determine the top three selections and the team that finished with the worst record could not have a draft pick lower than fourth. The remaining teams would then select in inverse order, but often the team with the worst record did not get the second selection either (see Tables 5.4 and 5.5).

Another change in the NBA Draft and NBA Lottery was adopted in 1989 with the creation of a weighted system to try to give the worst team the best opportunity and a team that had the best record not to qualify for the playoffs the least opportunity to get the first selection in the draft. For the 11 eligible franchises, the team with the worst record would get 11 of 66 total ping-pong balls, and the team with the best record of the non-playoff teams would only get one (see Table 5.6).

For the 1994 draft lottery, the league once again adjusted the system to increase the opportunity for the worst teams to get the top selections. The current system now has 1,000 ping-pong balls, which provides the worst team with a 36% chance of getting the top selection and the team with the best record a 5% possibility (see Table 5.7).

The NBA Draft and NBA Lottery provide television opportunities that the NBA has taken advantage of. The draft used to occur on a weekday and consisted of six—and in some years 10—rounds.

Table 5.4. Draft Lottery: 1985-2000.

Year	Team with worst finish	Record	Team that won lottery	Record
1985	Golden State and Indiana	22-60	New York	24-58
1986	New York	23-59	Cleveland	29-53
1987	L.A. Clippers	12-70	San Antonio	28-54
1988	L.A. Clippers	17-65	L.A. Clippers	17-65
1989	Miami	15-67	Sacramento	27-55
1990	New Jersey	17-65	New Jersey	17-65
1991	Denver	20-62	Charlotte	26-56
1992	Minnesota	15-67	Orlando	21-61
1993	Dallas	11-71	Orlando	41-41
1994	Dallas	13-69	Milwaukee	20-62
1995	L.A. Clippers	17-65	Golden State	26-56
1996	Vancouver	15-67	Philadelphia	18-64
1997	Vancouver	14-68	San Antonio	20-62
1998	Denver	11-71	L.A. Clippers	17-65
1999	Vancouver	8-42	Chicago	13-37
2000	L.A. Clippers	15-67	New Jersey	31-51

(Source: NBA)

Table 5.5. First and Second Selections in the NBA Draft: 1985-2000.

Year	1st Player Selected	Team	2nd Player Selected	Team
1985	Patrick Ewing	New York	Wayman Tisdale	Indiana
1986	Brad Daugherty	Cleveland	Len Bias	Boston
1987	David Robinson	San Antonio	Armon Gilliam	Phoenix
1988	Danny Manning	L.A. Clippers	Rik Smits	Indiana
1989	Pervis Ellison	Sacramento	Danny Ferry	L.A. Clippers
1990	Derek Coleman	New Jersey	Gary Payton	Seattle
1991	Larry Johnson	Charlotte	Kenny Anderson	New Jersey
1992	Shaquille O'Neal	Orlando	Alonzo Mourning	Charlotte
1993	Chris Webber	Orlando	Shawn Bradley	Philadelphia
1994	Glenn Robinson	Milwaukee	Jason Kidd	Dallas
1995	Joe Smith	Golden State	Antonio McDyess	L.A. Clippers
1996	Allen Iverson	Philadelphia	Marcus Camby	Toronto
1997	Tim Duncan	San Antonio	Keith Van Horn	New Jersey
1998	Michael Olowokandi	L.A. Clippers	Mike Bibby	Vancouver
1999	Elton Brand	Chicago	Steve Francis	Vancouver
2000	Kenyon Martin	New Jersey	Stromile Swift	Vancouver

(Source: NBA)

Table 5.6. Draft Lottery Opportunity with Draft Position—1993.

Team	Record	# of balls	Draft Position
Dallas	11-71	11	4
Minnesota	19-63	10	5
Washington	22-60	9	6
Sacramento	25-57	8	7
Philadelphia	26-56	7	2
Milwaukee	28-54	6	8
Golden State	34-48	5	3
Denver	36-46	4	9
Miami	36-46	3	10
Detroit	40-42	2	11
Orlando	41-41	1	1

(Source: NBA)

Table 5.7. Draft Lottery Opportunity with Draft Position—2000.

Team	Record	Chances	Pick 1%	Pick 2%	Pick 3%	Draft #
L.A. Clippers	15-67	250	25.00	21.55	17.84	3
Chicago	17-65	200	20.00	18.91	17.22	4
Orlando	41-41	157	15.70	15.84	15.70	5
Vancouver	22-60	120	12.00	12.71	13.43	2
Atlanta	28-54	89	8.90	9.77	10.82	6
Washington	29-53	64	6.40	7.21	8.26	7
New Jersey	31-52	44	4.40	5.06	5.93	1
Cleveland	32-50	29	2.90	3.38	4.03	8
Houston	34-48	18	1.80	2.12	2.56	9
Orlando	41-41	9	0.90	1.07	1.30	10
Boston	35-47	9	0.90	1.07	1.30	11
Dallas	40-42	6	0.60	0.71	0.87	12
Orlando	41-41	5	0.50	0.60	0.73	13

(Source: NBA)

The NBA Draft is now a prime-time event televised on TNT. The NBA Draft format has also been revised to two rounds, with each team having five minutes to make its first round selection and two minutes for its second round choice. Hubie Brown describes the televising of the draft as the toughest broadcasting assignment for Turner in terms of both the length of the broadcast (4 to 4 1/2 hours) and the preparation involved. Brown claims it is important to stay positive with a high energy level as you do not want to slight a player or a school because "every player drafted, whether they are selected number one or the last player, it is the biggest day in his life for himself, his family, and his college" (personal communication, January 27, 1999). For those reasons Brown claims he never downgrades the player or the pick by a team. The televising of the draft allows almost each player to be seen and heard as after a player is selected, he is interviewed on the TNT broadcast.

The NBA Draft Lottery, telecast during halftime of a playoff game on NBC, determines who obtains the first selection in the upcoming draft. Ted Shaker says that when CBS "televised the lottery for the first time, we split-screened two guys and it was the year that Ewing went to the Knicks and it was great television for six or seven minutes of the halftime" (personal communication, October 9, 1998). The NBA Draft allows the NBA to introduce, or reintroduce, the college stars who will be joining the league. As players are selected and walk up to the podium to be greeted by Commissioner Stern, they are given a cap, and some players get the team's jersey. This allows the NBA to introduce and market a new cap or jersey. The draft is thus an example of multiple agenda-setting initiatives of the NBA operating simultaneously.

The timing of the draft shortly after the NBA Finals helps make the NBA a league that demands year-round coverage. Fred Kerber, New Jersey Nets beat writer for the *New York Post*, describes the schedule of the NBA from a coverage perspective:

> There really is no off-season anymore because consider that the NBA Finals went to the end of June or mid-June, then you have a week leading up to the draft, then after the draft, July 1 is always a magical date in the NBA, it usually is the day that you can start signing free agents or at least start talking to free agents. If there is a downtime it's August, then what happens in September is sort of bargain basement time, all of your free agents who didn't get signed in July who want to play if they haven't struck a deal in Europe, they're looking to scramble and find a NBA roster spot. Because of the salary cap they may be apt to get less than what they were hoping for and so the teams are looking for bargains then. (personal communication, July 29, 1998)

The NBA has thus set a schedule in which the league does not go too long without news occurring and exposure continuing in the newspapers, or on ESPN *SportsCenter*.

The issue of competitive balance and its unwavering importance on the part of the league was a core issue in the NBA lockout, which cancelled 30 games from the NBA schedule for the 1998-99 season. The ability of the owners to lockout the players was provided in the previous collective bargaining agreement that had been ratified between the owners and the players' association. On August 8, 1995, owners and players reached an agreement giving the owners the right to toss out the agreement after three years if the percentage of basketball-related income devoted to players salaries exceeded 51.8%.

On March 23, 1998, the owners, by a vote of 27-2, elected to reopen the collective bargaining agreement at the conclusion of the season, and on July 1, 1998, the owners of the NBA's 29 franchises imposed the third lockout in NBA history, but the first that would cause the league to cancel regularly scheduled games (the first lockout was from July 1 to September 17 in 1985, whereas the second lasted only hours on July 11, 1996, in a dispute over television money).

The first contentious moment between the NBA and the players' association occurred in 1964. The efforts to unionize the players in the early 1960s were led by Tommy Heinsohn and Oscar Robertson, but the owners had not recognized the union as a bargaining unit. Heinsohn explained that the union wanted very basic things such as "improved playing conditions, a trainer for each team, which we didn't have, and if we had a Saturday night game, we wanted to do away with the Sunday afternoon game in another city. They were all things for the betterment of the game. Pensions were the only financial issue" (cited in D'Alessandro, November 3, 1998). With the help of the late lawyer Larry Fleisher, a man who was introduced to the NBA business after doing Heinsohn's tax return, the union decided to strike on January 14, 1964, immediately before ABC was about to broadcast the annual All-Star Game, an event in which players were not contractually bound to participate. Fearing the loss of the NBA on television, with ABC threatening to pull out of all its coverage of the NBA and the owners desperately needing the revenue of television, the owners gave in and promised the players a pension plan.

The NBA lockout of 1998-99, as all work stoppages, was essentially a dispute about money. In sports today, money and competitive balance have become synonymous. The new NBA collective bargaining agreement was approved by the players on January 6, 1999, and by the owners on January 7, 1999. It created a new system of rules to secure financial prosperity and competitive balance. The league and the players' association have created an escrow system in which there is no fixed number for the first three years, but beginning with the 2001-02 season, player salaries will be reduced to the extent that total salaries and benefits not exceed 55% of basketball-related income. If the owners exercise their option and extend the collective bargaining agreement to a seventh year, the escrow percentage will be 57%. This provision allows an aspect of cost containment for owners, as, if the total of salaries and benefits exceeds the escrow percentage by more than 10%, the team will pay a tax to the NBA equal to the amount of the excess. The players will decide who among them must pay the 10% escrow tax that goes to the owners. All current player contracts are reinstated at their present terms.

The collective bargaining agreement of 1999 is a six-year contract with a league option for a seventh year. The major provisions of the deal include the salary cap, which continues to be 48% of basketball-related income. The Larry Bird exceptions to the salary cap will remain unchanged: Bird contracts may increase by up to 12.5% and all other contracts may increase by up to 10%. There is, however, a limit to "high-end" contracts regardless of their Bird status. The limiting of "high-end" contracts was a major desire of the NBA owners. The new maximum salary for a player in the first year of a contract is 105% of their previous salary, or the salary is then subject to years played. For players with fewer than six years of service the maximum they can earn is $9 million or 25% of the salary cap, $11 million or 30% of the salary cap for players with seven to nine years of service, and for players with over 10 years of service, their maximum is $14 million or 35% of the salary cap.

The cap on maximum salaries was a major concession by the players' association as there will no longer be the extraordinary contracts, such as Michael Jordan's one year contract in excess of $30 million in his final season with the Bulls or the deal that Kevin Garnett signed with the Minnesota Timberwolves. In August 1997, Garnett turned down an offer from the Timberwolves for $103.5 million over six years. On October 1, 1997, Garnett did sign a contract extension with Minnesota that paid him $125 million over six years. The new cap on maximum salaries provides an advantage to the team that currently has the player under contract, as players will earn more money by signing with their current team. Milwaukee Bucks General Manager Ernie Grunfeld states, "the home team now has the edge in keeping its players." He adds "it gives an extra year, and annual raises are 12 percent instead of ten" (cited in D'Alessandro, 1999). Since the end of the lockout the following notable players have all signed long-term contracts to remain with their respective teams: Jayson Williams (Nets), Stephon Marbury (Nets), Kerry Kittles (Nets), Kobe Bryant (Lakers), Antoine Walker (Celtics), Zydrunas Ilgauskas (Cavaliers), Allen Iverson (76ers), Tim Duncan (Spurs), and Ray Allen (Bucks). With the stricter rules of the salary scale, Ray Allen did not even use an agent to negotiate his contract extension.

There are two other exceptions to the salary cap: (a) the $1 million exception that teams can exercise every other season to sign a player for $1 million without that money being counted against the team salary cap. This exception increases by $100,000 for each season of the agreement beginning in the 1999-2000 season, when it will then be $1.1 million. And (b) the "middle-class" exception that teams can exercise every season. This exception allows a team to sign a player for $1.75 million in 1998-99, $2 million in 1999-2000, $2.25 million in 2000-01, and then the average player salary for the remainder of the agreement without the team being penalized against its salary cap. Minimum salaries will also increase based on service. Players with five years of service will be paid a minimum of

$500,000, and players with more than 10 years of service will receive a minimum of $1 million, up from the league minimum of $250,000.

Another major issue settled in the collective bargaining agreement of 1999 was the rookie salary scale. The rookie salary scale began with players selected in the 1999 draft. Rookies are subject to a 3-year wage scale with teams holding the option for the fourth year and a right of first refusal for the fifth season. Rookie extensions will continue to be permitted in the last year of the player's contract (year four) but are subject to the "high-end" contract limits. The salaries for NBA rookies have substantially increased, creating a need for these new provisions (See Table 5.8).

In utilizing the cumulative inflation rate of just over 43% (.434) from 1987 to 1999 (as the contracts are signed prior to the actual season beginning) provided by the United States Department of Labor Bureau of Labor Statistics, the average of the top-ten rookie salaries in 1987 would equate to $860,335 instead of $2,231,397 in 1999. The top-ten rookie average represents a 284% increase in salaries. The average salary of the entire first round of players represents a 262% increase from 1987 to 1999.

The new financial agreements, with the limit on "high-end" contracts and the increase in the million dollar and middle-class exceptions and the league minimum, can be described as a redistribution of the wealth, with the majority of NBA players receiving more money, and the superstars earning a little less than they would have under the previous rules. The new financial agreement is also one designed to help create competitive balance among all of the NBA's 29 teams. To demonstrate the connection between the financial structure and the competitive balance of NBA basketball, Commissioner Stern commented on both areas in his initial remarks at the ratification of the collective bargaining agreement press conference on January 7, 1998. Stern stated,

> From the NBA's perspective, this reaffirms our partnership with our players. It gives 29 teams the opportunity to compete. It emphasizes continuity of rosters. Hopefully players will be encouraged to maximize their income and do it with the teams that they had previously played with. It gives well-managed teams the opportunity to have a return on their investment, and I believe guaranteed NBA players will remain the highest paid athletes in the world. Deservedly so. (press conference, January 7, 1998, see Table 5.9)

Table 5.8. NBA Rookie Salaries; 1987-88 and 1999-2000.

1987-1988			1999-2000		
Player	Team	Salary millions	Player	Team	Salary millions
1. David Robinson	San Antonio	$1.05	1. Elton Brand	Chicago	$3.38
2. Armon Gilliam	Phoenix	$ .7	2. Steve Francis	Houston	$3.02
3. Dennis Hopson	New Jersey	$ .4	3. Baron Davis	Charlotte	$2.71
4. Reggie Williams	L.A. Clippers	$ .6	4. Lamar Odom	L.A. Clippers	$2.45
5. Scottie Pippen	Seattle	$ .73	5. Jonathan Bender	Indiana	$2.21
6. Kenny Smith	Sacramento	$ .6	6. Wally Szczerbiak	Minnesota	$2.01
7. Kevin Johnson	Cleveland	$ .54	7. Richard Hamilton	Washington	$1.84
8. Olden Polynice	Chicago	$ .35	8. Andre Miller	Utah	$1.68
9. Derrick McKey	Seattle	$ .36	9. Shawn Marion	Phoenix	$1.55
10. Horace Grant	Chicago	$ .5	10. Jason Terry	Atlanta	$1.47

Average Top Ten: $581,000
Average First Round: $378,000

Average Top Ten: $2,231,397
Average First Round: $1,368,410

(Source 1987-88: *The Sporting News*)

(Source 1999-2000: *The Newark Star-Ledger*)

Table 5.9. Top Ten NBA Salaries; 1987-88 and 1999-2000.

	1987-1988			1999-2000	
Player	Team	Salary millions	Player	Team	Salary millions
1. Patrick Ewing	New York	$2.75	1. Shaquille O'Neal	Los Angeles	$17.14
2. Magic Johnson	Los Angeles	$2.5	2. Kevin Garnett	Minnesota	$16.81
3. Moses Malone	Washington	$2.07	3. Alonzo Mourning	Miami	$11.25
4. Robert Parrish	Boston	$2.04	4. Patrick Ewing	New York	$15.0
5. K. Abdul-Jabbar	Los Angeles	$2.0	5. Juwan Howard	Washington	$15.0
6. Larry Bird	Boston	$1.8	6. Scottie Pippen	Portland	$14.76
7. Ralph Sampson	Houston	$1.74	7. Hakeem Olajuwon	Houston	$14.30
8. Jack Sikma	Milwaukee	$1.6	8. Karl Malone	Utah	$14.0
9. Alex English	Denver	$1.5	9. Dikembe Mutombo	Atlanta	$12.8
10. Dom. Wilkins	Atlanta	$1.46	10. Jayson Williams	New Jersey	$12.38
Average Top Ten: $1,945,033			Average Top Ten: $14,724,684		

(Source 1987-88: *The Sporting News*)

(Source 1999-2000: *The Newark Star-Ledger*)

Adjusted to the approximately 43% increase in the rate of inflation, the average salary of the top ten NBA players of $1,945,033 in 1987 would grow to $2,880,240. Instead, the average salary of the top ten players in 1999 has increased 657% to $14,724,684.

Moreover, Stern stated,

> our players are going to get at least 55 percent, I would project, of an ever-increasing pie. That would push their average salaries to $5 million a year in the life of this deal. I would add that NBA teams will not be guaranteed a profit. They are guaranteed the opportunity to make a profit if they are well-managed. To me, that is the best win-win that you can come out of a sports collective bargaining agreement with. (press conference, January 7, 1998)

On the issue of competitive balance, Stern said, "we want the fans in all NBA cities, when the exhibition season is about to begin, to have a sense or to be able to have a sense over some period of years, that there's an opportunity for their teams to compete and possibly win, and that's very important" (press conference, January 7, 1998, see Table 5.10).

A comparison can be made between the NBA and major league baseball, which does not have as comprehensive a revenue sharing structure among its franchises (see Table 5.11).

The difference between the highest (Portland) and the lowest (L.A. Clippers) NBA salary is $47.6 million, whereas in major league baseball it is $77.29 million between the highest (New York Yankees) and lowest (Minnesota). A statistical correlation was conducted to further illustrate the relationship between team's players' salaries and winning percentage and the need for revenue sharing. The results of the correlation between team's players' salaries and winning percentage were statistically significant: An increase in the team's players' salaries relates to an increase in that particular team's winning percentage for both the NBA and major league baseball; however, the NBA showed a stronger relationship, NBA, $r = .54$, $p < .01$, and major league baseball, $r = .40$, $p < .05$. It is important to point out that the results of a correlation between team's players' salaries and winning percentage can differ from year-to-year. A correlation for the 1997-98 NBA and the 1998 major league baseball season reveals statistically significant correlations for both sports, however major league baseball is stronger, $r = .70$, $p < .01$, in comparison to the NBA, $r = .51$, $p < .01$.

Table 5.10. NBA Team Salaries; 1987-88 and 1999-2000.

1987-88		1999-2000	
Team	Salary in millions	Team	Salary in millions
1. Los Angeles Lakers	$9.10	1. Portland Trail Blazers	$73.9
2. Boston Celtics	$8.50	2. New York Knicks	$71.3
3. New York Knicks	$7.40	3. Indiana Pacers	$54.2
4. Houston Rockets	$7.00	4. Los Angeles Lakers	$54.1
5. Milwaukee Bucks	$6.60	5. New Jersey Nets	$52.7
6. New Jersey Nets	$6.55	6. Washington Wizards	$52.6
7. Atlanta Hawks	$6.50	7. Houston Rockets	$52.3
8. Washington Bullets	$6.35	8. Miami Heat	$51.0
9. Philadelphia 76ers	$6.20	9. Utah Jazz	$49.2
10. Los Angles Clippers	$6.10	10. Cleveland Cavaliers	$46.5
11. Detroit Pistons	$5.90	11. Phoenix Suns	$46.5
12. Denver Nuggets	$5.85	12. Boston Celtics	$46.1
13. Utah Jazz	$5.80	13. Milwaukee Bucks	$45.8
14. Sacramento Kings	$5.70	14. Atlanta Hawks	$44.2
15. Phoenix Suns	$5.25	15. Denver Nuggets	$43.3
16. Portland Trail Blazers	$5.20	16. Philadelphia 76ers	$42.7
17. Golden State Warriors	$5.15	17. San Antonio Spurs	$42.6
18. Seattle SuperSonics	$5.10	18. Minnesota Timberwolves	$42.1
19. Chicago Bulls	$5.00	19. Detroit Pistons	$42.0
20. Indiana Pacers	$4.95	20. Orlando Magic	$41.8
21. San Antonio Spurs	$4.90	21. Sacramento Kings	$40.1
22. Dallas Mavericks	$4.85	22. Dallas Mavericks	$39.4
23. Cleveland Cavaliers	$4.30	23. Seattle SuperSonics	$38.3
		24. Vancouver Grizzlies	$37.7
		25. Golden State Warriors	$36.3
		26. Charlotte Hornets	$36.0
		27. Toronto Raptors	$34.7
		28. Chicago Bulls	$27.0
		29. Los Angeles Clippers	$26.3

Average Top Ten: $7.03 million
Total Average: $6.01 million

Average Top Ten: $56.32 million
Total Average: $45.20 million

(Source 1987-88: *The Sporting News*)

(Source 1999-2000: *The Newark Star-Ledger*)

Table 5.11. Salary Comparison and Winning Percentage NBA and Baseball.

NBA-1999-2000			Major League Baseball-2000		
Team	Salary in millions	Win%	Team	Salary in millions	Win%
1. Portland Trail Blazers	$73.9	.720	1. New York Yankees	$92.9	.540
2. New York Knicks	$71.3	.610	2. Los Angeles Dodgers	$90.7	.531
3. Indiana Pacers	$54.2	.683	3. Atlanta Braves	$82.7	.586
4. Los Angeles Lakers	$54.1	.817	4. Baltimore Orioles	$82.7	.457
5. New Jersey Nets	$52.7	.378	5. Boston Red Sox	$81.2	.525
6. Washington Wizards	$52.6	.354	6. New York Mets	$79.8	.580
7. Houston Rockets	$52.3	.415	7. Arizona Diamondbacks	$77.8	.525
8. Miami Heat	$51.0	.634	8. Cleveland Indians	$76.5	.556
9. Utah Jazz	$49.2	.671	9. Texas Rangers	$70.8	.438
10. Cleveland Cavaliers	$46.5	.390	10. Tampa Bay Devil Rays	$64.4	.429
11. Phoenix Suns	$46.5	.646	11. Colorado Rockies	$64.1	.506
12. Boston Celtics	$46.1	.427	12. Saint Louis Cardinals	$64.0	.586
13. Milwaukee Bucks	$45.8	.512	13. Chicago Cubs	$62.1	.401
14. Atlanta Hawks	$44.2	.341	14. Detroit Tigers	$61.7	.488
15. Denver Nuggets	$43.3	.427	15. Seattle Mariners	$59.2	.562
16. Philadelphia 76ers	$42.7	.598	16. Anaheim Angels	$55.8	.506
17. San Antonio Spurs	$42.6	.646	17. San Diego Padres	$55.0	.469
18. Minnesota Timberwolves	$42.1	.610	18. San Francisco Giants	$53.5	.599
19. Detroit Pistons	$42.0	.512	19. Houston Astros	$47.0	.444
20. Orlando Magic	$41.8	.500	20. Philadelphia Phillies	$46.4	.401
21. Sacramento Kings	$40.1	.537	21. Toronto Blue Jays	$44.2	.512
22. Dallas Mavericks	$39.4	.488	22. Cincinnati Reds	$42.2	.525
23. Seattle SuperSonics	$38.3	.549	23. Milwaukee Brewers	$35.8	.451
24. Vancouver Grizzlies	$37.7	.268	24. Montreal Expos	$33.5	.414
25. Golden State Warriors	$36.3	.232	25. Oakland Athletics	$32.1	.565
26. Charlotte Hornets	$36.0	.598	26. Chicago White Sox	$31.1	.586
27. Toronto Raptors	$34.7	.549	27. Pittsburgh Pirates	$29.6	.426
28. Chicago Bulls	$27.0	.207	28. Kansas City Royals	$23.1	.475
29. Los Angeles Clippers	$26.3	.183	29. Florida Marlins	$19.9	.401
			30. Minnesota Twins	$15.7	.426

Average Top Ten: $56.32 million
Total Average: $45.20 million

Average Top Ten: $79.97 million
Total Average: $56.20 million

(Source 1999-2000: *The Newark Star-Ledger*)   (Source: *USA Today*)

This correlation does not represent causation between the variable of spending money and winning percentage. The relationship is not a perfect association, and spending more money on players' salaries does not guarantee a higher winning percentage. For example, in major league baseball the Baltimore Orioles had the fourth highest salary in 2000, but finished with a .457 winning percentage and had only the 20th best record in baseball. In the NBA, the New Jersey Nets had the fifth highest salary, finished with a .378 winning percentage, and had only the 23rd best record in the NBA. Other factors include of acquiring the proper players (not necessarily the most expensive), the chemistry the team develops, players staying healthy, younger players producing prior to their peak salary earning years [a factor most evident in the success of the 2000 Oakland Athletics and Chicago White Sox], and the coaching these players receive.

One of the strengths that the owners had in negotiating with the players was that the owners were receiving their regularly scheduled payments from their broadcast partners. The broadcast partners would not be required to continue to pay the NBA if the lockout had continued into a second season. Prior to the NBA lockout, NBC was scheduled to broadcast NBA games in 33 different time slots beginning with a double header on Christmas Day. After the lockout, NBC was only able to schedule games in 28 time slots. TNT had 52 games originally, but only broadcast 31 due to the lockout, and TBS had their allotment drop in half from 28 to 14. The NBA did make concessions to the broadcast partners by providing extra unscheduled games through double headers and by extending the season beyond its original date of completion. Dick Ebersol, President of NBC Sports, summarized, "it would be crazy to say there isn't damage, but traditionally, the greatest interest in the NBA as a national television product doesn't begin until this time of year" (cited in D'Alessandro, 1999).

THE NBA GIFTS

Most coaches in any sport will claim that great players and a little bit of luck are major ingredients in winning a championship. In the efforts of the NBA to become an elite league in the 1980s they received a fair amount of luck, and some of the game's best players. In 1924, the Notre Dame football team, led by legendary Head Coach Knute Rockne, defeated a powerful Army team, prompting sportswriter Grantland Rice to pen one of the most notable opening lines in sportswriting history: "Outlined against a blue-grey October sky, the Four Horsemen rode again. In dramatic lore they are known as Famine, Pestilence, Destruction, and Death. These are only aliases. Their real names are Stuhldreher, Miller, Crowley, and Layden" (e.g., Rader, 1984, p. 21). As the NBA in the late 1970s and early 1980s might have thought its league was playing under a similar blue-grey sky, Rice might have a written a passage that described a new group of Four Horsemen that would carry the NBA; their names were Erving, Bird, Johnson, and Jordan.

Julius Erving, Dr. J., joined the NBA when the league merged with the American Basketball Association in the 1976-77 season. After being traded by the then New York Nets to the Philadelphia 76ers, Erving immediately helped lead the 76ers to the NBA Finals in 1977 (losing four games to two to Bill Walton and the Portland Trail Blazers). Erving and the 76ers were perennial contenders for the NBA Championship, making four trips to the NBA Finals and winning the championship by sweeping the Lakers in 1983. Erving was a major attraction for the league due to his style of play, which would often feature high-flying slam dunks. Erving was also the major attraction in the first-ever NBA Slam Dunk Contest, although the contest was won by Larry Nance, then of the Phoenix Suns. Dr. J. would finish his career with one NBA and two ABA Championships and one NBA and two ABA MVP awards. He was named All-NBA first team five times and All-ABA first team four times, and he appeared in 11 NBA and five ABA All-Star Games.

Larry Bird and Erving "Magic" Johnson played in the highest rated collegiate basketball game ever (24.1, Nielsen) when Johnson's Michigan State team defeated the Bird-led Indiana State Sycamores in 1979. In his 13-year career with the Boston Celtics, Larry Bird would win three NBA Championships, three MVP awards, be named to the first team All-NBA nine times, and appear in 12 All-Star Games. Bird also won the All-Star Weekend Long Distance Shootout event three times. Johnson also played 13 years, winning five NBA Championships with the Los Angeles Lakers, three MVP awards, was named to the first team All-NBA nine times, and appeared in 12 All-Star Games. Tommy Heinsohn describes Larry Bird and Magic Johnson as two throwback players who were true artists on the basketball court. Heinsohn also claims he often referred to Bird as the "Bobby Fisher of basketball. He plays chess while others are playing checkers. It is the same board, but he is playing a different game" (personal communication, November 10, 1998).

Erving, Johnson, and Bird were able to recreate two of the greatest rivalries in sports: The Boston Celtics and the Los Angeles Lakers, and the Boston Celtics and the Philadelphia 76ers. At least one of these players participated in the NBA Finals every season from 1980 to 1989. It was game seven of the 1984 NBA Finals between the Lakers and the Celtics that received a then all-time high rating of 19.3. The game was the highest rated program on CBS in the month of June that year and began to demonstrate to the NBA that progress was being made. Two of the Bird, Erving, and Johnson trio were opposing one another in the Finals for 6 of the 10 seasons, only interrupted by trips to the Finals in 1981 and 1985 of the Western Conference Champion Houston Rockets. Houston had superstars such as Moses Malone in 1981 and Hakeem Olajuwon and Ralph Sampson in the 1985 Finals. Bird and Erving also met four times in the NBA playoffs with the Eastern Conference Championship at stake from 1980 until Erving retired after the 1986-87 season.

Ted Shaker alluded to a desire on the part of the NBA and CBS that other teams and other stars emerge to supplement the triad that was Boston, Philadelphia, and Los Angeles. The NBA received more player "luck"—in addition to Houston gaining two very popular college players in Sampson and Olajuwon, the New York Knicks won the lottery that gave them Patrick Ewing; one of the dominant college players of his generation was now going to be playing in the nation's largest television market. The Detroit Pistons, led by Isiah Thomas, emerged and challenged Bird's Celtics in the 1987 and 1988 playoffs, beating Boston in 1988 and challenging Johnson's Lakers in the 1988 and 1989 Finals. They won the NBA Championship in 1989 against Los Angeles and repeated as champions in 1990 by defeating Portland.

The NBA had its ultimate superstar when Michael Jordan joined in the 1984-85 season. Jordan and the Chicago Bulls would win six NBA Championships. Individually, Jordan earned the MVP award five times, was named first team All-NBA 10 times, and won two Slam Dunk Championships. One of the first of many memorable moments for Jordan occurred in 1986 against the Celtics when he poured in 63 points in a 135-131 double overtime playoff loss on a Sunday afternoon in Boston that was broadcast on CBS. Jordan began to cement his image for last second heroics at the professional level by hitting a jump shot against the Cleveland Cavaliers in the decisive game five in 1989 broadcast by CBS on a Sunday afternoon. Jordan had already established himself as a clutch player at the collegiate level in the 1982 NCAA Championship Game when he hit a 17-foot jump shot with seconds left to give his North Carolina Tar Heels a 63-62 win over Patrick Ewing and the Georgetown Hoyas. That game was also broadcast on CBS.

NBC also was lucky in the first year that they had the broadcast rights to the NBA by getting a dream match-up of the Bulls with Jordan against Johnson and the Lakers, a four games to one Bulls win. Jordan's return from his initial retirement took place during a Sunday afternoon game on March 19, 1995, against the Indiana Pacers on NBC. This game produced a rating of 10.9, well above what had been an average rating of 5.0 for that year's broadcasts (Coe, 1995). In his last professional game in the 1998 NBA Finals, it was Jordan again creating another memorable NBA on NBC moment when he hit the winning game shot to give the Bulls their sixth NBA championship. Ricky Diamond tries to put the role of Jordan into some perspective, stating:

> There really is no underestimating the impact he has had on the ratings, it is a singularly unusual thing. I guess we all would have been interested since Babe Ruth played in the pre-television era what impact he would have had on television ratings. The seventh game of a NBA Finals is not going to do what the seventh game of the World Series is going to do, it hasn't grown to that yet despite Michael Jordan. But for what basketball is, Jordan can provide some unbelievable numbers and there is no question that when you take him out of the equation the numbers are less. Anyone who says anything to the contrary just isn't reading the numbers right. (personal communication, October 21, 1998)

To support Diamond's assertion regarding Jordan's impact on the television ratings, the average ratings for the six years that Jordan and the Bulls were in the NBA Finals (all on NBC) were 36% higher and the average share increased 38% more than the years Jordan and the Bulls were not in the Finals. The NBA Finals with Jordan and the Bulls produced a mean of 16.7 ($SD = 1.6$). The ratings for the four years that Jordan and the Bulls were not in the NBA Finals on NBC produced a mean of 12.3 ($SD = 1.2$). The share for the six years that Jordan and the Bulls were in the NBA Finals produced a mean of 31.0 ($SD = 2.3$). The share for the four years that Jordan and the Bulls were not in the NBA Finals on NBC produced a mean of 22.5 ($SD = 1.9$).

Mike Francesca, notable radio talk show host from WFAN in New York, comments on the impact of Michael Jordan: "Michael Jordan cuts across all barriers, he cuts across all economic stratas, he cuts across all demographics. He brings people who are not basketball fans to the telecasts. He is an American hero, he is an American icon (personal communication, November 20, 1998). Francesca also points out that Jordan had built on the foundation that had been established by Larry Bird and Magic Johnson:

> Basketball's emergence or re-emergence, but really its emergence, started with the Bird-Magic NCAA Championship game that still is the highest rated college game of all-time. Bird and Magic then took what they had into the NBA. They became enormously successful, they became very, very big figures. A couple of years later Jordan joined them and became kind of a holy trinity and these three guys lifted the league. They were stars, but they were stars who wanted to win. They were stars who weren't selfish. They were stars who tried to make their teams better. So when all of that happened, I think that it really carried the league and then Jordan carried it to another level. He brought people who are not regular basketball fans or sports fans to the telecast because of who he was. He was like a rock star, he was an icon. He was a person of that kind of ability of that kind of appeal and that was why the NBA did so well. (personal communication, November 20, 1998)

Long-time Bulls' teammate Bill Wennington commented: "Every guest I've ever had in Chicago wanted to eat at Michael Jordan's Restaurant. The food is, you know, okay. The beer tastes the same as anywhere else. But everyone wants to go there, to get some piece of him" (cited in D'Alessandro, 1998).

Ricky Diamond comments on the future of the NBA without Michael Jordan playing: "He has an impact and we will miss his impact, but hopefully all of us will help grow the game and the popularity and Jordan helped grow the game and its popularity and hopefully there will be someone else that people will want to watch, but I'm not sure it will be with the same fervor that they watch him now" (personal communication, October 21, 1998). Steve Grubbs, senior vice president/director of network television buying for BBDO, claims the NBA does a great job of marketing their product, stating, "there's concern over Michael Jordan leaving, but something tells me they'll find someone to replace him. They probably have somebody waiting in the wings who could assume a greater leadership role. If not, they'll create one" (cited in Schlosser, 1998, p. 32).

From a "luck" perspective, the emergence of the NBA nicely coincided with the growth of the cable industry, which created a need for more programming. Although Superstations created an exposure conflict for the NBA, the true root cause was that only one team was

profiting from the cable bonanza rather than the entire league. Once
the NBA created a system that made a clear distinction between
national and local broadcasting and the distribution of rights fees,
cable then became an essential asset for the NBA. It is the growth of
cable in terms of the sheer number of channels that not only provides
a national vehicle for exposure, but also a local outlet for each individual team. The development of cable simply allows for every NBA
game to be on television. Commissioner Stern comments that the
growth of cable has created a thirst for sports programming, not only
in the televising of NBA games, but in the creation of sports news
organizations such as ESPN, CNNSI, and Fox Sports. Stern states:

> When Michael Jordan retired, the comparison to his audience
> and Wilt Chamberlain's audience would cause you to believe that
> Wilt Chamberlain played in relative obscurity, compared to
> Michael Jordan. It wasn't real obscurity because there were
> national newspapers, magazines and all that, but it was obscuri-
> ty in terms of the amount of time that people got to see them.
> Now our broadcast partners are NBC and Turner, between them
> we are on the air three times a week on Turner and probably
> twice a week between January and May on NBC and then five
> times a week on NBC and Turner. So we are with our broadcast
> partners bringing our fans the greatest amount of pro basketball
> in the history of the sport. (personal communication, April 14,
> 1999)

It is the utilization of cable and other satellite technology,
such as the Direct Broadcast package offered through NBA initiatives, that helped set the agenda. Commissioner Stern explains:

> At that point [the perception of the NBA had improved] it was
> not about our strategy, but more about the development of com-
> munications that we rode. So we were predominantly an over-
> the-air network sport, then we became with our teams predomi-
> nantly over-the-air in their markets, then we became an over-the-
> air network sport with a major cable exposure, and our teams
> became over-the-air and cable in their local market and then we
> became an over-the-air, cable, and satellite delivery and our
> teams became over-the-air, cable, and satellite in their markets.
> Now we are knocking on the door to digital cable and the Internet
> as another mode of delivery and we are now involved in deliver-
> ing NBA content over the Internet. So I would just call it the self
> effectuating brand, which is what happened. It happens as we fol-

low communications development, we just sort of, when you are riding behind a truck, you get the jet stream, that is what is happening to us. (personal communication, April 14, 1999)

Ed Desser adds:

It's not just that people pay more attention all the time, but it's both the multiplicity of shelf space exponentially expanding together with the creation of a plethora of additional programming, support programming. It has been a struggle to establish all of that programming, get it on the air, create an audience, produce it in a first class way, and nurture and sell sponsors who want to be associated with it. (personal communication, August 26, 1998)

What might distinguish great teams from others, however, is how they take advantage of the opportunities and gifts they have been given, capitalizing on the "luck." The NBA had the right leader to design a system to take advantage of these opportunities in Commissioner David Stern.

David Stern was unanimously elected as Commissioner on February 1, 1984, after having been involved with the NBA since 1966 as outside counsel. Stern, a graduate of Rutgers University and Columbia Law School, joined the NBA in 1978 as General Counsel and became the Executive Vice President of the league in 1980. In these positions, Stern was instrumental in the future of the NBA, including the settlement in 1976 that helped create player free agency, the collective bargaining agreement that introduced the salary cap and revenue sharing, and professional sports' first anti-drug policy. Stern also helped develop the marketing divisions of NBA Properties and NBA Entertainment. Since his election as commissioner, the NBA has added six franchises, its revenues have quadrupled, television exposure has greatly increased, and the international interest in the NBA has led to the opening of league offices in Barcelona, Hong Kong, London, Melbourne, Mexico City, Miami (serving Latin America), Paris, Singapore, Taiwan, Tokyo, and Toronto.

Hubie Brown describes David Stern as a brilliant lawyer and a brilliant man. The NBA always had great players, but "none of this [the success of the NBA] would have happened without him first" (personal communication, January 27, 1999). Ted Shaker claims David Stern is a major reason for the growth of the NBA, particularly the relationship between the NBA and the television networks.

Shaker says that if a network was going to make a commitment to the NBA in the form of a rights fees contract, Stern and the NBA were going to equal that commitment and provide its broadcast partners whatever accommodation necessary to best televise the NBA. Shaker offers an example of the constant effort of Stern to enhance the image of the NBA:

> I remember there was one game where it was a Saturday playoff game, somebody was playing at the Knicks and for some reason on Saturday afternoon I was up at our office on 6th Avenue and not at the Garden and I had the game on. I don't remember what I was doing, but I was there on Saturday afternoon and the game ended and there was some time to kill and we went off the air with credits over a big wide shot of an empty Madison Square Garden because everybody had left. He found me, the phone rings and it was David Stern, he said what are you doing here, you are making us look like there is nobody, like we had no fans, why are you doing that and I thought it was a pretty fair point, regardless of if there are fans or not, it is boring television. So what Mike and Sandy [producer, Mike Burks and director, Sandy Grossman] came up with off of the bat was the idea of taking still frames of video and putting the credits against them and there would be a new picture, a new credit with each page turn. That was the first time that was ever done and it was a direct result of David Stern pushing to try to make it a more compelling telecast. (personal communication, October 9, 1998)

In a 1997 interview Stern stated the two main principles that guided the development of the league: "the number one principle never changes: that the game is king—that no matter what the marketplace demanded, we never screwed around with the basic integrity of the game." The second principle was "the understanding that nobody was going to care about the NBA as much as we cared about ourselves. And so we were fiercely protective to the point of combativeness. That's why I wouldn't hesitate to call an executive producer and complain about the way he'd presented a certain game on TV" (cited in Rosen, 1997, pp. 40-44).

John Andariese believes Stern's impact cannot be underestimated, not only from a television perspective but regarding the entire marketing approach of the NBA. Andariese credits Stern with his ability to gauge the thinking of other companies from a marketing and sponsorship perspective. He states:

David Stern deservedly gets credit for his astute understanding of the marketing forces. I tell people knowing David Stern as I do that I have trouble in my career, which is selling television advertising, keeping up with the trades advertising and media public relations and I always say David Stern reads them before probably any of you do, people in the business, that's the kind of guy he is. He's very much on top of what's happening, how companies are thinking, what are they looking for, who their target audience is and he took a league that was dissipating in many ways as a national sport. It is because of the leadership of somebody who was sensitive to how companies were thinking. (personal communication, August 3, 1998)

Ricky Diamond, producer of *NBA Showtime* on NBC, adds:

I think the league in general became a much more credible league under David Stern's leadership. I don't think there is really any question. If you go back and you look at the history of the league there is no quarreling with the fact that there were great players before this era. There have always been great players since the league started, but it wasn't nearly as organized a business as it is today under David Stern. Since they have sort of gotten their house in order under Stern, they have taken steps to do things that would make it a more viable television property. Also they have nurtured every aspect of the game, not just as a television property, but the in-arena experience. They are just very savvy as marketers. (personal communication, October 21, 1998)

Regarding his own role, Stern stated in 1985, after he had been Commissioner for one year, "no fan has ever bought a ticket or watched a game on TV because of an owner, a general manager, or a commissioner. What is going to excite our fans are the great athletes and the breathtaking plays they make. It's my job to help provide a stage for that" (Associated Press, 1985, pp. 1, 19).

6

THE CONNECTION BETWEEN THE NBA STRATEGY AND AN INTEGRATED MASS COMMUNICATION APPROACH

The analysis of television's influence on the growth of the NBA begins with the simple fact that the NBA did not always enjoy the economic and popular culture status it has currently attained. The simple questions are how and why did this growth in acceptance of the NBA by the public and advertising community occur and what role did television networks play? There are multiple responses, but the claim here is that the broadcast strategies employed by both television networks and the NBA through exposure and portrayal framing methods and the NBA's management of its own product are among the primary reasons for the growth of the league.

The NBA strategy is fundamentally a communication strategy that can be explained through an integrative approach. My assumption that television network and communication strategies influenced the growth of the NBA is more strongly confirmed having completed this book. Through the claim that television networks critically influence the operations of a sports league, and that there have been new broadcast strategies employed to help grow the sport of NBA basketball indicates the author's leaning toward the more powerful, direct-effects perspective. Media power research is often associated with the study of media effects on the audience. The mass media effects form of power can be debated, but the media power to select and frame messages cannot be debated for that power always exists.

The leaning toward powerful, direct mass media effects is, however, tempered by the idea that the audience has to be receptive to the media content, even with all these broadcast strategies designed to make the broadcast more appealing.

In debating mass media effects there are two aspects that are difficult to reconcile. The first stems from a more direct-effects perspective—that the media have the power to select and frame their content. The second stems from an indirect-effects perspective—the audience having the power to select, interpret, and subsequently behave as they choose in relation to the messages that are available to them through the media. It is this notion—that these two components of mass communication cannot act independently of one another—that serves as the impetus to integrate these perspectives. A more integrated approach that encompasses the message producer, message producer constituency groups (i.e., advertisers), message content, message medium, and the audience must be utilized for analyzing mass communication, and specifically the topic of the NBA and television relationship. It is my hope that the integration model that was utilized and the evidence gathered will contribute to the mass media effects debate (see Figures 6.1 and 6.2).

Certain aspects of the integration model contribute more than others to the NBA and television relationship. Although the direct-effects and agenda-setting approaches are emphasized through the interviewing of the content producers, neither direct nor indirect perspectives provide an ultimate explanation as both need to be considered. In the case of the NBA, however, a modified agenda-setting approach focusing on both exposure and portrayal broadcast strategies and a strong consideration of a media dependency model provide the best understanding.

In addition to the transfer of salience regarding an issue, at its core agenda-setting is a theory about decision making on the part of the producers, directors, and editors of a media organization. The approach of this book was to understand the NBA from the perspective of the decision makers from both the NBA and the television networks. The decision making includes which stories or events receive exposure, where they are placed in a media production, and the amount of time devoted to them. Key aspects are the objectives of the decisions of mass media personnel. The objectives are multiple: (a) to report news and events, (b) to attract an audience—readers, viewers, or listeners, and (c) to attract advertisers. In reaching these objectives the NBA and television network partnership is performing an agenda-setting function for their own agenda.

The evidence in the NBA case suggests that agenda-setting goes beyond the media as the sole agenda-setting entity and includes

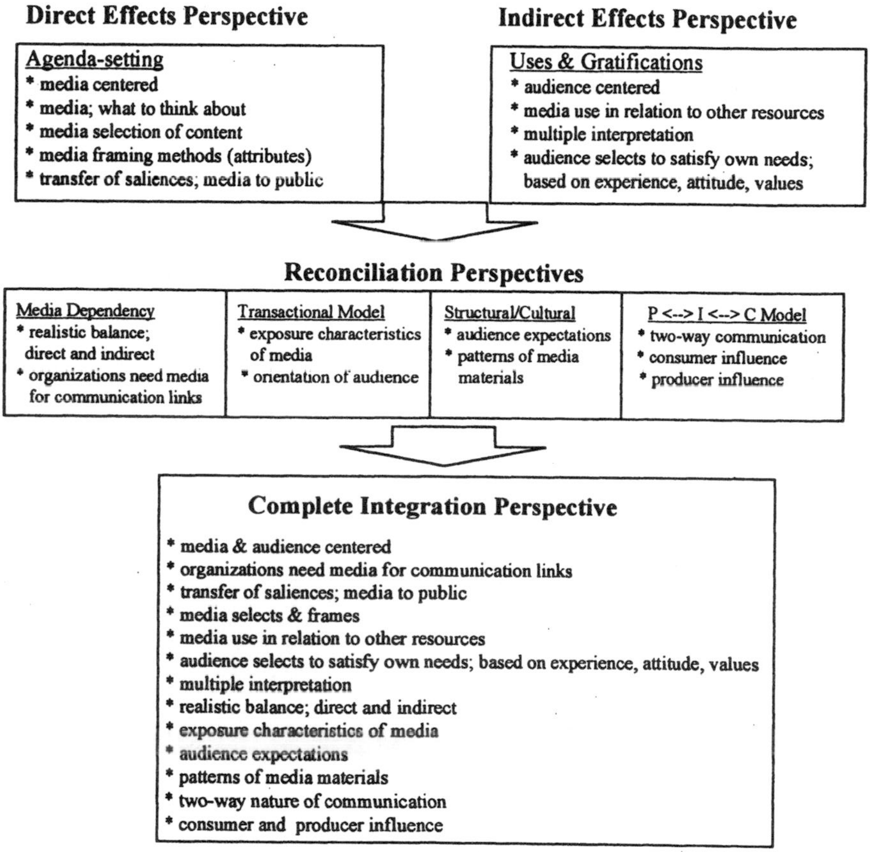

Direct Effects Perspective   **Indirect Effects Perspective**

<u>Agenda-setting</u>
* media centered
* media; what to think about
* media selection of content
* media framing methods (attributes)
* transfer of saliences; media to public

<u>Uses & Gratifications</u>
* audience centered
* media use in relation to other resources
* multiple interpretation
* audience selects to satisfy own needs;
  based on experience, attitude, values

Reconciliation Perspectives

<u>Media Dependency</u>	<u>Transactional Model</u>	<u>Structural/Cultural</u>	<u>P <--> I <--> C Model</u>
* realistic balance; direct and indirect * organizations need media for communication links	* exposure characteristics of media * orientation of audience	* audience expectations * patterns of media materials	* two-way communication * consumer influence * producer influence

Complete Integration Perspective

* media & audience centered
* organizations need media for communication links
* transfer of saliences; media to public
* media selects & frames
* media use in relation to other resources
* audience selects to satisfy own needs; based on experience, attitude, values
* multiple interpretation
* realistic balance; direct and indirect
* exposure characteristics of media
* audience expectations
* patterns of media materials
* two-way nature of communication
* consumer and producer influence

Figure 6.1. Mass media integration model

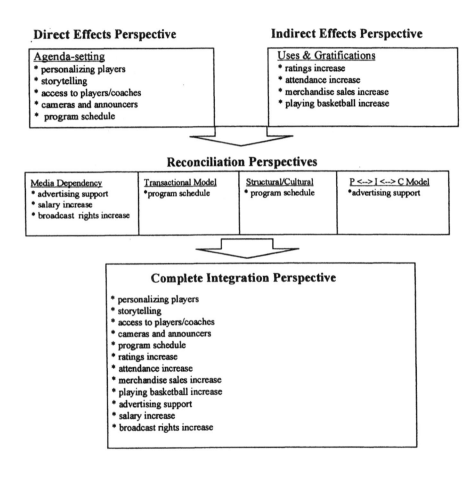

Figure 6.2. Mass media integration model with NBA strategy

the person or organization that has an agenda or a message to promote. In studying the relationship between the NBA and its broadcast partners and their strategies for televising NBA basketball, it
became apparent that the NBA itself was the impetus for many initiatives that changed how the league was broadcast. It is the NBA
that demonstrates an understanding of the power of television and
the dependency of television networks to assist in growing the sport.
The NBA assists television networks in constructing the message
and in transferring its message (its agenda) to the audience. The best
evidence is the coordination between the NBA and its broadcast partners in establishing the television game programming schedule, the
most important product item because of the revenue and exposure it
generates. It is the NBA that demonstrates an understanding of the
need for different television programming vehicles, such as NBA
Inside Stuff, which help personalize players and create storylines,
but more importantly appeal to different niche audiences and different niche advertisers.

The NBA is constantly performing its own agenda-setting
function through multiple initiatives:

1. Facilitating media access to players and coaches
2. Providing information to reporters and announcers.
3. Creating the proper space in arenas for cameras
4. Production of its own support programming that attracts a
    niche audience and a niche advertiser
5. Educating players about the media
6. Educating television personnel
7. Sing new technology such as on-line or direct broadcast
    television services
8. Marketing NBA merchandise
9. Implementing initiatives of competitive balance such as
    revenue sharing and the draft so that each team has an
    opportunity to compete for a championship
10. Recruiting advertisers. Media power exists in their ability to
    select and frame messages; however, if the organization is
    instrumental in the selecting and framing of messages, this
    could diminish the power of the media considered earlier.

Schiller (1989) would probably contend that the true agenda-
setters for the NBA are the advertisers who sponsor the league and
its games on television. In examining the NBA, however, advertisers
were not interested in the NBA until ratings increased, an increase
argued here assisted by the broadcast strategies employed through
the NBA and television relationship. It was the audience who ulti-

mately determined the NBA in the proper circumstances (i.e., the right spot in the program schedule with the best teams and players and enhanced through the numerous broadcast strategies) to be gratifying. This adds two new sources as potential agenda-setters: not only the media, as argued by McCombs and Shaw and most agenda-setting research, or the organization that has an agenda to promote, especially pronounced in the case of the NBA. Now, advertisers who validate programming and the audience through behaviors of viewing NBA games, attending NBA games, and purchasing NBA merchandise, also act as agenda-setting forces. In examining who sets the public agenda, the media, even if only in its "potential to influence," invariably become an answer. The media, and in particular television in this situation, serve as the main conduit between the NBA and the audience. An interesting area of investigation in the future to complement the agenda-setting effects studies might be the setting of the media agenda, as the multiple agenda-section factions for the NBA lend credibility to the suggestion that there needs to be a better understanding of how the media agenda is set (e.g., Carragee et al., 1987; Danielian & Reese, 1989; Roberts, 1997; Rogers et al., 1993; Roberts, 1997; Takeshita, 1997). For the NBA, the agenda is transferred to the television networks through the signing of a long-term contract, an inherent characteristic in a sports league and television network relationship that creates a mutual agenda.

Regarding agenda-setting research, Kosicki (1993) claims that a twin focus on media content and audience perception is necessary. Regardless of the intent of the initial agenda-setting study and its roots in a direct-effects tradition, one of the appeals of agenda-setting is its evolution to also include the audience as an evaluator of content before an effect can be measured. For an industry to grow, perception must then translate into behavior. Positive perception, without the supportive individual behavior that can be recognized and that concretely contributes economically is not adequate to any industry's growth. It is in the idea that the audience always has the ability to reject the NBA, or any other message to which they are exposed, where the uses and gratifications concept of how people utilize television resources within their environment begins to emerge.

It is the audience's ability to select and interpret messages and behave accordingly that diminishes the arguments of direct-media effects and necessitates a limited-effects approach into the integration model utilized in this book. The audience is thus a critical component of this story of television's influence on the growth of the NBA. The NBA and television network partnership could have implemented any broadcast strategy they chose and still not be accepted by the audience if they did not desire NBA basketball and behave accordingly. If a major problem of the NBA in the late 1970s and early 1980s was a poor perception, it was in the minds of the audience where this negative perception existed and it was revealed through their behavior. For the NBA, necessary behavior includes watching games, attending games, purchasing NBA-licensed merchandise, and purchasing the products of the NBA's sponsors. The most important behavior is the watching of games because the broadcast contracts for the rights to televise NBA games are the largest revenue source and greatest exposure for the NBA. Viewing is essential for the broadcast partners: It is the only way a television network makes any money as it is the number and demographic of viewers that they are selling to advertisers.

A key aspect to uses and gratifications is the concept of people's behavior in relation to "the other resources available." For the NBA, the audience does not have that many resources to satisfactorily participate in the games. For people who do not possess a ticket to the game, which is obviously a great majority of the audience as a NBA arena can only hold approximately 20,000 people, television becomes the most complete alternative to see a game live in terms of visual content enhanced with camera replays, statistical graphics, and announcers providing storylines, information about the players, and game analysis. It is this unobtrusive characteristic that creates the multiple dependencies that are involved in the NBA, television network, advertiser, and audience relationship. The NBA is dependent on television networks for its largest source of revenue and exposure as it is the vehicle to best transfer the NBA agenda to the audience. The NBA understands the unobtrusive nature of the league, so television becomes the major vehicle for providing games and creating the image of the league. The NBA also needs advertisers for revenue and advertisers become dependent on both the NBA and its broadcast partners in reaching a certain demographic audience. Dependency also occurs on the individual level with NBA fans utilizing television as the means for them to most frequently participate in an activity they enjoy: watching NBA basketball.

Television networks position themselves in the middle of both organizational and individual dependency, serving as the conduit for the NBA agenda. Television networks are dependent on sports leagues to provide a type of programming that generates consistent ratings and attracts advertisers who might not sponsor other types of programming. In addition to the consistency of ratings with sports, the television network receives a type of programming with the beneficial characteristics of: (a) the ability to influence the program schedule, (b) the potential advertising possibilities, (c) the potential promotion possibilities, and (d) the real-life qualities of sports events. The

NBA has additional beneficial characteristics of: (a) proximity to the court for cameras, (b) seeing the players' faces, (c) seeing the superstars and all 10 players continuously throughout the game, and (d) the timing of the NBA playoffs, which occur at a time of the year when it is the major sporting event and the major advertising event, as other networks are not offering original programming.

Whereas the NBA always had a dependency on television for revenue and exposure, it was television networks and advertisers who did not need the NBA because it was not drawing an audience. The audience did not have a dependency on television as the medium to experience the NBA because they had a poor perception of the league and little desire to watch its games. The availability of the product must match the desire and availability of the audience. It appears as though the properly executed agenda-setting function of the NBA and television relationship has created the media dependency, both organizational and individual. For the NBA, media dependency occurs only because of the status that the NBA has attained.

The mass communication process, and the potential direct or indirect effects that may result, occurs within a larger cultural context of ideas, topics, and societal situations. Zillmann et al. (1989) offer a simplistic and interesting point in their statements that people enjoy watching sports and because of this enjoyment that experience has some value. The agenda-setting function that was performed made watching the NBA on television an enjoyable experience. The audience gratifications that can be derived from watching sports on television had presumably existed, but it had to be demonstrated that these gratifications could be derived through viewing NBA basketball. The NBA's status creates multiple dependencies that now exist within the NBA relationships. The direct and indirect media effects perspectives help provide a communicative explanation for television's influence in the growth of the NBA, and the specific case of the NBA helps reveal ideas about the integrated model (see Tables 6.1 and 6.2).

Table 6.1. What Does the Theory Reveal About the Case of the NBA and Television.

Agenda-setting:	The agenda-setting function does not begin with television networks, but with the initiatives of the NBA, who understands and utilizes the power of television networks. The initiatives of the partnership include new broadcast strategies that involve both exposure, placement of games in the programming schedule; and portrayal, enhancing the broadcast with camera replays, statistical graphics, analysis, creation of storylines, and the personalizing of players. In addition to transfer of salience, decision making of producers, directors, announcers, and editors is at the core of agenda-setting.
Uses and gratifications:	The audience will determine how it responds to NBA content, regardless of the broadcast strategies employed. The best product must be broadcast in a way that is appealing to the audience—placed at a time of convenience, enhanced through camera replays, statistical graphics, analysis, creation of storylines, and personalizing of players so the audience is more informed, more entertained, and can learn about the game and its participants and experience gratifications such as to thrill in victory.
Media dependency:	The NBA needs television networks for revenue and exposure. Television networks need the type of programming that the NBA offers to reach a niche audience and attract a niche advertiser. Advertisers need television networks and programming such as the NBA for expo-sure of their products to the target audience they are trying to reach. The audience needs television networks as the major vehicle for experiencing the NBA.

Table 6.2. What Does the Case of the NBA and Television Reveal About the Theory.

Agenda-setting:	The media have the power to select and frame through both exposure and portrayal framing methods (broadcast strategies).
Uses and gratifications:	Audiences must be considered in determining the influence of mass media messages.
Media dependency:	Organizations need the media for exposure. Advertisers need the media for exposure. The audience needs the media to learn about issues, products, and for entertainment. Television networks need certain types of programming to reach a niche audience and attract a niche advertiser.

7

DISCUSSION AND CONCLUSION

Sports maintain a secure place within the entire culture because people can relate to the games and events. The experience of watching sports on television evokes emotions of rooting, thrilling in victory or suffering in defeat, witnessing the excellence of skill, and connecting to community. Sports contain the real-life characteristics that provide a piece of entertainment not found in other entertainment-culture industries. Sports contests are constantly available and each game presents a new, unknown drama that the fan can watch unfold live.

Television helps convey, create, and best capture the emotion and the skill of these games and their players. The visions that are emblazoned in the memories of sports fans are those not only of events they attended, but those seen on television: the simple camera shot of Michael Jordan rising to the basket, then switching the ball into his left hand and banking it off of the backboard while in mid-air during game two of the 1991 NBA Finals against the Lakers; or Carlton Fisk of the Boston Red Sox waving fair his 12th inning home run in game six of the 1975 World Series. It is not only the visions that are created, but the memorable announcer commentary: Al Michaels description of the United States Mens' Hockey team upsetting the Soviet Union at the 1980 Winter Olympics with the comment, "Do you believe in miracles? Yes!;" or Howard Cosell screaming "down goes Frazier, down goes Frazier" when George Foreman scored a second round knockout against Joe Frazier in 1973 to win the Heavyweight Championship of the World. These sports moments captured on television evoke the emotions that sports can provide at any given moment. They become cultural events that make people remember where they were and who they were with when they occurred.

From any standpoint, the growth of the NBA is a major success story in sports and in business. The demonstration that so much of this growth was through the utilization of television speaks to the power of the medium and the effects of the mass media in general. The exposure and portrayal framing methods are deemed by television and NBA personnel to be effective, and the audience's receptivity, a vital component of this success story, is through behavior measures of ratings, attendance, and merchandise sales that reflect the growth of the NBA. However, could it be that the product sells itself; it is intrinsically appealing to consumers. The greatness of the game of basketball and its players cannot be underestimated in the growth of the NBA. There was an already-great product of NBA basketball to sell. As former two-time All-Star Kelly Tripucka simply comments, "the entertainment is the 10 guys running around in shorts out there" (personal communication, December 4, 1998).

A great product and great players can be enhanced. The major claim, and the impetus for this book, is that the NBA and television partnership were not able to transform their mutual agenda to the public agenda until they changed the general broadcast strategies or framing methods for their coverage in order to change the damaged perception of the league. The overall goal of this book was to identify and explain the multiple broadcast strategies utilized to televise NBA basketball and ultimately influence the growth of the NBA. I claim that the NBA success story occurred not only because of the greatness of the game of NBA basketball, but because the league and its television partners were able to translate this greatness to the audience.

Some of the greatest players (Wilt Chamberlain, Oscar Robertson, and Bill Russell), greatest teams, and one of sport's greatest dynasties (the Boston Celtics winning 11 NBA Championships in 13 years from 1957 to 1969) existed before the tremendous popular growth of the NBA. In the late 1970s and early 1980s the NBA had a poor public perception and was receiving poor exposure on network television. The challenge of the NBA and its broadcast partners was to change the perception about what they believed to be a quality product, one that had been receiving poor exposure and was not properly portrayed to the audience. The utilization of television resources became a major foundation of the overall NBA communication strategy for enhancing its image and growing the league. Regarding the overall thesis of there being new broadcast strategies behind the way the NBA was televised to help grow the sport, Commissioner Stern comments:

> I agree with the thesis. I think that we number one understood the importance of the quality of production of our network telecasts. We anticipated well. I think the promise of cable as an ancillary means of getting our games out to an audience that became increasingly larger as cable grew. We appreciate the ability of all of the other outlets to furnish our image by additional programming and we understand the advances in technology that enable our image and those images that we communicated to an even broader audience and in many cases picking out the niche that would furnish our image to a particular audience. So it is very much a communication-based strategy for growth aided to a considerable measure by things over which we have no control which is the growth of technology and the ability to get it to fans. But we are very conscious of its [communication strategy] ever being there. (personal communication, April 14, 1999)

The main strategic initiatives of the NBA in coordination with its broadcast partners was to better manage the exposure of NBA games on television. McChesney (1989) claims that "virtually every surge in the popularity of sport has been accompanied by a dramatic increase in the coverage provided sport by the media" (p. 13). For the NBA, however, an increase in coverage at the point of its poor perception would not have helped. Rather than continuing to have a product with a poor perception saturate the market, the NBA was more concerned with the quality of the exposure the games were receiving. The NBA implemented a "less is more" strategy, which was a three-part plan that simultaneously entailed: (a) limiting the number of NBA games available on national television and cable television, (b) placing the games that were available in the most attractive spot in the programming schedule for both a potential audience and advertisers, and (c) having the best teams and the best players participating in the games that were televised. The NBA thus had its product in the best location with the best features of the product being shown to the audience.

The "less is more" strategy enabled each NBA network telecast to take on the connotation of a special event, as another game might not be broadcast on network television in the immediate future. The broadcasts featured the best players and best teams and created a sense of urgency because it might have been the only opportunity for a fan to see Larry Bird, Julius Erving, or Magic Johnson. More importantly, exposure was adjusted for the playoffs with a programming schedule that eliminated tape delay broadcasts and, eventually in 1995, every NBA playoff game was broadcast on national television. As the exposure strategy worked and an increase in ratings could be demonstrated, sponsors could be more easily persuaded to advertise their products during NBA games. Overall, the "less is more" strategy simply involved putting the best games into the program schedule location where they would be more apt to thrive in the ratings.

The issue of exposure is one of how much or how often a product is available to the audience so that it manages the supply and demand in the market and the product maintains its greatest value. The issue of exposure is basically one of product placement: Where, when, and how an organization makes its product available. The issue of product exposure in terms of the amount and the placement of a product is a decision-making endeavor that every company must confront in maximizing profitability. For example, a company such as McDonald's must determine how many restaurants to open and in which communities without saturating the market. The placement (exposure) of the NBA product on television was therefore the initial strategy of the NBA.

Once a product is in the right spot to reach an audience, it must still be portrayed in the most positive, attractive manner. The NBA had to be portrayed in a positive way for the audience to change its negative perception and understand the entertaining value of its games. The portrayal framing methods of television and the NBA include educating the audience to the game of NBA basketball through camera placement around the court and the initiative of slow-motion instant replays that could be obtained to visually demonstrate the strategy of NBA basketball and the athletic talent of the players. These visual images were continuously supplemented with the analysis of announcers who could explain the importance of what they were seeing to the audience. Announcers such as Tommy Heinsohn educated the viewers and CBS television personnel so they would understand what to look for when broadcasting a NBA game. Education not only included teaching the game, but personalizing the players and visually demonstrating the passion, emotion, endurance, and athletic skill involved in playing the game of basketball at the NBA level. Camera placement, such as court-side low angle cameras, was again vital in showing the tight face shots and the physical aspects that demonstrate the emotion involved in NBA basketball.

Personalizing players was a broadcast strategy that was designed to create images of the players as stars who the audience would want to see perform. NBC would then have the broadcast rights to Michael Jordan, as it did any other actor or actress who appeared on its network. Personalizing strategies allowed the audience to learn about the players as more than people with large salaries, and they emphasized the more human characteristics of these people: incredibly talented at playing the game, but otherwise like every one else.

Closely related to personalizing players is the creation of storylines—which are explained to the audience through promotion, the opening game tease, and updated throughout the game through replays—and statistical graphics to help create the importance and the impact of a game. The storyline of the game and learning the human side of the players and coaches involved "hooks" the attention of the audience and provides them with a rooting interest. The access provided media, particularly the broadcast media, to players and coaches through initiatives of the NBA helps facilitate interviews with players and coaches to better personalize them and create and explain storylines.

These exposure and portrayal broadcast strategies were designed to change the perception of the audience and grow the sport of NBA basketball. Although executives at the NBA and television networks are not aware of it, they have implicitly followed the agenda-setting research model: the exposure framing idea has been successful in telling people what to think about; the portrayal framing idea has been successful in telling people how to think about an issue. Although different, the exposure and portrayal framing methods are closely related, and it is their simultaneous deployment which gives the NBA its best opportunity for economic and popular growth. Both the exposure and portrayal framing methods are designed to attract and engage the audience, particularly the target audience. Utilizing one method without the other would eliminate an important strategic component.

AT THE BUZZER: CONCLUSION

On October 15, 1958, Edward R. Murrow delivered a speech to the Radio and Television News Directors Association in Chicago. In speaking of the challenges of working in commercial television, Murrow stated: "This instrument can teach, it can illuminate; yes, and it can even inspire. But it can do so only to the extent that humans are determined to use it to those ends. Otherwise it is merely wires and lights in a box. There is a great and perhaps decisive battle to be fought against ignorance, intolerance, and indifference. This weapon of television could be useful" (cited in Rather, 1994). Murrow is speaking of the power and potential influence of television, but also importantly stressing the talent and skill of the people who work in television and create its content.

When investing in a sports property, there must be faith and confidence in the product on the part of the television network. Personnel from television networks must also have the belief that even the best product can be enhanced. From the league perspective, there must also be a sense that the network can enhance the product. Everyone involved in the NBA and television relationship acknowledge the quality of the product, the greatness of the game of basketball. The goal of the broadcast is then to translate this greatness of the game to the audience and make the watching of the NBA more enjoyable.

The NBA is very fortunate for the talent of the people who cover the league and the passion they have in their work of broadcasting the games. Mike Burks claims there was a tremendous bond between people at CBS and the NBA. Burks states that "there was a mutual agenda between CBS and the NBA to make the game better" and the relationship was a true partnership with people working toward the same goals to "make a great television show and grow a sport" (personal communication, December 1, 1998). Burks also points out that "the NBA was totally in step with what we [CBS] needed" (personal communication, December 1, 1998). In not underestimating the importance of Larry Bird, Magic Johnson, and Michael Jordan, Burks claims that the passions of the people on the NBA side and the television side toward the presentation of the broadcast had as much to do with the growth of the game.

Ted Shaker describes his overall philosophy of the NBA coverage on CBS: "I thought our responsibility was to show this was a great game. We weren't making stuff up, this was the real thing. It wasn't there before, we didn't do a good job of it before so it took some re-tooling and it took an effort where we worked closely with the NBA" (personal communication, October 9, 1998). Tommy Heinsohn adds that "television put the game in the living room and expanded knowledge to people who had never watched before" (personal communication, November 10, 1998).

Kevin Smollon, NBC Producer, comments:

> I just think because we get so much cooperation from them [the NBA] that we in turn put so much more from our end into it

because we see it is such a good feeling, the cooperation. We will put the facilities into it. Our NBA telecasts are probably the most sophisticated shows on television now as far as effects and the look of everything. So I think and in the fact with football you are doing seven games where here you are doing two, we use our best trucks, we use our best equipment, our best crews because it is such a confined area as far as only two games. I think I would put those telecasts up against anything out there, just the quality of them and the technology and just the storylines we deal with and the way we analyze the games. It's a good feeling to do because you know you are getting cooperation and everybody is working together on the same page. (personal communication, September 23, 1998)

Chuck Daly, Hall-of-Fame Head Coach, understands television is vital in enhancing the NBA, but points out that the game itself and its outcome must remain the primary attraction. Daly offers three guidelines that he believes networks should abide by when broadcasting a NBA game: (a) report the game in as objective and as exciting a way possible, (b) inform and educate the audience to understand what teams, players, and coaches are trying to do, and (c) let the game and its players be the stars, not the announcers.

Howie Singer, New York Knicks Producer, also describes his philosophy of the how production and framing methods allow the fan to better enjoy a NBA game. He claims:

I think reaction shots and reaction replays add something to the game. I think really good graphics, well-researched graphics; you want a fan to say, wow I didn't know that. I think when you get fans, whether it's the announcer saying something or you putting up a graphic or somebody telling a story. I think anybody can show a basketball game, you can follow the ball up and down, and you know what probably 50% of the audience will be fine, maybe more. We may be kidding ourselves and saying people really notice that stuff. But I know I watched games with my father, or friends, and they watch the game and say wow I didn't know that—that is what you want to do—or make people say wow that was a great replay, that's cool did you see that. That's what you can do to add to the game and that's where your subtle knowledge of the game may help or just being observant about things, anticipating things. That's where you hope you can make a fan better enjoy the game, because that is what it is all about, you want the fan to have enjoyed their three hours of basketball. (personal communication, August 26, 1998)

Ted Shaker summarizes the greatness of the game and the television relationship with the NBA, in which television can make or break a sport. When the NBA was not successful, part of the reason was television not portraying it properly. Shaker states:

> The power of the medium, the way the NBA came off the floor so to speak says so much about the power of television and when it's used correctly and you have something that is really good. If the NBA wasn't all the good things that the NBA is we couldn't have gone on pulling the wool over everybody's eyes. The greatness of the game is really the heart of the whole thing and the power of television is shown in being able to capture that greatness. I would say the power of the medium and the greatness of the game crossed and this is what happens. (personal communication, October 9, 1998)

Television network and NBA personnel measure the success of the broadcast strategies that they utilize in terms of behavior by the audience. There is not a myopic evaluation of each strategic communication initiative in terms of causation, but rather an evaluation of overall performance. The increase in the major economic audience feedback measures of television ratings, attendance, and merchandise sales are indicators of audience acceptance and serve as a validation of the overall NBA communication strategy. Because of the focus on overall revenue-related feedback measures, there is no analysis or determination of the effect for each individual broadcast strategy. Although the nature of exposure can directly relate to ratings, the portrayal framing methods might not even be a factor as the NBA and television networks might simply be beneficiaries of a dependent relationship between the NBA and its fans.

The NBA and its broadcast partners were simply successful in utilizing the potential of television to influence by performing an agenda-setting function for the topic of NBA basketball. This agenda-setting attempt could have faltered at multiple points in the process: (a) television networks no longer having faith in the quality of the product of NBA basketball, nor its own ability to enhance the presentation of the game to attract and maintain an audience; (b) the audience, had it not desired the content of NBA basketball, could have rejected any agenda-setting attempts; and (c) sponsors could have derailed the agenda-setting function had certain demographic audiences been available elsewhere. For the NBA, all these various constituencies aligned and each, at some point in the growth of the NBA, accepted and contributed to the agenda-setting process because of the financial or entertainment benefits they received.

The audience gratifications, the media dependency (both organizational [advertising] and individual [audience]), and the position the NBA currently maintains within the popular culture are all very much a result of the agenda-setting function performed by the NBA and its broadcast partners. The agenda-setting function, through exposure and portrayal framing methods, demonstrated to the audience the quality of NBA basketball, and it continues to enhance the product today. The exposure and portrayal framing methods that have been described here are, however, not meant to be depicted in terms of direct causality in the growth of the NBA. People can argue that various factors were the cause of the growth of the NBA and not be wrong. The greatness of the game of NBA basketball as a product that provides excitement and entertainment may have caused the success regardless of any new strategy in broadcasting the league. This is an important distinction because it cannot be concluded with absolute certainty that new broadcast strategies would create a growth for other sports, such as professional soccer, although the overall belief is that television is a necessary and vital component of the growth of any sport or sports league. The quality of the product of NBA basketball and the greatness of its players should not be questioned. There will also never be an exact percentage of accountability distributed to these various factors. The influence of framing methods, both exposure and portrayal, employed through the relationship of the NBA and the television networks (The Ultimate Assist), however, appears to be substantiated and must be included near the top of any list of reasons for the NBA's growth.

APPENDIX A

KEY INFORMANT INTERVIEW SUMMARY

Informant	Title	Organization
1. John Andariese	Knicks Analyst	MSG Network
2. Mike Breen	Announcer	NBC & MSG
3. Chris Brienza	Former Director Media Relations	NBA
4. Hubie Brown	Analyst, Head Coach	TNT
5. Mike Burks	Producer	CBS & TNT
6. P. J. Carlesimo	Former Head Coach	Golden St. Warriors
7. Dave CHecketts	President & CEO	MSG
8. Dave Coskey	Vice President Marketing/Comm.	Philadelphia 76ers
9. Vincent Costello	Feature Producer	NBC
10. Chuck Daly	Former Head Coach	Orlando Magic
11. Ed Desser	President, Television	NBA
12. Ricky Diamond	Producer, Showtime	NBC
13. Ian Eagle	Announcer	Fox Sports NY
14. Tom Fox	V. P. Sports Markt.	Gatorade
15. Mike Francesca	Radio Talk Show Host	WFAN
16. Joe Gangone	Executive V. P. Ad. Sales	MSG
17. Tom Heinsohn	Player/Coach/Analyst	Boston Celtics
18. Fred Kerber	Nets Beat Writer	New York Post
19. Brian McIntyre	Vice President Communications	NBA
20. John Mertz	PR Director	New Jersey Nets
21. Mike Pearl	Senior Vice President & Executive Producer	Turner Sports
22. Tommy Roy	Executive Producer, NBA	NBC
23. Bob Ryan	Writer	Boston Globe
24. Ted Shaker	Executive Producer	CBS

Informant	Title	Organization
25. Adam Silver	President	NBA Entertainment
26. Howie Singer	Knicks Producer	MSG Network
27. Kevin Smollon	Game Producer	NBC
28. David Stern	Commissioner	NBA
29. Kelly Tripucka	Player/Announcer	Detroit Pistons
30. Stephen Ulrich	Director, Talent & Promotion	NBC
31. Greg Winik	Vice President Broadcast	NBA

APPENDIX B

NBA PLAYOFFS TELEVISION SCHEDULE—1977

Day	Date	Network	Time		Game	
Fri	4/15	CBS	11:30	Reg	Portland at Chicago	- Game 2-tape
Sun	4/17	CBS	1:30	Reg	Boston at Philadelphia	- Game 1
					Cleveland at Washington	- Game 3
		CBS	3:30	Reg	Chicago at Portland	- Game 3
					Detroit at Golden State	- Game 3
Fri	4/22	CBS	11:30		Golden State at Los Angeles	- Game 2
Sun	4/24	CBS	1:30	Reg	Philadelphia at Boston	- Game 4
					Houston at Washington	Game 3
					Denver at Portland	- Game 3
Fri	4/29	CBS	11:30		Golden State at Los Angeles	- Game 5
Sun	5/1	CBS	1:30	Reg	Boston at Philadelphia	- Game 7
					Houston at Washington	- Game 6
		CBS	3:45		Los Angeles at Golden State	- Game 6
Weds	5/4	CBS	11:30		Golden State at Los Angeles	- Game 7
Fri	5/6	CBS	11:30		Portland at Los Angeles	- Game 1
Sun	5/8	CBS	1:30		Houston at Philadelphia	- Game 2
		CBS	3:45		Portland at Los Angeles	- Game 2
Fri	5/13	CBS	11:30		Los Angeles at Portland	- Game 4
Sun	5/15	CBS	1:30		Houston at Philadelphia	- Game 5

NBA Finals

Sun	5/22	CBS	1:30	Portland at Philadelphia	- Game 1
Thur	5/26	CBS	9:00	Portland at Philadelphia	- Game 2
Sun	5/29	CBS	3:30	Philadelphia at Portland	- Game 3
Tue	5/31	CBS	9:00	Philadelphia at Portland	- Game 4
Fri	6/3	CBS	9:00	Portland at Philadelphia	- Game 5
Sun	6/5	CBS	3:00	Philadelphia at Portland	- Game 6

NBA PLAYOFFS TELEVISION SCHEDULE—1978

Day	Date	Network	Time		Game	
Wed	4/12	CBS	11:30		Los Angeles at Seattle	- Game 1
Fri	4/14	CBS	11:30		Los Angeles at Seattle	- Game 2
Sun	4/16	CBS	1:00		New York at Philadelphia	- Game 1
		CBS	3:30	Reg	Los Angeles at Seattle	- Game 3
					Washington at San Antonio	- Game 1
Fri	4/21	CBS	11:30		Seattle at Portland	- Game 2
Sun	4/23	CBS	1:00		Philadelphia at New York	- Game 4
			3:45		Portland at Seattle	- Game 3
Fri	4/28	CBS	11:30		Milwaukee at Denver	- Game 5
Sun	4/30	CBS	1:30		Washington at Philadelphia	- Game 1
			3:45		Denver at Milwaukee	- Game 6
Fri	5/5	CBS	11:30		Seattle at Denver	- Game 1
Sun	5/7	CBS	1:30		Philadelphia at Washington	- Game 4
			3:45		Seattle at Denver	- Game 2
Fri	5/12	CBS	11:30		Denver at Seattle	- Game 4
Sun	5/14	CBS	4:00		Seattle at Denver	- Game 5

NBA Finals

Sun	5/21	CBS	3:00	Washington at Seattle	- Game 1
Thur	5/25	CBS	9:00	Seattle at Washington	- Game 2
Sun	5/28	CBS	1:30	Seattle at Washington	- Game 3
Tue	5/30	CBS	9:00	Washington at Seattle	- Game 4
Fri	6/2	CBS	9:00	Washington at Seattle	- Game 5
Sun	6/4	CBS	1:30	Seattle at Washington	- Game 6
Wed	6/7	CBS	9:00	Washington at Seattle	- Game 7

NBA PLAYOFFS TELEVISION SCHEDULE—1979

Day	Date	Network	Time		Game	
Fri	4/13	CBS	11:30		Phoenix at Portland	- Game 2
Sun	4/15	CBS	1:00	Reg	Atlanta at Washington	- Game 1
					Philadelphia at San Antonio	- Game 1
Fri	4/20	CBS	11:30		Seattle at Los Angeles	- Game 3
Sun	4/22	CBS	1:30		Washington at Atlanta	- Game 4
			3:45		Seattle at Los Angeles	- Game 4
Fri	4/27	CBS	11:30		Kansas City at Phoenix	- Game 5

Sun	4/29	CBS	1:30	San Antonio at Philadelphia	- Game 6
			3:45	Atlanta at Washington	- Game 7
Fri	5/4	CBS	11:30	Phoenix at Seattle	- Game 2
Sun	5/6	CBS	1:30	San Antonio at Washington	- Game 2
			3:45	Seattle at Phoenix	- Game 3
Fri	5/11	CBS	11:30	Phoenix at Seattle	- Game 5
Sun	5/13	CBS	1:30	San Antonio at Washington	- Game 5
			3:45	Seattle at Phoenix	- Game 6

NBA Finals

Sun	5/20	CBS	1:30	Seattle at Washington	- Game 1
Thur	5/24	CBS	9:00	Seattle at Washington	- Game 2
Sun	5/27	CBS	3:00	Washington at Seattle	- Game 3
Tue	5/29	CBS	11:30	Washington at Seattle	- Game 4
Fri	6/1	CBS	9:00	Seattle at Washington	- Game 5

NBA PLAYOFFS TELEVISION SCHEDULE—1980

Day	Date	Network	Time		Game	
Fri	4/4	CBS	11:30		Seattle at Portland	- Game 2
Sun	4/6	CBS	1:00		Atlanta at Philadelphia	- Game 1
			3:30	Reg	Kansas City at Phoenix	- Game 3
					Portland at Seattle	- Game 3
Fri	4/11	CBS	11:30		Los Angeles at Phoenix	- Game 3
Sun	4/13	CBS	1:00		Boston at Houston	- Game 3
Fri	4/18	CBS	11:30		Seattle at Milwaukee or	- Game 6-tape
					Philadelphia at Boston	- Game 1
Sun	4/20	CBS	1:00		Philadelphia at Boston	- Game 2
			3:30		Milwaukee at Seattle	- Game 7
Wed	4/23		11:30		Seattle at Los Angeles	- Game 2
Fri	4/25	CBS	11:30		Los Angeles at Seattle	- Game 3
Sun	4/27	CBS	1:00		Philadelphia at Boston	- Game 5
			3:30		Los Angeles at Seattle	- Game 4
Wed	4/30	CBS	11:30		Seattle at Los Angeles	- Game 5

NBA Finals

Sun	5/4	CBS	3:30	Philadelphia at Los Angeles	- Game 1
Wed	5/7	CBS	11:30	Philadelphia at Los Angeles	- Game 2
Sat	5/10	CBS	3:30	Los Angeles at Philadelphia	- Game 3
Sun	5/11	CBS	3:00	Los Angeles at Philadelphia	- Game 4
Wed	5/14	CBS	11:30	Philadelphia at Los Angeles	- Game 5
Fri	5/16	CBS	9:00	Los Angeles at Philadelphia	- Game 6

NBA PLAYOFFS TELEVISION SCHEDULE—1981

Day	Date	Network	Time	Game	
Wed	4/1	CBS	11:30	Houston at Los Angeles	- Game 1
Fri	4/3	USA	8:00	New York at Chicago	- Game 2
		CBS	11:30	Los Angeles at Houston	- Game 2
Sun	4/5	CBS	1:00	Milwaukee at Philadelphia *or*	- Game 1
				Chicago at Boston	- Game 1
			3:15	Houston at Los Angeles	- Game 3
Tue	4/7	USA	8:00	Milwaukee at Philadelphia *or*	- Game 2
				Chicago at Boston	- Game 2
		CBS	11:30	Kansas City at Phoenix	- Game 1-tape
				Houston at San Antonio	- Game 1
Wed	4/8	USA	8:00	Houston at San Antonio	- Game 2
		CBS	11:30	Kansas City at Phoenix	- Game 2-tape
Fri	4/10	CBS	11:30	Boston at Chicago	- Game 3-tape
Sun	4/12	CBS	1:00	Philadelphia at Milwaukee *or*	- Game 4
				Boston at Chicago	- Game 4
Wed	4/15	CBS	11:30	Milwaukee at Philadelphia	- Game 5-tape
Fri	4/17	CBS	11:30	Philadelphia at Milwaukee	- Game 6-tape
Sun	4/19	CBS	1:00	Milwaukee at Philadelphia	- Game 7
			3:30	Kansas City at Phoenix	- Game 7
Tue	4/21	CBS	11:30	Houston at Kansas City	- Game 1-tape
Wed	4/22	CBS	11:30	Houston at Kansas City	- Game 2-tape
Fri	4/24	CBS	11:30	Kansas City at Houston	- Game 3-tape
Sun	4/26	CBS	1:00	Boston at Philadelphia	- Game 4
			3:30	Kansas City at Houston	- Game 4
Wed	4/29	CBS	11:30	Philadelphia at Boston	- Game 5-tape
Fri	5/1	CBS	11:30	Boston at Philadelphia	- Game 6-tape
Sun	5/3	CBS	3:30	Philadelphia at Boston	- Game 7

NBA Finals

Day	Date	Network	Time	Game	
Tue	5/5	CBS	11:30	Houston at Boston	- Game 1-tape
Thur	5/7	CBS	11:30	Houston at Boston	- Game 2-tape
Sat	5/9	CBS	3:30	Boston at Houston	- Game 3
Sun	5/10	CBS	3:30	Boston at Houston	- Game 4
Tue	5/12	CBS	11:30	Houston at Boston	- Game 5-tape
Thur	5/14	CBS	11:30	Boston at Houston	- Game 6-tape

NBA PLAYOFFS TELEVISION SCHEDULE—1982

Day	Date	Network	Time	Game	
Wed	4/21	USA	11:00	Houston at Seattle	- Game 1
Fri	4/23	CBS	11:30	Seattle at Houston	- Game 2-tape
Sun	4/25	CBS	1:00	Washington at Boston	- Game 1
			3:00	Houston at Seattle	- Game 3
Wed	4/28	USA	8:00	Washington at Boston	- Game 2
		USA	10:30	Phoenix at Los Angeles	- Game 2

Fri	4/30	USA	8:00		Seattle at San Antonio	- Game 3
		CBS	11:30		Los Angeles at Phoenix	- Game 3
Sat	5/1	CBS	1:00		Boston at Washington	- Game 3
			3:30		Philadelphia at Milwaukee	- Game 3
Sun	5/2	CBS	1:00		Boston at Washington	- Game 4
			3:30	Reg	Seattle at San Antonio	- Game 4
					Los Angeles at Phoenix	- Game 4
Wed	5/5	USA	7:30		Washington at Boston	- Game 5
			10:30		San Antonio at Seattle	- Game 5
Fri	5/7	CBS	11:30		Philadelphia at Milwaukee	- Game 6-tape
Sun	5/9	CBS	1:00		Philadelphia at Boston	- Game 1
			3:30		San Antonio at Los Angeles	- Game 1
Wed	5/12	USA	7:30		Philadelphia at Boston	- Game 2
Fri	5/14	CBS	11:30		Los Angeles at San Antonio	- Game 3-tape
Sat	5/15	CBS	2:30		Boston at Philadelphia	- Game 3
		USA	8:30		Los Angeles at San Antonio	- Game 4
Sun	5/16	CBS	1:00		Boston at Philadelphia	- Game 4
Wed	5/19	USA	8:00		Philadelphia at Boston	- Game 5
Fri	5/21	CBS	11:30		Boston at Philadelphia	- Game 6-tape
Sun	5/23	CBS	3:30		Philadelphia at Boston	- Game 7

NBA Finals

Thur	5/27	CBS	9:00	Los Angeles at Philadelphia	- Game 1
Sun	5/30	CBS	1:00	Los Angeles at Philadelphia	- Game 2
Tue	6/1	CBS	9:00	Philadelphia at Los Angeles	- Game 3
Thur	6/3	CBS	9:00	Philadelphia at Los Angeles	- Game 4
Sun	6/6	CBS	2:00	Los Angeles at Philadelphia	- Game 5
Tue	6/8	CBS	9:00	Philadelphia at Los Angeles	- Game 6

NBA PLAYOFFS TELEVISION SCHEDULE—1983

Day	Date	Network	Time		Game	
Tue	4/19	USA	8:00		Atlanta at Boston	- Game 1
		ESPN	10:00		Denver at Phoenix	- Game 1
Wed	4/20	USA	11:00		Portland at Seattle	- Game 1
Thur	4/21	USA	8:00		New Jersey at New York	- Game 2
Fri	4/22	ESPN	8:00		Boston at Atlanta	- Game 2
		CBS	11:30		Seattle at Portland	- Game 2
Sun	4/24	CBS	1:00		Atlanta at Boston	- Game 3
			3:30	Reg	New York at Philadelphia	- Game 1
					Portland at Los Angeles	- Game 1
Tue	4/26	ESPN	8:30		Denver at San Antonio	- Game 1
		USA	11:00		Portland at Los Angeles	- Game 2
Wed	4/27	USA	8:00		Milwaukee at Boston	- Game 1
Fri	4/29	USA	8:00		Milwaukee at Boston	- Game 2
		CBS	11:30		Los Angeles at Portland	- Game 3
Sat	4/30	CBS	2:00		Philadelphia at New York	- Game 3
Sun	5/1	CBS	1:00		Boston at Milwaukee	- Game 3
			3:30	Reg	Philadelphia at New York	- Game 4
					Los Angeles at Portland	- Game 4

Sun	5/8	CBS	1:00		Milwaukee at Philadelphia	- Game 1
			3:30		San Antonio at Los Angeles	- Game 1
Tue	5/10	CBS	11:30		San Antonio at Los Angeles	- Game 2
Wed	5/11	USA	8:00		Milwaukee at Philadelphia	- Game 2
Fri	5/13	CBS	11:30		Los Angeles at San Antonio	- Game 3-tape
Sat	5/14	CBS	2:30		Philadelphia at Milwaukee	- Game 3
Sun	5/15	CBS	1:00	Reg	Philadelphia at Milwaukee	- Game 4
					Los Angeles at San Antonio	- Game 4
Wed	5/18	ESPN	8:00		Milwaukee at Philadelphia	- Game 5
		CBS	11:30		San Antonio at Los Angeles	- Game 5
Fri	5/20	CBS	11:30		Los Angeles at San Antonio	- Game 6-tape

NBA Finals

Sun	5/22	CBS	3:30	Los Angeles at Philadelphia	- Game 1
Thur	5/26	CBS	9:00	Los Angeles at Philadelphia	- Game 2
Sun	5/29	CBS	3:30	Philadelphia at Los Angeles	- Game 3
Tue	5/31	CBS	9:00	Philadelphia at Los Angeles	- Game 3

NBA PLAYOFFS TELEVISION SCHEDULE—1984

Day	Date	Network	Time		Game	
Tue	4/17	USA	8:00		Washington at Boston	- Game 1
		ESPN	10:30		Denver at Utah	- Game 1
Wed	4/18	ESPN	8:00		New Jersey at Philadelphia	- Game 1
		USA	11:00		Kansas City at Los Angeles	- Game 1
Thur	4/19	USA	8:00		New York at Detroit	- Game 2
Fri	4/20	ESPN	8:00		New Jersey at Philadelphia	- Game 2
		ESPN	10:30		Kansas City at Los Angeles	- Game 2
Sat	4/21	CBS	3:30	Reg	Boston at Washington	- Game 3
					Dallas at Seattle	- Game 3
Sun	4/22	CBS	1:00	Reg	Philadelphia at New Jersey	- Game 3
					Los Angeles at Kansas City	- Game 3
Tue	4/24	ESPN	8:00		Boston at Washington	- Game 4
Wed	4/25	USA	8:00		Detroit at New York	- Game 4
Thur	4/26	ESPN	7:30		New Jersey at Philadelphia	- Game 5
		USA	10:30		Phoenix at Portland	- Game 5
Fri	4/27	USA	8:00		New York at Detroit	- Game 5
Sat	4/28	CBS	3:30		Dallas at Los Angeles	- Game 1
Sun	4/29	CBS	1:00		New York at Boston	- Game 1
			3:30	Reg	New Jersey at Milwaukee	- Game 1
					Phoenix at Utah	- Game 1
Tue	5/1	ESPN	8:00		New Jersey at Milwaukee	- Game 2
Wed	5/2	USA	8:00		New York at Boston	- Game 2
		ESPN	9:30		Phoenix at Utah	- Game 2
Thur	5/3	ESPN	7:30		Milwaukee at New Jersey	- Game 3
Fri	5/4	ESPN	8:00		Boston at New York	- Game 3
Sat	5/5	CBS	2:00		Milwaukee at New Jersey	- Game 4
Sun	5/6	CBS	1:00		Boston at New York	- Game 4
			3:30		Los Angeles at Dallas	- Game 4
Tue	5/8	ESPN	8:00		New Jersey at Milwaukee	- Game 5
		USA	10:30		Phoenix at Utah	- Game 5

Weds	5/9	USA	8:00	New York at Boston	- Game 5
Thur	5/10	CBS	11:30	Utah at Phoenix	- Game 6-tape
Fri	5/11	ESPN	8:00	Boston at New York	- Game 6
Sat	5/12	CBS	3:30	Phoenix at Los Angeles	- Game 1
Sun	5/13	CBS	1:00	New York at Boston	- Game 7
Tue	5/15	ESPN	8:00	Milwaukee at Boston	- Game 1
Thur	5/17	ESPN	8:00	Milwaukee at Boston	- Game 2
Fri	5/18	CBS	11:30	Los Angeles at Phoenix	- Game 3
Sat	5/19	CBS	2:00	Boston at Milwaukee	- Game 3
Sun	5/20	CBS	3:30	Los Angeles at Phoenix	- Game 4
Mon	5/21	USA	8:00	Boston at Milwaukee	- Game 4
Wed	5/23	USA	8:00	Milwaukee at Boston	- Game 5
		CBS	11:30	Phoenix at Los Angeles	- Game 5
Fri	5/25	CBS	11:30	Los Angeles at Phoenix	- Game 6

NBA Finals

Sun	5/27	CBS	1:00	Los Angeles at Boston	- Game 1
Thur	5/31	CBS	9:00	Los Angeles at Boston	- Game 2
Sun	6/3	CBS	3:30	Boston at Los Angeles	- Game 3
Wed	6/6	CBS	9:00	Boston at Los Angeles	- Game 4
Fri	6/8	CBS	9:00	Los Angeles at Boston	- Game 5
Sun	6/10	CBS	3:30	Boston at Los Angeles	- Game 6
Tue	6/12	CBS	9:00	Los Angeles at Boston	- Game 7

NBA PLAYOFFS TELEVISION SCHEDULE—1985

Day	Date	Network	Time		Game	
Wed	4/17	TBS	8:00		Washington at Philadelphia	- Game 1
Thur	4/18	TBS	8:00		Cleveland at Boston	- Game 1
		TBS	10:30		Phoenix at Los Angeles	- Game 1
Sat	4/20	TBS	1:00		Portland at Dallas	- Game 2
		CBS	3:30	Reg	Cleveland at Boston	- Game 2
					Phoenix at Los Angeles	- Game 2
		TBS	10:30		San Antonio at Denver	- Game 2
Sun	4/21	CBS	1:00	Reg	Washington at Philadelphia	- Game 2
					Chicago at Milwaukee	- Game 2
		TBS	5:30		Utah at Houston	- Game 2
		TBS	8:00		New Jersey at Detroit	- Game 2
Tue	4/23	TBS	7:30		Boston at Cleveland	- Game 3
Wed	4/24	TBS	7:30		Philadelphia at Washington	- Game 3
Fri	4/26	TBS	8:00		Milwaukee at Chicago	- Game 4
		TBS	10:30		Houston at Utah	- Game 4
Sat	4/27	CBS	3:30		Portland at Los Angeles	- Game 1
Sun	4/28	CBS	3:30		Detroit at Boston	- Game 1
		CBS	1:00	Reg	Philadelphia at Milwaukee	- Game 1
					Utah at Houston	- Game 5
		TBS	10:00		San Antonio at Denver	- Game 5
Tue	4/30	TBS	10:30		Portland at Los Angeles	- Game 2
Thur	5/2	TBS	8:00		Boston at Detroit	- Game 3

Day	Date	Network	Time		Game	
Fri	5/3	TBS	8:00		Milwaukee at Philadelphia	- Game 3
		TBS	10:30		Los Angeles at Portland	- Game 3
Sat	5/4	CBS	2:30		Denver at Utah	- Game 3
Sun	5/5	CBS	1:00		Boston at Detroit	- Game 4
		CBS	3:30	Reg	Milwaukee at Philadelphia	- Game 4
					Los Angeles at Portland	- Game 4
		TBS	10:00		Denver at Utah	- Game 4
Tue	5/7	TBS	10:30		Portland at Los Angeles	- Game 5
Wed	5/8	TBS	8:00		Detroit at Boston	- Game 5
Fri	5/10	CBS	7:30		Boston at Detroit	- Game 6
Sat	5/11	CBS	3:30		Denver at Los Angeles	- Game 1
Sun	5/12	CBS	1:00		Philadelphia at Boston	- Game 1
Tue	5/14	TBS	8:30		Philadelphia at Boston	- Game 2
		TBS	11:00		Denver at Los Angeles	- Game 2
Fri	5/17	CBS	11:30		Los Angeles at Denver	- Game 3-tape
Sat	5/18	CBS	3:30		Boston at Philadelphia	- Game 3
Sun	5/19	CBS	1:00		Boston at Philadelphia	- Game 4
		CBS	6:00	Reg	Los Angeles at Denver	- Game 4
Wed	5/22	TBS	8:00		Philadelphia at Boston	- Game 5
		CBS	11:30		Denver at Los Angeles	- Game 5

NBA Finals

Mon	5/27	CBS	3:00	Los Angeles at Boston	- Game 1
Thur	5/30	CBS	9:00	Los Angeles at Boston	- Game 2
Sun	6/2	CBS	3:30	Boston at Los Angeles	- Game 3
Wed	6/5	CBS	9:00	Boston at Los Angeles	- Game 4
Fri	6/7	CBS	9:00	Boston at Los Angeles	- Game 5
Sun	6/9	CBS	1:00	Los Angeles at Boston	- Game 6

NBA PLAYOFFS TELEVISION SCHEDULE—1986

Day	Date	Network	Time		Game	
Thur	4/17	TBS	8:00		Chicago at Boston	- Game 1
		TBS	10:30		San Antonio at Los Angeles	- Game 1
Fri	4/18	TBS	10:30		Portland at Denver	- Game 1
Sat	4/19	CBS	3:30	Reg	Detroit at Atlanta	- Game 2
					San Antonio at Los Angeles	- Game 2
		TBS	8:00		Sacramento at Houston	- Game 2
Sun	4/20	CBS	1:00	Reg	Chicago at Boston	- Game 2
					Washington at Philadelphia	- Game 2
		TBS	5:30		New Jersey at Milwaukee	- Game 2
		TBS	8:00		Utah at Dallas	- Game 2
Tue	4/22	TBS	10:30		Houston at Sacramento	- Game 3
Wed	4/23	TBS	8:30		Los Angeles at San Antonio	- Game 3
Fri	4/25	TBS	8:00		Atlanta at Detroit	- Game 4
Sat	4/26	CBS	3:30		Denver at Houston	- Game 1
Sun	4/27	CBS	1:00		Atlanta at Boston	- Game 1
		CBS	3:30	Reg	Washington at Philadelphia	- Game 5
					Dallas at Los Angeles	- Game 1

Tue	4/29	TBS	8:30		Atlanta at Boston	- Game 2
Wed	4/30	TBS	10:30		Dallas at Los Angeles	- Game 2
Thur	5/1	TBS	8:30		Philadelphia at Milwaukee	- Game 2
Fri	5/2	TBS	10:30		Houston at Denver	- Game 3
Sat	5/3	CBS	2:30		Milwaukee at Philadelphia	- Game 3
Sun	5/4	CBS	1:00		Boston at Atlanta	- Game 4
		CBS	3:30	Reg	Houston at Denver	- Game 4
					Los Angeles at Dallas	- Game 4
Mon	5/5	TBS	7:30		Milwaukee at Philadelphia	- Game 4
Tue	5/6	TBS	7:30		Atlanta at Boston	- Game 5
		TBS	10:30		Dallas at Los Angeles	- Game 5
Wed	5/7	TBS	8:00		Philadelphia at Milwaukee	- Game 5
Thur	5/8	CBS	11:30		Los Angeles at Dallas	- Game 6-tape
Fri	5/9	TBS	8:30		Milwaukee at Philadelphia	- Game 6
Sat	5/10	CBS	3:30		Houston at Los Angeles	- Game 1
Sun	5/11	CBS	1:00		Philadelphia at Milwaukee	- Game 7
Tue	5/13	TBS	10:30		Houston at Los Angeles	- Game 2
Thur	5/15	TBS	8:00		Milwaukee at Boston	- Game 2
Fri	5/16	CBS	11:30		Los Angeles at Houston	- Game 3-tape
Sat	5/17	CBS	2:00		Boston at Milwaukee	- Game 3
Sun	5/18	CBS	3:30	Reg	Boston at Milwaukee	- Game 4
					Los Angeles at Houston	- Game 4
Wed	5/21	CBS	11:30		Houston at Los Angeles	- Game 5

NBA Finals

Mon	5/26	CBS	3:00	Houston at Boston	- Game 1
Thur	5/29	CBS	9:00	Houston at Boston	- Game 2
Sun	6/1	CBS	3:30	Boston at Houston	- Game 3
Tue	6/3	CBS	9:00	Boston at Houston	- Game 4
Thur	6/5	CBS	9:00	Boston at Houston	- Game 5
Sun	6/8	CBS	1:00	Houston at Boston	- Game 6

NBA PLAYOFFS TELEVISION SCHEDULE—1987

Day	Date	Network	Time	Game	
Thur	4/23	TBS	8:00	Chicago at Boston	- Game 1
			10:30	Denver at Los Angeles	- Game 1
Fri	4/24	TBS	8:30	Washington at Detroit	- Game 1
			11:00	Houston at Portland	- Game 1
Sat	4/25	CBS	3:30	Denver at Los Angeles	- Game 2
Sun	4/26	CBS	1:00	Chicago at Boston	- Game 2
			3:30	Philadelphia at Milwaukee	- Game 2
Tue	4/28	TBS	10:30	Dallas at Seattle	- Game 3
Wed	4/29	TBS	10:30	Los Angeles at Denver	- Game 3
Thur	4/30	TBS	8:00	Portland at Houston	- Game 4
			10:30	Dallas at Seattle	- Game 4
Fri	5/1	TBS	8:30	Milwaukee at Philadelphia	- Game 4
			11:00	Utah at Golden State	- Game 4
Sat	5/2	CBS	3:30	Seattle at Houston	- Game 1

Sun	5/3	CBS	1:30		Philadelphia at Milwaukee	- Game 5
			3:30	Reg	Detroit at Atlanta	- Game 1
					Golden State at Utah	- Game 5
Tue	5/5	TBS	8:30		Detroit at Atlanta	- Game 2
			11:00		Golden State at Los Angeles	- Game 1
Wed	5/6	TBS	7:30		Milwaukee at Boston	- Game 1
Thur	5/7	TBS	10:00		Houston at Seattle	- Game 3
Fri	5/8	TBS	7:30		Atlanta at Detroit	- Game 3
Sat	5/9	CBS	3:30		Los Angeles at Golden State	- Game 3
Sun	5/10	CBS	1:00		Boston at Milwaukee	- Game 4
		TBS	6:00		Los Angeles at Golden State	- Game 4
Tue	5/12	TBS	10:30		Golden State at Los Angeles	- Game 5
Wed	5/13	TBS	7:30		Milwaukee at Boston	- Game 5
Sat	5/16	CBS	3:30		Seattle at Los Angeles	- Game 1
Sun	5/17	CBS	1:00		Milwaukee at Boston	- Game 7
Tue	5/19	TBS	10:30		Seattle at Los Angeles	- Game 2
Thur	5/21	TBS	8:30		Detroit at Boston	- Game 2
Sat	5/23	CBS	3:30		Boston at Detroit	- Game 3
		TBS	7:00		Los Angeles at Seattle	- Game 3
Sun	5/24	CBS	3:30		Boston at Detroit	- Game 4
Mon	5/25	CBS	3:30		Los Angeles at Seattle	- Game 4
Tue	5/26	TBS	8:00		Detroit at Boston	- Game 5
Thur	5/28	TBS	9:00		Boston at Detroit	- Game 5
Sat	5/30	CBS	3:30		Detroit at Boston	- Game 7

NBA Finals

Tue	6/2	CBS	9:00	Boston at Los Angeles	- Game 1
Thur	6/4	CBS	9:00	Boston at Los Angeles	- Game 2
Sun	6/7	CBS	1:30	Los Angeles at Boston	- Game 3
Tue	6/9	CBS	9:00	Los Angeles at Boston	- Game 4
Thur	6/11	CBS	9:00	Los Angeles at Boston	- Game 5
Sun	6/14	CBS	3:30	Boston at Los Angeles	- Game 6

NBA PLAYOFFS TELEVISION SCHEDULE—1988

Day	Date	Network	Time	Game	
Thur	4/28	TBS	8:00	Cleveland at Chicago	- Game 1
		TBS	10:30	Utah at Portland	- Game 1
Fri	4/29	TBS	8:00	New York at Boston	- Game 1
			10:30	San Antonio at Los Angeles	- Game 1
Sat	4/30	CBS	3:30	Houston at Dallas	- Game 2
			8:00	Washington at Detroit	- Game 2
Sun	5/1	CBS	1:00	New York at Boston	- Game 2
			3:30	Cleveland at Chicago	- Game 2
Tue	5/3	TBS	8:00	Chicago at Cleveland	- Game 3
			10:30	Denver at Seattle	- Game 3
Wed	5/4	TBS	8:00	Boston at New York	- Game 3
Thur	5/5	TBS	8:00	Chicago at Cleveland	- Game 4
			10:30	Denver at Seattle	- Game 4
Fri	5/6	TBS	8:30	Boston at New York	- Game 4

Day	Date	Network	Time		Matchup	
Sat	5/7	CBS	3:30		Seattle at Denver	- Game 5
Sun	5/8	CBS	1:00		Cleveland at Chicago	- Game 5
			3:30	Reg	Washington at Detroit	- Game 5
					Utah at Los Angeles	- Game 1
		TBS	7:00		Milwaukee at Atlanta	- Game 5
Tue	5/10	TBS	8:30		Chicago at Detroit	- Game 1
		TBS	11:00		Utah at Los Angeles	- Game 1
Wed	5/11	TBS	8:30		Atlanta at Boston	- Game 1
Thur	5/12	TBS	10:00		Dallas at Denver	- Game 2
Fri	5/13	TBS	8:00		Atlanta at Boston	- Game 2
			10:30		Los Angeles at Utah	- Game 3
Sat	5/14	CBS	1:00		Detroit at Chicago	- Game 3
			3:30		Denver at Dallas	- Game 3
Sun	5/15	CBS	1:00		Boston at Atlanta	- Game 3
			3:30	Reg	Detroit at Chicago	- Game 4
					Los Angeles at Utah	- Game 4
Mon	5/16	TBS	8:00		Boston at Atlanta	- Game 4
Tue	5/17	TBS	11:00		Utah at Los Angeles	- Game 5
Wed	5/18	TBS	8:00		Chicago at Detroit	- Game 5
Thur	5/19	TBS	8:00		Denver at Dallas	- Game 6
			10:30		Los Angeles at Utah	- Game 6
Fri	5/20	TBS	8:00		Boston at Atlanta	- Game 6
Sat	5/21	CBS	3:30		Utah at Los Angeles	- Game 7
Sun	5/22	CBS	1:00		Atlanta at Boston	- Game 7
Mon	5/23	TBS	10:00		Dallas at Los Angeles	- Game 1
Wed	5/25	TBS	8:00		Detroit at Boston	- Game 1
			10:30		Dallas at Los Angeles	- Game 2
Thur	5/26	TBS	8:00		Detroit at Boston	- Game 2
Fri	5/27	TBS	8:00		Los Angeles at Dallas	- Game 3
Sat	5/28	CBS	3:30		Boston at Detroit	- Game 3
Sun	5/29	CBS	3:30		Los Angeles at Dallas	- Game 4
Mon	5/30	CBS	3:00		Boston at Detroit	- Game 4
Tue	5/31	CBS	11:30		Dallas at Los Angeles	- Game 5
Wed	6/1	TBS	8:00		Detroit at Boston	- Game 5
Thur	6/2	TBS	9:00		Los Angeles at Dallas	- Game 6
Fri	6/3	CBS	9:00		Boston at Detroit	- Game 6
Sat	6/4	CBS	3:30		Dallas at Los Angeles	- Game 7

NBA Finals

Day	Date	Network	Time	Matchup	
Tue	6/7	CBS	9:00	Detroit at Los Angeles	- Game 1
Thur	6/9	CBS	9:00	Detroit at Los Angeles	- Game 2
Sun	6/12	CBS	3:30	Los Angeles at Detroit	- Game 3
Tue	6/14	CBS	9:00	Los Angeles at Detroit	- Game 4
Thur	6/16	CBS	9:00	Los Angeles at Detroit	- Game 5
Sun	6/19	CBS	3:30	Detroit at Los Angeles	- Game 6
Tue	6/21	CBS	9:00	Detroit at Los Angeles	- Game 7

NBA PLAYOFFS TELEVISION SCHEDULE—1989

Day	Date	Network	Time		Game	
Thur	4/27	TBS	8:00		Philadelphia at New York	- Game 1
			10:30		Portland at Los Angeles	- Game 1
Fri	4/28	TBS	8:00		Boston at Detroit	- Game 1
			10:30		Denver at Phoenix	- Game 1
Sat	4/29	CBS	3:30		Philadelphia at New York	- Game 2
		TBS	8:00		Milwaukee at Atlanta	- Game 2
Sun	4/30	CBS	1:00		Chicago at Cleveland	- Game 2
			3:30	Reg	Boston at Detroit	- Game 2
					Portland at Los Angeles	- Game 2
Tue	5/2	TBS	8:00		Detroit at Boston	- Game 3
			10:30		Utah at Golden State	- Game 3
Wed	5/3	TBS	8:00		Cleveland at Chicago	- Game 3
		TBS	10:30		Los Angeles at Portland	- Game 3
Fri	5/5	TBS	8:00		Cleveland at Chicago	- Game 4
Sat	5/6	CBS	3:30		Golden State at Phoenix	- Game 1
Sun	5/7	CBS	1:00		Milwaukee at Atlanta	- Game 5
			3:30	Reg	Chicago at Cleveland	- Game 5
					Seattle at Los Angeles	- Game 1
Tue	5/9	TBS	8:00		Chicago at New York	- Game 1
			10:30		Golden State at Phoenix	- Game 2
Wed	5/10	TBS	8:00		Milwaukee at Detroit	- Game 1
			10:30		Seattle at Los Angeles	- Game 1
Thur	5/11	TBS	8:00		Chicago at New York	- Game 2
			10:30		Phoenix at Golden State	- Game 3
Fri	5/12	TBS	8:00		Milwaukee at Detroit	- Game 2
			10:30		Los Angeles at Seattle	- Game 3
Sat	5/13	CBS	1:00		New York at Chicago	- Game 3
			3:30		Phoenix at Golden State	- Game 4
Sun	5/14	CBS	1:00		New York at Chicago	- Game 4
			3:30	Reg	Detroit at Milwaukee	- Game 3
					Los Angeles at Seattle	- Game 4
Mon	5/15	TBS	8:00		Detroit at Milwaukee	- Game 4
Tue	5/16	TBS	8:00		Chicago at New York	- Game 5
			10:30		Golden State at Phoenix	- Game 5
Fri	5/19	TBS	8:00		New York at Chicago	- Game 6
Sat	5/20	CBS	3:30		Phoenix at Los Angeles	- Game 1
Sun	5/21	CBS	1:00		Chicago at Detroit	- Game 1
Tue	5/23	TBS	8:00		Chicago at Detroit	- Game 2
			10:30		Phoenix at Los Angeles	- Game 2
Fri	5/26	TBS	10:00		Los Angeles at Phoenix	- Game 3
Sat	5/27	CBS	2:00		Detroit at Chicago	- Game 3
Sun	5/28	CBS	3:30		Los Angeles at Phoenix	- Game 4
Mon	5/29	CBS	3:00		Detroit at Chicago	- Game 4
Wed	5/31	TBS	8:00		Chicago at Detroit	- Game 5
Fri	6/2	CBS	9:00		Detroit at Chicago	- Game 6

NBA Finals

Tue	6/6	CBS	9:00	Los Angeles at Detroit	- Game 1
Thur	6/8	CBS	9:00	Los Angeles at Detroit	- Game 2
Sun	6/11	CBS	3:30	Detroit at Los Angeles	- Game 3
Tue	6/13	CBS	9:00	Detroit at Los Angeles	- Game 4

NBA PLAYOFFS TELEVISION SCHEDULE—1990

Day	Date	Network	Time		Game	
Thur	4/26	TNT	8:00		New York at Boston	- Game 1
			10:30		Dallas at Portland	- Game 1
Fri	4/27	TNT	8:00		Milwaukee at Chicago	- Game 1
			10:30		Houston at Los Angeles	- Game 1
Sat	4/28	CBS	1:00		New York at Boston	- Game 2
			3:30		Indiana at Detroit	- Game 2
		TNT	8:00		Denver at San Antonio	- Game 2
			10:30		Dallas at Portland	- Game 2
Sun	4/29	CBS	1:00		Milwaukee at Chicago	- Game 2
			3:30		Houston at Los Angeles	- Game 2
		TNT	7:30		Cleveland at Philadelphia	- Game 2
Tue	5/1	TNT	8:00		Chicago at Milwaukee	- Game 3
			10:30		San Antonio at Denver	- Game 3
Wed	5/2	TNT	8:00		Boston at New York	- Game 3
			10:30		Utah at Phoenix	- Game 3
Thur	5/3	TNT	8:00		Los Angeles at Houston	- Game 4
Fri	5/4	TNT	8:00		Boston at New York	- Game 4
			10:30		Utah at Phoenix	- Game 4
Sat	5/5	CBS	1:00		Cleveland at Philadelphia	- Game 5
			3:30		San Antonio at Portland	- Game 1
Sun	5/6	CBS	1:00		New York at Boston	- Game 5
			3:30		Phoenix at Utah	- Game 5
Mon	5/7	TNT	8:00		Philadelphia at Chicago	- Game 1
Tue	5/8	TNT	8:00		New York at Detroit	- Game 1
			10:30		Phoenix at Los Angeles	- Game 1
Wed	5/9	TNT	8:00		Philadelphia at Chicago	- Game 2
Thur	5/10	TNT	8:00		New York at Detroit	- Game 2
			10:30		Phoenix at Los Angeles	- Game 2
Fri	5/11	TNT	8:00		Chicago at Philadelphia	- Game 3
Sat	5/12	CBS	1:00		Detroit at New York	- Game 3
			3:30	Reg	Portland at San Antonio	- Game 4
					Los Angeles at Phoenix	- Game 3
Sun	5/13	CBS	1:00		Chicago at Philadelphia	- Game 4
			3:30	Reg	Detroit at New York	- Game 4
					Los Angeles at Phoenix	- Game 4
Tue	5/15	TNT	8:00		New York at Detroit	- Game 5
			10:30		Phoenix at Los Angeles	- Game 5
Wed	5/16	TNT	8:00		Philadelphia at Chicago	- Game 5
Thur	5/17	TNT	8:00		Portland at San Antonio	- Game 6
Sat	5/19	CBS	3:30		San Antonio at Portland	- Game 7

Day	Date	Network	Time	Game	
Sun	5/20	CBS	1:00	Chicago at Detroit	- Game 1
Mon	5/21	TNT	10:00	Phoenix at Portland	- Game 1
Tue	5/22	TNT	8:00	Chicago at Detroit	- Game 2
Wed	5/23	TNT	10:00	Phoenix at Portland	- Game 2
Fri	5/25	TNT	10:00	Portland at Phoenix	- Game 3
Sat	5/26	CBS	2:00	Detroit at Chicago	- Game 3
Sun	5/27	CBS	3:30	Portland at Phoenix	- Game 4
Mon	5/28	CBS	3:00	Detroit at Chicago	- Game 4
Tue	5/29	CBS	9:00	Phoenix at Portland	- Game 5
Wed	5/30	TNT	8:00	Chicago at Detroit	- Game 5
Thur	5/31	CBS	9:00	Portland at Phoenix	- Game 6
Fri	6/1	CBS	9:00	Detroit at Chicago	- Game 6
Sun	6/3	CBS	1:00	Chicago at Detroit	- Game 7

NBA Finals

Day	Date	Network	Time	Game	
Tue	6/5	CBS	9:00	Portland at Detroit	- Game 1
Thur	6/7	CBS	9:00	Portland at Detroit	- Game 2
Sun	6/10	CBS	3:30	Detroit at Portland	- Game 3
Tue	6/12	CBS	9:00	Detroit at Portland	- Game 4
Thur	6/14	CBS	9:00	Detroit at Portland	- Game 5

NBA PLAYOFFS TELEVISION SCHEDULE—1991

Day	Date	Network	Time	Game	
Thur	4/25	TNT	8:00	New York at Chicago	- Game 1
			10:30	Houston at Los Angeles	- Game 1
Fri	4/26	TNT	8:00	Indiana at Boston	- Game 1
			10:30	Seattle at Portland	- Game 1
Sat	4/27	NBC	1:00	Golden State at San Antonio	- Game 2
			3:30	Houston at Los Angeles	- Game 2
		TNT	6:00	Utah at Phoenix	- Game 2
			8:30	Philadelphia at Milwaukee	- Game 2
Sun	4/28	NBC	1:00	Indiana at Boston	- Game 2
			3:30	New York at Chicago	- Game 2
			7:00	Atlanta at Detroit	- Game 2
			9:30	Seattle at Portland	- Game 2
Tue	4/30	TNT	8:00	Los Angeles at Houston	- Game 3
			10:30	Phoenix at Utah	- Game 3
Wed	5/1	TNT	8:00	Boston at Indiana	- Game 3
			10:30	San Antonio at Golden State	- Game 3
Thur	5/2	TNT	8:00	Detroit at Atlanta	- Game 4
			10:30	Phoenix at Utah	- Game 4
Fri	5/3	TNT	8:00	Boston at Indiana	- Game 4
			10:30	San Antonio at Golden State	- Game 4
Sat	5/4	NBC	1:00	Philadelphia at Chicago	- Game 1
			3:30	Seattle at Portland	- Game 5
Sun	5/5	NBC	1:00	Indiana at Boston	- Game 5
			3:30	Atlanta at Detroit	- Game 5
		TNT	8:00	Golden State at Los Angeles	- Game 1

Mon	5/6	TNT	8:00	Philadelphia at Chicago	- Game 2
Tue	5/7	TNT	8:00	Detroit at Boston	- Game 1
			10:30	Utah at Portland	- Game 1
Wed	5/8	TNT	10:30	Golden State at Los Angeles	- Game 2
Thur	5/9	TNT	1:00	Detroit at Boston	- Game 2
			10:00	Utah at Portland	- Game 2
Fri	5/10	TNT	8:00	Chicago at Philadelphia	- Game 3
			10:30	Los Angeles at Golden State	- Game 3
Sat	5/11	NBC	1:00	Boston at Detroit	- Game 3
			3:30	Portland at Utah	- Game 3
Sun	5/12	NBC	1:00	Chicago at Philadelphia	- Game 4
			3:30	Los Angeles at Golden State	- Game 4
		TNT	8:00	Portland at Utah	- Game 4
Mon	5/13	TNT	8:00	Boston at Detroit	- Game 4
Tue	5/14	TNT	8:00	Philadelphia at Chicago	- Game 5
			10:30	Golden State at Los Angeles	- Game 5
Wed	5/15	TNT	8:00	Detroit at Boston	- Game 5
Fri	5/17	TNT	8:00	Boston at Detroit	- Game 6
Sat	5/18	NBC	3:30	Los Angeles at Portland	- Game 1
Sun	5/19	NBC	3:30	Detroit at Chicago	- Game 1
Tue	5/21	TNT	8:00	Detroit at Chicago	- Game 2
			10:30	Los Angeles at Portland	- Game 2
Fri	5/24	TNT	10:00	Portland at Los Angeles	- Game 3
Sat	5/25	NBC	3:30	Chicago at Detroit	- Game 3
Sun	5/26	NBC	3:30	Portland at Los Angeles	- Game 4
Mon	5/27	NBC	3:30	Chicago at Detroit	- Game 4
Tue	5/28	NBC	9:00	Los Angeles at Portland	- Game 5
Thur	5/30	NBC	9:00	Portland at Los Angeles	- Game 6

NBA Finals

Sun	6/2	NBC	3:30	Los Angeles at Chicago	- Game 1
Wed	6/5	NBC	9:00	Los Angeles at Chicago	- Game 2
Fri	6/7	NBC	9:00	Chicago at Los Angeles	- Game 3
Sun	6/9	NBC	7:00	Chicago at Los Angeles	- Game 4
Wed	6/12	NBC	9:00	Chicago at Los Angeles	- Game 5

NBA PLAYOFFS TELEVISION SCHEDULE—1992

Day	Date	Network	Time	Game	
Thur	4/23	TNT	8:00	Indiana at Boston	- Game 1
			10:30	Los Angeles at Portland	- Game 1
Fri	4/24	TNT	8:00	Miami at Chicago	- Game 1
			10:30	L.A. Clippers at Utah	- Game 1
Sat	4/25	NBC	1:00	Indiana at Boston	- Game 2
			3:30	Los Angeles at Portland	- Game 2
		TNT	6:00	Seattle at Golden State	- Game 2
			8:30	New Jersey at Cleveland	- Game 2
Sun	4/26	NBC	1:00	Miami at Chicago	- Game 2
			3:30	Detroit at New York	- Game 2
		TNT	7:00	L.A. Clippers at Utah	- Game 2
			9:30	San Antonio at Phoenix	- Game 2

Mon	4/27	TNT	8:00	Boston at Indiana	- Game 3
Tue	4/28	TNT	8:00	New York at Detroit	- Game 3
			10:30	Golden State at Seattle	- Game 3
Wed	4/29	TNT	8:00	Chicago at Miami	- Game 3
			10:30	Portland at Los Angeles	- Game 3
Thur	4/30	TNT	8:00	Cleveland at New Jersey	- Game 4
			10:30	Golden State at Seattle	- Game 4
Fri	5/1	TNT	8:00	New York at Detroit	- Game 4
Sat	5/2	NBC	1:00	Boston at Cleveland	- Game 1
Sun	5/3	NBC	1:00	Detroit at New York	- Game 5
			3:30	Portland at Los Angeles	- Game 4
		TNT	6:00	Utah at L.A. Clippers	- Game 4
Mon	5/4	TNT	8:00	Boston at Cleveland	- Game 2
		TNT	10:30	L.A. Clippers at Utah	- Game 5
Tue	5/5	TNT	8:00	New York at Chicago	- Game 1
			10:30	Phoenix at Portland	- Game 1
Wed	5/6	TNT	9:00	Seattle at Utah	- Game 1
Thur	5/7	TNT	8:00	New York at Chicago	- Game 2
			10:30	Phoenix at Portland	- Game 2
Fri	5/8	TNT	8:00	Cleveland at Boston	- Game 3
			10:30	Seattle at Utah	- Game 2
Sat	5/9	NBC	1:00	Chicago at New York	- Game 3
			3:30	Portland at Phoenix	- Game 3
Sun	5/10	NBC	12:30	Cleveland at Boston	- Game 4
			3:00	Utah at Seattle	- Game 3
			6:30	Chicago at New York	- Game 4
Mon	5/11	TNT	9:00	Portland at Phoenix	- Game 4
Tue	5/12	TNT	8:00	New York at Chicago	- Game 5
			10:30	Utah at Seattle	- Game 4
Wed	5/13	TNT	8:00	Boston at Cleveland	- Game 5
Thur	5/14	TNT	8:00	Chicago at New York	- Game 6
			10:30	Phoenix at Portland	- Game 5
Fri	5/15	TNT	8:00	Cleveland at Boston	- Game 6
Sat	5/16	NBC	3:30	Utah at Portland	- Game 1
Sun	5/17	NBC	2:00	Boston at Cleveland	- Game 7
			4:30	New York at Chicago	- Game 7
Tue	5/19	TNT	8:00	Cleveland at Chicago	- Game 1
			10:30	Utah at Portland	- Game 2
Thur	5/21	TNT	8:00	Cleveland at Chicago	- Game 2
Fri	5/22	TNT	8:00	Portland at Utah	- Game 3
Sat	5/23	NBC	3:30	Chicago at Cleveland	- Game 3
Sun	5/24	NBC	3:30	Portland at Utah	- Game 4
Mon	5/25	NBC	3:30	Chicago at Cleveland	- Game 4
Tue	5/26	NBC	9:00	Utah at Portland	- Game 5
Wed	5/27	NBC	9:00	Cleveland at Chicago	- Game 5
Thur	5/28	NBC	9:00	Portland at Utah	- Game 6
Fri	5/29	NBC	9:00	Chicago at Cleveland	- Game 6

NBA Finals

Wed	6/3	NBC	9:00	Portland at Chicago	- Game 1
Fri	6/5	NBC	9:00	Portland at Chicago	- Game 2
Sun	6/7	NBC	7:00	Chicago at Portland	- Game 3

Day	Date	Network	Time	Game	
Wed	6/10	NBC	9:00	Chicago at Portland	- Game 4
Fri	6/12	NBC	9:00	Chicago at Portland	- Game 5
Sun	6/14	NBC	7:00	Portland at Chicago	- Game 6

NBA PLAYOFFS TELEVISION SCHEDULE—1993

Day	Date	Network	Time	Game	
Thur	4/29	TNT	8:00	Charlotte at Boston	- Game 1
			10:30	San Antonio at Portland	- Game 1
Fri	4/30	TNT	8:00	Atlanta at Chicago	- Game 1
			10:30	Los Angeles at Phoenix	- Game 1
Sat	5/1	NBC	1:00	Charlotte at Boston	- Game 2
			3:30	San Antonio at Portland	- Game 2
		TNT	7:00	New Jersey at Cleveland	- Game 2
			9:30	L.A. Clippers at Houston	- Game 2
Sun	5/2	NBC	12:30	Indiana at New York	- Game 2
			3:00	Los Angeles at Phoenix	- Game 2
			5:30	Atlanta at Chicago	- Game 2
		TNT	9:00	Utah at Seattle	- Game 2
Mon	5/3	TNT	8:00	Boston at Charlotte	- Game 3
			10:30	Houston at L.A. Clippers	- Game 3
Tue	5/4	TNT	8:00	Chicago at Atlanta	- Game 3
			10:30	Phoenix at Los Angeles	- Game 3
Wed	5/5	TNT	8:00	Boston at Charlotte	- Game 4
			10:30	Houston at L.A. Clippers	- Game 4
Thur	5/6	TNT	8:00	New York at Indiana	- Game 4
			10:30	Phoenix at Los Angeles	- Game 4
Fri	5/7	TNT	7:00	Cleveland at New Jersey	- Game 4
			9:30	Portland at San Antonio	- Game 4
Sat	5/8	NBC	1:00	L.A. Clippers at Houston	- Game 5
			3:30	Utah at Seattle	- Game 5
Sun	5/9	NBC	12:30	New Jersey at Cleveland	- Game 5
			3:00	Charlotte at New York	- Game 1
			5:30	Los Angeles at Phoenix	- Game 5
Mon	5/10	TNT	9:00	Houston at Seattle	- Game 1
Tue	5/11	TNT	8:00	Cleveland at Chicago	- Game 1
			10:30	San Antonio at Phoenix	- Game 1
Wed	5/12	TNT	8:00	Charlotte at New York	- Game 2
			10:30	Houston at Seattle	- Game 2
Thur	5/13	TNT	8:00	Cleveland at Chicago	- Game 2
			10:30	San Antonio at Phoenix	- Game 2
Fri	5/14	TNT	8:00	New York at Charlotte	- Game 3
Sat	5/15	NBC	1:00	Phoenix at San Antonio	- Game 3
			3:30	Chicago at Cleveland	- Game 3
		TNT	9:00	Seattle at Houston	- Game 3
Sun	5/16	NBC	1:00	New York at Charlotte	- Game 4
			3:30	Phoenix at San Antonio	- Game 4
		TNT	9:00	Seattle at Houston	- Game 4
Mon	5/17	TNT	8:00	Chicago at Cleveland	- Game 4

Tue	5/18	TNT	8:00	Charlotte at New York	- Game 5
			10:30	San Antonio at Phoenix	- Game 5
Thur	5/20	TNT	7:00	Phoenix at San Antonio	- Game 6
			9:30	Seattle at Houston	- Game 6
Sat	5/22	NBC	3:30	Houston at Seattle	- Game 7
Sun	5/23	NBC	3:30	Chicago at New York	- Game 1
Mon	5/24	TNT	9:00	Seattle at Phoenix	- Game 1
Tue	5/25	TNT	8:00	Chicago at New York	- Game 2
Wed	5/26	TNT	9:00	Seattle at Phoenix	- Game 2
Fri	5/28	TNT	9:00	Phoenix at Seattle	- Game 3
Sat	5/29	NBC	3:30	New York at Chicago	- Game 3
Sun	5/30	NBC	3:30	Phoenix at Seattle	- Game 4
Mon	5/31	NBC	3:30	New York at Chicago	- Game 4
Tue	6/1	NBC	9:00	Seattle at Phoenix	- Game 5
Wed	6/2	NBC	9:00	Chicago at New York	- Game 5
Thur	6/3	NBC	9:00	Phoenix at Seattle	- Game 6
Fri	6/4	NBC	9:00	New York at Chicago	- Game 6
Sat	6/5	NBC	3:30	Seattle at Phoenix	- Game 7

NBA Finals

Wed	6/9	NBC	9:00	Chicago at Phoenix	- Game 1
Fri	6/11	NBC	9:00	Chicago at Phoenix	- Game 2
Sun	6/13	NBC	7:00	Phoenix at Chicago	- Game 3
Wed	6/16	NBC	9:00	Phoenix at Chicago	- Game 4
Fri	6/18	NBC	9:00	Phoenix at Chicago	- Game 5
Sun	6/20	NBC	7:00	Chicago at Phoenix	- Game 6

NBA PLAYOFFS TELEVISION SCHEDULE—1994

Day	Date	Network	Time	Game	
Thur	4/28	TBS	7:00	Miami at Atlanta	- Game 1
		TNT	8:00	Indiana at Orlando	- Game 1
		TBS	9:30	Utah at San Antonio	- Game 1
		TNT	10:30	Denver at Seattle	- Game 1
Fri	4/29	TBS	7:00	New Jersey at New York	- Game 1
		TNT	8:00	Cleveland at Chicago	- Game 1
		TBS	9:30	Portland at Houston	- Game 1
		TNT	10:30	Golden State at Phoenix	- Game 1
Sat	4/30	NBC	1:00	Utah at San Antonio	- Game 2
			3:30	Indiana at Orlando	- Game 2
		TNT	8:00	Miami at Atlanta	- Game 2
			10:30	Denver at Seattle	- Game 2
Sun	5/1	NBC	12:30	New Jersey at New York	- Game 2
			3:00	Cleveland at Chicago	- Game 2
			5:30	Golden State at Phoenix	- Game 2
		TNT	9:00	Portland at Houston	- Game 2
Mon	5/2	TNT	8:00	Orlando at Indiana	- Game 3
		TNT	10:30	Seattle at Denver	- Game 3

Day	Date	Net	Time	Matchup	Game
Tue	5/3	TNT	8:00	Atlanta at Miami	- Game 3
		TBS	10:30	Houston at Portland	- Game 3
		TNT	10:30	San Antonio at Utah	- Game 3
Wed	5/4	TNT	8:00	New York at New Jersey	- Game 3
			10:30	Phoenix at Golden State	- Game 3
Thur	5/5	TNT	8:00	Atlanta at Miami	- Game 4
		TNT	10:30	San Antonio at Utah	- Game 4
Fri	5/6	TNT	8:00	New York at New Jersey	- Game 4
			10:30	Houston at Portland	- Game 4
Sat	5/7	NBC	3:30	Denver at Seattle	- Game 5
Sun	5/8	NBC	12:30	Miami at Atlanta	- Game 5
			3:00	Phoenix at Houston	- Game 1
			5:30	Chicago at New York	- Game 1
Tue	5/10	TNT	8:00	Indiana at Atlanta	- Game 1
			10:30	Denver at Utah	- Game 1
Wed	5/11	TNT	7:00	Chicago at New York	- Game 2
			9:30	Phoenix at Houston	- Game 2
Thur	5/12	TNT	8:00	Indiana at Atlanta	- Game 2
			10:30	Denver at Utah	- Game 2
Fri	5/13	TNT	8:00	New York at Chicago	- Game 3
			10:30	Houston at Phoenix	- Game 3
Sat	5/14	NBC	1:00	Atlanta at Indiana	- Game 3
			3:30	Utah at Denver	- Game 3
Sun	5/15	NBC	1:00	Atlanta at Indiana	- Game 4
			3.00	Houston at Phoenix	- Game 4
			5:30	New York at Chicago	- Game 4
		TNT	9:00	Utah at Denver	- Game 4
Tue	5/17	TNT	8:00	Indiana at Atlanta	- Game 5
			9:45	Phoenix at Houston	- Game 5
				Denver at Utah	- Game 5
Wed	5/18	TNT	8:00	Chicago at New York	- Game 5
Thur	5/19	TNT	7:00	Atlanta at Indiana	- Game 6
			9:00	Utah at Denver	- Game 6
			11:30	Houston at Phoenix	- Game 6
Fri	5/20	TNT	8:00	New York at Chicago	- Game 6
Sat	5/21	NBC	1:00	Phoenix at Houston	- Game 7
			3:30	Denver at Utah	- Game 7
Sun	5/22	NBC	3:30	Chicago at New York	- Game 7
Mon	5/23	TNT	9:00	Utah at Houston	- Game 1
Tue	5/24	TNT	8:00	Indiana at New York	- Game 1
Wed	5/25	TNT	9:00	Utah at Houston	- Game 2
Thur	5/26	TNT	8:00	Indiana at New York	- Game 2
Fri	5/27	TNT	9:00	Houston at Utah	- Game 3
Sat	5/28	NBC	3:30	New York at Indiana	- Game 3
Sun	5/29	NBC	3:30	Houston at Utah	- Game 4
Mon	5/30	NBC	3:30	New York at Indiana	- Game 4
Tue	5/31	NBC	9:00	Utah at Houston	- Game 5
Wed	6/1	NBC	9:00	Indiana at New York	- Game 5
Fri	6/3	NBC	9:00	New York at Indiana	- Game 6
Sun	6/5	NBC	7:00	Indiana at New York	- Game 7

NBA Finals

Day	Date	Network	Time	Game	
Wed	6/8	NBC	9:00	New York at Houston	- Game 1
Fri	6/10	NBC	9:00	New York at Houston	- Game 2
Sun	6/12	NBC	7:00	Houston at New York	- Game 3
Wed	6/15	NBC	9:00	Houston at New York	- Game 4
Fri	6/17	NBC	9:00	Houston at New York	- Game 5
Sun	6/19	NBC	7:00	New York at Houston	- Game 6
Wed	6/22	NBC	9:00	New York at Houston	- Game 7

NBA PLAYOFFS TELEVISION SCHEDULE—1995

Day	Date	Network	Time	Game	
Thur	4/27	TBS	7:00	Cleveland at New York	- Game 1
		TNT	8:00	Atlanta at Indiana	- Game 1
		TBS	9:30	Houston at Utah	- Game 1
		TNT	10:30	Los Angeles at Seattle	- Game 1
Fri	4/28	TBS	7:00	Chicago at Charlotte	- Game 1
		TNT	8:00	Boston at Orlando	- Game 1
		TBS	9:30	Denver at San Antonio	- Game 1
		TNT	10:30	Portland at Phoenix	- Game 1
Sat	4/29	NBC	1:00	Cleveland at New York	- Game 2
		NBC	3:30	Los Angeles at Seattle	- Game 2
		TNT	1:00	Atlanta at Indiana	- Game 2
		TNT	10:00	Houston at Utah	- Game 2
Sun	4/30	NBC	12:30	Boston at Orlando	- Game 2
			3:00	Portland at Phoenix	- Game 2
			5:30	Chicago at Charlotte	- Game 2
		TNT	9:00	Denver at San Antonio	- Game 2
Mon	5/1	TNT	8:00	New York at Cleveland	- Game 3
			10:30	Seattle at Los Angeles	- Game 3
Tue	5/2	TBS	7:00	Indiana at Atlanta	- Game 3
		TNT	8:00	Charlotte at Chicago	- Game 3
		TBS	9:30	San Antonio at Denver	- Game 3
		TNT	10:30	Phoenix at Portland	- Game 3
Wed	5/3	TNT	8:00	Orlando at Boston	- Game 3
			9:30	Utah at Houston	- Game 3
Thur	5/4	TNT	7:00	New York at Cleveland	- Game 4
			9:30	Charlotte at Chicago	- Game 4
		TBS	10:30	Seattle at Los Angeles	- Game 4
Fri	5/5	TNT	7:00	Orlando at Boston	- Game 4
			9:30	Utah at Houston	- Game 4
Sat	5/6	NBC	3:30	Los Angeles at San Antonio	- Game 1
Sun	5/7	NBC	12:30	Indiana at New York	- Game 1
			3:00	Houston at Utah	- Game 5
			5:30	Chicago at Orlando	- Game 1
Mon	5/8	TNT	8:00	Los Angeles at San Antonio	- Game 2
Tue	5/9	TNT	8:00	Indiana at New York	- Game 2
			10:30	Houston at Phoenix	- Game 1
Wed	5/10	TNT	8:00	Chicago at Orlando	- Game 2

Thur	5/11	TNT	8:00	New York at Indiana	- Game 3
			10:30	Houston at Phoenix	- Game 2
Fri	5/12	TNT	8:00	Orlando at Chicago	- Game 3
			10:30	San Antonio at Los Angeles	- Game 3
Sat	5/13	NBC	1:00	Phoenix at Houston	- Game 3
			3:30	New York at Indiana	- Game 4
Sun	5/14	NBC	1:00	Phoenix at Houston	- Game 4
			3:00	San Antonio at Los Angeles	- Game 4
			5:30	Orlando at Chicago	- Game 4
Tue	5/16	TNT	7:00	Chicago at Orlando	- Game 5
			9:30	Los Angeles at San Antonio	- Game 5
			10:30	Houston at Phoenix	- Game 5
Wed	5/17	TNT	8:00	Indiana at New York	- Game 5
Thur	5/18	TBS	8:00	Orlando at Chicago	- Game 6
		TNT	8:30	Phoenix at Houston	- Game 6
			11:00	San Antonio at Los Angeles	- Game 6
Fri	5/19	TNT	8:00	New York at Indiana	- Game 6
Sat	5/20	NBC	3:30	Houston at Phoenix	- Game 7
Sun	5/21	NBC	3:30	Indiana at New York	- Game 7
Mon	5/22	TNT	8:30	Houston at San Antonio	- Game 1
Tue	5/23	TNT	8:00	Indiana at Orlando	- Game 1
Wed	5/24	TNT	8:30	Houston at San Antonio	- Game 2
Thur	5/25	TNT	8:00	Indiana at Orlando	- Game 2
Fri	5/26	TNT	9:00	San Antonio at Houston	- Game 3
Sat	5/27	NBC	3:30	Orlando at Indiana	- Game 3
Sun	5/28	NBC	3:30	San Antonio at Houston	- Game 4
Mon	5/29	NBC	3:30	Orlando at Indiana	- Game 4
Tue	5/30	NBC	9:00	Houston at San Antonio	- Game 5
Wed	5/31	NBC	9:00	Indiana at Orlando	- Game 5
Thur	6/1	NBC	9:00	San Antonio at Houston	- Game 6
Fri	6/2	NBC	9:00	Orlando at Indiana	- Game 6
Sun	6/4	NBC	7:00	Indiana at Orlando	- Game 7

NBA Finals

Wed	6/7	NBC	9:00	Houston at Orlando	- Game 1
Fri	6/9	NBC	9:00	Houston at Orlando	- Game 2
Sun	6/11	NBC	7:30	Orlando at Houston	- Game 3
Wed	6/14	NBC	9:00	Orlando at Houston	- Game 4

NBA PLAYOFFS TELEVISION SCHEDULE—1996

Day	Date	Network	Time	Game	
Thur	4/25	TBS	7:00	New York at Cleveland	- Game 1
		TNT	8:00	Atlanta at Indiana	- Game 1
		TBS	9:30	Portland at Utah	- Game 1
		TNT	10:30	Houston at Los Angeles	- Game 1
Fri	4/26	TBS	7:00	Detroit at Orlando	- Game 1
		TNT	8:00	Phoenix at San Antonio	- Game 1
		TBS	9:30	Miami at Chicago	- Game 1
		TNT	10:30	Sacramento at Seattle	- Game 1

Sat	4/27	NBC	1:00	New York at Cleveland	- Game 2
			3:30	Houston at Los Angeles	- Game 2
		TNT	8:00	Atlanta at Indiana	- Game 2
			10:30	Portland at Utah	- Game 2
Sun	4/28	NBC	12:30	Detroit at Orlando	- Game 2
			3:00	Phoenix at San Antonio	- Game 2
			5:30	Miami at Chicago	- Game 2
		TNT	9:00	Sacramento at Seattle	- Game 2
Mon	4/29	TNT	8:00	Indiana at Atlanta	- Game 3
			10:30	Utah at Portland	- Game 3
Tue	4/30	TNT	8:00	Orlando at Detroit	- Game 3
		TBS	9:00	Los Angeles at Houston	- Game 3
		TNT	10:30	Seattle at Sacramento	- Game 3
Wed	5/1	TBS	7:00	Cleveland at New York	- Game 3
		TNT	8:00	Chicago at Miami	- Game 3
		TBS	9:30	Utah at Portland	- Game 3
		TNT	10:30	San Antonio at Phoenix	- Game 3
Thur	5/2	TNT	7:00	Indiana at Atlanta	- Game 4
		TNT	9:30	Los Angeles at Houston	- Game 4
		TBS	10:30	Seattle at Sacramento	- Game 4
Fri	5/3	TNT	9:00	San Antonio at Phoenix	- Game 4
Sat	5/4	NBC	3:30	Houston at Seattle	- Game 1
Sun	5/5	NBC	1:00	Atlanta at Indiana	- Game 5
			3:00	Portland at Utah	- Game 5
			5:30	New York at Chicago	- Game 1
Mon	5/6	TNT	9:00	Houston at Seattle	- Game 2
Tue	5/7	TNT	7:00	Utah at San Antonio	- Game 1
			9:30	New York at Chicago	- Game 2
Wed	5/8	TNT	8:00	Atlanta at Orlando	- Game 1
Thur	5/9	TNT	8:00	Utah at San Antonio	- Game 2
Fri	5/10	TNT	7:00	Atlanta at Orlando	- Game 2
			9:30	Seattle at Houston	- Game 3
Sat	5/11	NBC	1:00	Chicago at New York	- Game 3
			3:30	San Antonio at Utah	- Game 3
Sun	5/12	NBC	12:30	Orlando at Atlanta	- Game 3
			3:00	Seattle at Houston	- Game 4
			5:30	Chicago at New York	- Game 4
		TNT	8:30	San Antonio at Utah	- Game 4
Mon	5/13	TNT	8:00	Orlando at Atlanta	- Game 4
Tue	5/14	TNT	8:00	New York at Chicago	- Game 5
		TBS	9:00	Utah at San Antonio	- Game 5
Wed	5/15	TNT	8:00	Atlanta at Orlando	- Game 5
Thur	5/16	TNT	9:00	San Antonio at Utah	- Game 6
Sat	5/18	NBC	3:30	Utah at Seattle	- Game 1
Sun	5/19	NBC	3:30	Orlando at Chicago	- Game 1
Mon	5/20	TNT	9:00	Utah at Seattle	- Game 2
Tue	5/21	TNT	8:30	Orlando at Chicago	- Game 2
Fri	5/24	TNT	8:30	Seattle at Utah	- Game 3
Sat	5/25	NBC	3:30	Chicago at Orlando	- Game 3
Sun	5/26	NBC	3:30	Seattle at Utah	- Game 4
Mon	5/27	NBC	3:30	Chicago at Orlando	- Game 4
Tue	5/28	NBC	9:00	Utah at Seattle	- Game 5

| Thur | 5/30 | NBC | 9:00 | Seattle at Utah | - Game 6 |
| Sun | 6/2 | NBC | 7:00 | Utah at Seattle | - Game 7 |

NBA Finals

Wed	6/5	NBC	9:00	Seattle at Chicago	- Game 1
Fri	6/7	NBC	9:00	Seattle at Chicago	- Game 2
Sun	6/9	NBC	7:30	Chicago at Seattle	- Game 3
Wed	6/12	NBC	9:00	Chicago at Seattle	- Game 4
Fri	6/14	NBC	9:00	Chicago at Seattle	- Game 5
Sun	6/16	NBC	7:30	Seattle at Chicago	- Game 6

NBA PLAYOFFS TELEVISION SCHEDULE—1997

Day	Date	Network	Time	Game	
Thur	4/24	TBS	7:00	Charlotte at New York	- Game 1
		TNT	8:00	Orlando at Miami	- Game 1
		TBS	9:30	Minnesota at Houston	- Game 1
		TNT	10:30	L.A. Clippers at Utah	- Game 1
Fri	4/25	TBS	7:00	Detroit at Atlanta	- Game 1
		TNT	8:00	Washington at Chicago	- Game 1
		TBS	9:30	Phoenix at Seattle	- Game 1
		TNT	10:30	Portland at Los Angeles	- Game 1
Sat	4/26	NBC	1:30	Minnesota at Houston	- Game 2
			3:30	Charlotte at New York	- Game 2
		TNT	8:30	L.A. Clippers at Utah	- Game 2
Sun	4/27	NBC	12:30	Orlando at Miami	- Game 2
			3:00	Portland at Los Angeles	- Game 2
			5:30	Washington at Chicago	- Game 2
		TNT	8:00	Detroit at Atlanta	- Game 2
		TNT	10:30	Phoenix at Seattle	- Game 2
Mon	4/28	TNT	8:00	New York at Charlotte	- Game 3
			10:30	Utah at L.A. Clippers	- Game 3
Tue	4/29	TBS	7:00	Miami at Orlando	- Game 3
		TNT	8:00	Atlanta at Detroit	- Game 3
		TBS	9:30	Houston at Minnesota	- Game 3
		TNT	10:30	Seattle at Phoenix	- Game 3
Wed	4/30	TNT	8:00	Chicago at Washington	- Game 3
			10:30	Los Angeles at Portland	- Game 3
Thur	5/1	TNT	8:00	Miami at Orlando	- Game 4
			10:30	Seattle at Phoenix	- Game 4
Fri	5/2	TNT	8:00	Atlanta at Detroit	- Game 4
			10:30	Los Angeles at Portland	- Game 4
Sat	5/3	NBC	3:30	Phoenix at Seattle	- Game 4
Sun	5/4	NBC	12:30	Orlando at Miami	- Game 5
			3:00	Detroit at Atlanta	- Game 5
			5:30	Los Angeles at Utah	- Game 1
Mon	5/5	TNT	8:00	Seattle at Houston	- Game 1
Tue	5/6	TNT	8:00	Atlanta at Chicago	- Game 1
			10:30	Los Angeles at Utah	- Game 2

Wed	5/7	TNT	7:00	New York at Miami	- Game 1
			9:30	Seattle at Houston	- Game 2
Thur	5/8	TNT	8:00	Atlanta at Chicago	- Game 2
			10:30	Utah at Los Angeles	- Game 3
Fri	5/9	TNT	8:00	New York at Miami	- Game 2
			10:30	Houston at Seattle	- Game 3
Sat	5/10	NBC	1:00	Chicago at Atlanta	- Game 3
			3:30	Utah at Los Angeles	- Game 4
Sun	5/11	NBC	12:30	Miami at New York	- Game 3
			3:00	Houston at Seattle	- Game 4
			5:30	Chicago at Atlanta	- Game 4
Mon	5/12	TNT	8:00	Miami at New York	- Game 4
			10:30	Los Angeles at Utah	- Game 5
Tue	5/13	TNT	7:00	Seattle at Houston	- Game 5
			9:30	Atlanta at Chicago	- Game 5
Wed	5/14	TNT	8:00	New York at Miami	- Game 5
Thur	5/15	TNT	9:00	Houston at Seattle	- Game 6
Fri	5/16	TNT	8:00	Miami at New York	- Game 6
Sat	5/17	NBC	3:30	Seattle at Houston	- Game 7
Sun	5/18	NBC	3:30	New York at Miami	- Game 7
Mon	5/19	TNT	8:30	Houston at Utah	- Game 1
Tue	5/20	TNT	8:30	Miami at Chicago	- Game 1
Wed	5/21	TNT	8:30	Houston at Utah	- Game 2
Thur	5/22	TNT	8:30	Miami at Chicago	- Game 2
Fri	5/23	TNT	8:30	Utah at Houston	- Game 3
Sat	5/24	NBC	3:30	Chicago at Miami	- Game 3
Sun	5/25	NBC	3:30	Utah at Houston	- Game 4
Mon	5/26	NBC	3:30	Chicago at Miami	- Game 4
Tue	5/27	NBC	9:00	Houston at Utah	- Game 5
Wed	5/28	NBC	9:00	Miami at Chicago	- Game 5
Thur	5/29	NBC	9:00	Utah at Houston	- Game 6

NBA Finals

Sun	6/1	NBC	7:30	Utah at Chicago	- Game 1
Wed	6/4	NBC	9:00	Utah at Chicago	- Game 2
Fri	6/6	NBC	9:00	Chicago at Utah	- Game 3
Sun	6/8	NBC	7:30	Chicago at Utah	- Game 4
Wed	6/11	NBC	9:00	Chicago at Utah	- Game 5
Fri	6/13	NBC	9:00	Utah at Chicago	- Game 6

NBA PLAYOFFS TELEVISION SCHEDULE—1998

Day	Date	Network	Time	Game	
Thur	4/23	TBS	7:00	Atlanta at Charlotte	- Game 1
		TNT	8:00	Cleveland at Indiana	- Game 1
		TBS	9:30	Houston at Utah	- Game 1
		TNT	10:30	San Antonio at Phoenix	- Game 1
Fri	4/24	TBS	7:00	New York at Miami	- Game 1
		TNT	8:00	New Jersey at Chicago	- Game 1
		TBS	9:30	Minnesota at Seattle	- Game 1
		TNT	10:30	Portland at Los Angeles	- Game 1

Sat	4/25	NBC	1:00	Cleveland at Indiana	- Game 2
			3:30	San Antonio at Phoenix	- Game 2
		TNT	8:00	Atlanta at Charlotte	- Game 2
		TNT	10:30	Houston at Utah	- Game 2
Sun	4/26	NBC	12:30	New York at Miami	- Game 2
			3:00	Portland at Los Angeles	- Game 2
			5:30	New Jersey at Chicago	- Game 2
		TNT	9:00	Minnesota at Seattle	- Game 2
Mon	4/27	TNT	7:00	Indiana at Cleveland	- Game 3
			9:30	Phoenix at San Antonio	- Game 3
Tue	4/28	TBS	7:00	Miami at New York	- Game 3
		TNT	8:00	Charlotte at Atlanta	- Game 3
		TBS	9:30	Seattle at Minnesota	- Game 3
		TNT	10:30	Los Angeles at Portland	- Game 3
Wed	4/29	TNT	7:00	Chicago at New Jersey	- Game 3
		TBS	8:00	Phoenix at San Antonio	- Game 4
		TNT	9:30	Utah at Houston	- Game 3
Thur	4/30	TBS	7:00	Indiana at Cleveland	- Game 4
		TNT	8:00	Miami at New York	- Game 4
		TBS	9:30	Seattle at Minnesota	- Game 4
		TNT	10:30	Los Angeles at Portland	- Game 4
Fri	5/1	TNT	7:00	Charlotte at Atlanta	- Game 4
			9:30	Utah at Houston	- Game 4
Sat	5/2	NBC	3:30	Minnesota at Seattle	- Game 5
Sun	5/3	NBC	12:30	New York at Miami	- Game 5
			3:00	Houston at Utah	- Game 5
			5:30	Charlotte at Chicago	- Game 1
Mon	5/4	TNT	9:00	Los Angeles at Seattle	- Game 1
Tue	5/5	TNT	8:00	New York at Indiana	- Game 1
			10:30	San Antonio at Utah	- Game 1
Wed	5/6	TNT	8:00	Charlotte at Chicago	- Game 2
			10:30	Los Angeles at Seattle	- Game 2
Thur	5/7	TNT	8:00	New York at Indiana	- Game 2
			10:30	San Antonio at Utah	- Game 2
Fri	5/8	TNT	8:00	Chicago at Charlotte	- Game 3
			10:30	Seattle at Los Angeles	- Game 3
Sat	5/9	NBC	1:00	Indiana at New York	- Game 3
			3:30	Utah at San Antonio	- Game 3
Sun	5/10	NBC	12:30	Indiana at New York	- Game 4
			3:00	Seattle at Los Angeles	- Game 4
			5:30	Chicago at Charlotte	- Game 4
		TNT	9:00	Utah at San Antonio	- Game 4
Tue	5/12	TNT	8:00	San Antonio at Utah	- Game 5
			10:30	Los Angeles at Seattle	- Game 5
Wed	5/13	TNT	7:00	New York at Indiana	- Game 5
			9:30	Charlotte at Chicago	- Game 5
Sat	5/16	NBC	3:30	Los Angeles at Utah	- Game 1
Sun	5/17	NBC	3:30	Indiana at Chicago	- Game 1
Mon	5/18	TNT	8:30	Los Angeles at Utah	- Game 2
Tue	5/19	TNT	8:30	Indiana at Chicago	- Game 2
Fri	5/22	TNT	10:00	Utah at Los Angeles	- Game 3
Sat	5/23	NBC	3:30	Chicago at Indiana	- Game 3

Sun	5/24	NBC	3:30	Utah at Los Angeles	- Game 4
Mon	5/25	NBC	3:30	Chicago at Indiana	- Game 4
Wed	5/27	NBC	9:00	Indiana at Chicago	- Game 5
Fri	5/29	NBC	9:00	Chicago at Indiana	- Game 6
Sun	5/31	NBC	7:30	Indiana at Chicago	- Game 7

NBA Finals

Wed	6/3	NBC	9:00	Chicago at Utah	- Game 1
Fri	6/5	NBC	9:00	Chicago at Utah	- Game 2
Sun	6/7	NBC	7:30	Utah at Chicago	- Game 3
Wed	6/10	NBC	9:00	Utah at Chicago	- Game 4
Fri	6/12	NBC	9:00	Utah at Chicago	- Game 5
Sun	6/14	NBC	7:30	Chicago at Utah	- Game 6

NBA PLAYOFFS TELEVISION SCHEDULE—1999

Day	Date	Network	Time	Game	
Sat	5/8	NBC	12:30	New York at Miami	- Game 1
			3:00	Phoenix at Portland	- Game 1
			5:30	Sacramento at Utah	- Game 1
		TNT	8:30	Detroit at Atlanta	- Game 1
Sun	5/9	NBC	12:30	Philadelphia at Orlando	- Game 1
			3:00	Minnesota at San Antonio	- Game 1
			5:30	Houston at Los Angeles	- Game 1
		TNT	8:30	Milwaukee at Indiana	- Game 1
Mon	5/10	TBS	7:00	New York at Miami	- Game 2
		TNT	8:00	Detroit at Atlanta	- Game 2
		TBS	9:30	Sacramento at Utah	- Game 2
		TNT	10:30	Phoenix at Portland	- Game 2
Tue	5/11	TBS	7:00	Philadelphia at Orlando	- Game 2
		TNT	8:00	Minnesota at San Antonio	- Game 2
		TBS	9:30	Milwaukee at Indiana	- Game 2
		TNT	10:30	Houston at Los Angeles	- Game 2
Wed	5/12	TBS	7:00	Atlanta at Detroit	- Game 3
		TNT	8:00	Miami at New York	- Game 3
		TBS	9:30	Portland at Phoenix	- Game 3
		TNT	10:30	Utah at Sacramento	- Game 3
Thur	5/13	TBS	6:30	Orlando at Philadelphia	- Game 3
		TNT	7:00	San Antonio at Minnesota	- Game 3
		TBS	9:00	Indiana at Milwaukee	- Game 3
		TNT	9:30	Los Angeles at Houston	- Game 3
Fri	5/14	TBS	7:00	Atlanta at Detroit	- Game 4
		TNT	8:00	Miami at New York	- Game 4
			10:30	Utah at Sacramento	- Game 4
Sat	5/15	NBC	12:30	Orlando at Philadelphia	- Game 4
			3:00	San Antonio at Minnesota	- Game 4
			5:30	Los Angeles at Houston	- Game 4
Sun	5/16	NBC	3:00	New York at Miami	- Game 5
			5:00	Sacramento at Utah	- Game 5
		TNT	8:00	Detroit at Atlanta	- Game 5

Mon	5/17	TNT	7:00	Philadelphia at Indiana	- Game 1
			9:30	Los Angeles at San Antonio	- Game 1
Tue	5/18	TNT	8:00	New York at Atlanta	- Game 1
			10:30	Portland at Utah	- Game 1
Wed	5/19	TNT	7:00	Philadelphia at Indiana	- Game 2
			9:30	Los Angeles at San Antonio	- Game 2
Thur	5/20	TNT	8:00	New York at Atlanta	- Game 2
			10:30	Portland at Utah	- Game 2
Fri	5/21	TNT	8:00	Indiana at Philadelphia	- Game 3
Sat	5/22	NBC	3:00	Utah at Portland	- Game 3
			5:30	San Antonio at Los Angeles	- Game 3
Sun	5/23	NBC	12:30	Indiana at Philadelphia	- Game 4
			3:00	Atlanta at New York	- Game 3
			5:30	San Antonio at Los Angeles	- Game 4
		TNT	8:30	Utah at Portland	- Game 4
Mon	5/24	TNT	8:00	Atlanta at New York	- Game 4
Tue	5/25	TNT	8:00	Portland at Utah	- Game 5
Thur	5/27	TNT	8:00	Utah at Portland	- Game 6
Sat	5/29	NBC	5:30	Portland at San Antonio	- Game 1
Sun	5/30	NBC	5:30	New York at Indiana	- Game 1
Mon	5/31	TNT	5:30	Portland at San Antonio	- Game 2
Tue	6/1	TNT	8:30	New York at Indiana	- Game 2
Fri	6/4	NBC	9:00	San Antonio at Portland	- Game 3
Sat	6/5	NBC	6:30	Indiana at New York	- Game 3
Sun	6/6	NBC	6:30	San Antonio at Portland	- Game 4
Mon	6/7	NBC	9:00	Indiana at New York	- Game 4
Wed	6/9	NBC	9:00	New York at Indiana	- Game 5
Fri	6/11	NBC	9:00	Indiana at New York	- Game 6

NBA Finals

Wed	6/16	NBC	9:00	New York at San Antonio	- Game 1
Fri	6/18	NBC	9:00	New York at San Antonio	- Game 2
Mon	6/21	NBC	9:30	San Antonio at New York	- Game 3
Wed	6/23	NBC	9:00	San Antonio at New York	- Game 4
Fri	6/25	NBC	9:00	San Antonio at New York	- Game 5

NBA PLAYOFFS TELEVISION SCHEDULE—2000

Day	Date	Network	Time	Game	
Sat	4/22	NBC	12:30	Detroit at Miami	- Game 1
			3:00	Phoenix at San Antonio	- Game 1
			5:30	Seattle at Utah	- Game 1
		TNT	8:30	Philadelphia at Charlotte	- Game 1
Sun	4/23	NBC	12:30	Toronto at New York	- Game 1
			3:00	Minnesota at Portland	- Game 1
			5:30	Sacramento at Los Angeles	- Game 1
		TNT	8:30	Milwaukee at Indiana	- Game 1
Mon	4/24	TBS	8:00	Philadelphia at Charlotte	- Game 2
			10:30	Seattle at Utah	- Game 2

Tue	4/25	TNT	7:00	Detroit at Miami	- Game 2
			9:30	Phoenix at San Antonio	- Game 2
Wed	4/26	TNT	8:00	Toronto at New York	- Game 2
			10:30	Minnesota at Portland	- Game 2
Thur	4/27	TNT	8:00	Milwaukee at Indiana	- Game 2
			10:30	Sacramento at Los Angeles	- Game 2
Fri	4/28	TNT	8:00	Charlotte at Philadelphia	- Game 3
Sat	4/29	NBC	12:30	Miami at Detroit	- Game 3
			3:00	San Antonio at Phoenix	- Game 3
			5:30	Utah at Seattle	- Game 3
		TNT	8:30	Indiana at Milwaukee	- Game 3
Sun	4/30	NBC	12:30	New York at Toronto	- Game 3
			3:00	Portland at Minnesota	- Game 3
			5:30	Los Angeles at Sacramento	- Game 3
Mon	5/1	TBS	7:00	Charlotte at Philadelphia	- Game 4
			9:30	Indiana at Milwaukee	- Game 4
Tue	5/2	TNT	8:00	Portland at Minnesota	- Game 4
		TBS	9:00	San Antonio at Phoenix	- Game 4
		TNT	10:30	Los Angeles at Sacramento	- Game 4
Wed	5/3	TNT	9:00	Utah at Seattle	- Game 4
Thur	5/4	TNT	8:00	Milwaukee at Indiana	- Game 5
Fri	5/5	TNT	8:00	Seattle at Utah	- Game 5
			10:30	Sacramento at Los Angeles	- Game 5
Sat	5/6	NBC	3:30	Philadelphia at Indiana	- Game 1
Sun	5/7	NBC	12:30	New York at Miami	- Game 1
			3:00	Utah at Portland	- Game 1
			5:30	Phoenix at Los Angeles	- Game 1
Mon	5/8	TBS	8:00	Philadelphia at Indiana	- Game 2
Tue	5/9	TNT	8:00	New York at Miami	- Game 2
			10:30	Utah at Portland	- Game 2
Wed	5/10	TNT	8:00	Indiana at Philadelphia	- Game 3
			10:30	Phoenix at Los Angeles	- Game 2
Thur	5/11	TNT	8:00	Portland at Utah	- Game 3
Fri	5/12	TNT	8:00	Miami at New York	- Game 3
			10:30	Los Angeles at Phoenix	- Game 3
Sat	5/13	NBC	3:30	Indiana at Philadelphia	- Game 4
Sun	5/14	NBC	12:30	Miami at New York	- Game 4
			3:00	Portland at Utah	- Game 4
			5:30	Los Angeles at Phoenix	- Game 4
Mon	5/15	TBS	8:00	Philadelphia at Indiana	- Game 5
Tue	5/16	TNT	8:00	Utah at Portland	- Game 5
			10:30	Phoenix at Los Angeles	- Game 5
Wed	5/17	TNT	8:00	New York at Miami	- Game 5
Fri	5/19	TNT	6:30	Indiana at Philadelphia	- Game 6
			9:00	Miami at New York	- Game 6
Sat	5/20	NBC	3:30	Portland at Los Angeles	- Game 1
Sun	5/21	NBC	3:30	New York at Miami	- Game 7
Mon	5/22	TNT	9:30	Portland at Los Angeles	- Game 2
Tue	5/23	TNT	8:30	New York at Indiana	- Game 1
Thur	5/25	TNT	8:30	New York at Indiana	- Game 2
Fri	5/26	NBC	9:00	Los Angeles at Portland	- Game 3
Sat	5/27	NBC	3:30	Indiana at New York	- Game 3

Sun	5/28	NBC	3:30	Los Angeles at Portland	- Game 4
Mon	5/29	NBC	5:30	Indiana at New York	- Game 4
Tue	5/30	NBC	9:00	Portland at Los Angeles	- Game 5
Wed	5/31	NBC	9:00	New York at Indiana	- Game 5
Fri	6/2	NBC	7:00	Indiana at New York	- Game 6
			9:30	Los Angeles at Portland	- Game 6
Sun	6/4	NBC	7:30	Portland at Los Angeles	- Game 7

NBA Finals

Wed	6/7	NBC	9:00	Indiana at Los Angeles	- Game 1
Fri	6/9	NBC	9:00	Indiana at Los Angeles	- Game 2
Sun	6/11	NBC	7:30	Los Angeles at Indiana	- Game 3
Wed	6/14	NBC	9:00	Los Angeles at Indiana	- Game 4
Fri	6/16	NBC	9:00	Los Angeles at Indiana	- Game 5
Mon	6/19	NBC	9:00	Indiana at Los Angeles	- Game 6

APPENDIX C

NBA ON NBC 2000-2001 SCHEDULE

Day	Date	Game	Game Time
Mon	12/25	Orlando at Indiana	3:00
		Portland at L.A. Lakers	5:30
Sat	12/30	San Antonio at Indiana	7:30
		New York at Minnesota	7:30
		Toronto at Phoenix	7:30
		Philadelphia at Sacramento	7:30
Sat	1/13	Portland at New York	5:30
		Miami at Indiana	5:30
Sat	1/20	Orlando at San Antonio	5:30
		Sacramento at Portland	5:30
Sun	1/21	Indiana at New York	12:00
		Toronto at Philadelphia	2.30
		Phoenix at Utah	2:30
		Miami at L.A. Lakers	5:00
Sat	1/27	Miami at Orlando	3:00
		San Antonio at Utah	3:00
		Toronto at Chicago	5:30
		Portland at Minnesota	5:30
Sun	1/28	Philadelphia at Indiana	12:00
		L.A. Lakers at New York	2:30
Sun	2/4	New York at Miami	1:00
		Sacramento at L.A. Lakers	3:30
Sun	2/11	*All-Star Game*	

237

Sun	2/18	New York at Orlando	12:30
		Phoenix at Philadelphia	3:00
		Utah at Sacramento	3:00
		L.A. Lakers at Indiana	5:30
Sun	2/25	Sacramento at New York	12:30
		Minnesota at Indiana	3:00
		Utah at Phoenix	3:00
		Orlando at L.A. Lakers	5:30
Sun	3/4	New York at Toronto	12:30
		Orlando at Detroit	12:30
Sun	3/11	Philadelphia at Boston	12:30
		Miami at New York	12:30
Sun	3/18	L.A. Lakers at Orlando	12:00
Sun	3/25	Chicago at Boston	12:00
		Indiana at Orlando	12:00
		San Antonio at Miami	12:00
		L.A. Lakers at Sacramento	6:30
Sun	4/1	Indiana at Philadelphia	12:30
		Orlando at Toronto	12:30
		New York at L.A. Lakers	5:30
Sun	4/8	New York at Miami	12:30
		Chicago at Toronto	3:00
		Portland at Sacramento	3:00
		L.A. Lakers at Minnesota	5:30
Sun	4/15	New Jersey at Boston	12:30
		Orlando at Miami	12:30
		Indiana at Chicago	3:00
		Utah at Minnesota	3:00
		Sacramento at Phoenix	3:00
		Portland at L.A. Lakers	5:30

NBA ON TNT 2000-2001 SCHEDULE

Day	Date	Game	Game Time
Wed	11/1	Orlando at Miami	8:00
Thur	11/2	Minnesota at San Antonio	8:00
Wed	11/8	L.A. Lakers at San Antonio	8:00
Thur	11/9	Philadelphia at Minnesota	8:00
Wed	11/15	Miami at New Jersey	8:00
Thur	11/16	L.A. Lakers at Sacramento	8:00
Thur	11/23	Toronto at Indiana	8:00
Wed	11/29	Miami at New York	8:00
Wed	12/6	Cleveland at Chicago	8:00
Thur	12/7	New York at San Antonio	8:00
Wed	12/13	San Antonio at Phoenix	8:00
		L.A. Lakers at Portland	10:30
Thur	12/14	New York at Toronto	8:00
Wed	12/20	Utah at Philadelphia	8:00
		Minnesota at L.A. Clippers	10:30
Thur	12/21	Boston at New York	8:00

Day	Date	Game	Game Time
Wed	12/27	Indiana at Miami	8:00
Thur	12/28	Portland at Utah	8:00
Thur	1/4	Orlando at New York	8:00
Wed	1/10	Portland at Philadelphia	8:00
Thur	1/11	Indiana at Phoenix	8:00
Wed	1/17	Minnesota at Utah	8:00
		Phoenix at Seattle	10:30
Thru	1/18	Miami at Portland	8:00
Wed	1/24	New York at Charlotte	8:00
Thur	1/25	Portland at Indiana	8:00
		San Antonio at Sacramento	10:30
Wed	1/31	L.A. Lakers at Minnesota	8:00
Thur	2/1	Philadelphia at New York	8:00
Wed	2/7	Sacramento at Minnesota	8:00
Thur	2/8	San Antonio at New Jersey	8:00
Wed	2/14	L.A. Lakers at Philadelphia	8:00
Thur	2/15	Miami at Toronto	8:00
Wed	2/21	L.A. Lakers at San Antonio	8:00
Thur	2/22	Utah at Portland	8:00
Wed	2/28	Miami at Philadelphia	8:00
		Orlando at Phoenix	10:30
Thur	3/1	Phoenix at San Antonio	8:00
Wed	3/7	Sacramento at Phoenix	8:00
		Toronto at L.A. Lakers	10:30
Thur	3/8	San Antonio at Portland	8:00
Wed	3/14	Minnesota at San Antonio	8:00
Wed	3/21	L.A. Lakers at Milwaukee	8:00
Wed	3/28	Orlando at Philadelphia	8:00
		Sacramento at L.A. Lakers	10:30
Thur	3/29	Utah at San Antonio	8:00
Wed	4/4	Portland at Minnesota	8:00
Thur	4/5	Sacramento at Utah	8:00
Wed	4/11	New York at Indiana	8:00
Thur	4/12	Philadelphia at Orlando	8:00
Wed	4/18	Miami at Orlando	8:00
		Utah at Phoenix	10:30

NBA ON TBS 2000-2001 SCHEDULE

Day	Date	Game	Game Time
Tue	10/31	Philadelphia at New York	8:00
		L.A. Lakers at Portland	10:30
Tue	11/7	New York at Milwaukee	8:00
Tue	11/14	Orlando at Sacramento	8:00
Tue	11/21	New York at Orlando	8:00
Tue	11/28	Toronto at Dallas	8:00
		Indiana at L.A. Lakers	10:30
Tue	12/5	San Antonio at Sacramento	8:00
		Philadelphia at L.A. Lakers	10:30
Tue	12/12	Sacramento at Atlanta	8:00

Tue	12/19	L.A. Lakers at Miami	8:00
Tue	12/26	Toronto at Minnesota	8:00
		Phoenix at Vancouver	10:30
Tue	1/9	San Antonio at Orlando	8:00
Tue	1/16	Toronto at Houston	8:00
Tue	1/23	L.A. Lakers at Seattle	8:00
Tue	1/30	Indiana at Orlando	8:00
Tue	2/6	Indiana at Miami	8:00
Tue	2/13	Sacramento at Utah	8:00
Tue	2/20	Miami at New York	8:00
Tue	2/27	Seattle at New York	8:00
Tue	3/6	Indiana at New York	8:00
Tue	3/13	Sacramento at Orlando	8:00
Tue	3/20	Indiana at Toronto	8:00
Tue	3/27	Toronto at Miami	8:00
Tue	4/3	L.A. Lakers at Utah	8:00
Tue	4/10	Philadelphia at Miami	8:00
Tue	4/17	Philadelphia at Indiana	8:00

BIBLIOGRAPHY

Andersen, R. (1995). *Consumer culture and TV programming*. Boulder, CO: Westview Press.

Ang, I. (1990). Culture & communication. *European Journal of Communication, 5*(2-3), 239-261.

Associated Press. (1985, February 3). David Stern, a little man among giants, stands tall. *Los Angeles Times,* pp. 1, 19.

Associated Press. (1997, November 11). NBA about to make $2.4B. *Newark Star-Ledger,* p. 57.

Ball-Rokeach, S.J. (1985). The origins of individual media-system dependency: A sociological framework. *Communication Research, 12*(4), 485-510.

Ball-Rokeach, S.J., & DeFleur, M.L. (1976). A dependency model of mass-media effects. *Communication Research, 3*(1), 3-21.

Ball-Rokeach, S.J., & DeFleur, M.L. (1986). The interdependence of the media and other social systems. In G. Gumpert & R. Cathcart (Eds.), *Inter / Media: Interpersonal communication in a media world* (Vol. 3, pp. 81-96). New York: Oxford.

Ball-Rokeach, S.J., Rokeach, M., & Grube, J.W. (1984). *The great American values test: Influencing behavior and belief through television*. New York: The Free Press.

Becker, L.B., & Kosicki, G.M. (1995). Understanding the message-producer/message receiver transaction. *Research in Political Sociology, 7,* 33-62.

241

Bellamy, R.V., Jr. (1989). Professional sports organizations: Media strategies. In L.A. Wenner (Ed.), *Media, sports, and society* (pp. 120-133). Newbury Park: Sage.

Blumler, J.G. (1979). The role of theory in uses and gratifications studies. *Communication Research, 6*(1), 9-36.

Blumler, J.G., & Katz, E. (Eds.). (1974). *The uses of mass communication: Current perspectives on gratifications research.* Newbury Park, CA: Sage.

Blumler, J.G., Gurevitch, M., & Katz, E. (1985). Reaching out: A future of gratifications research. In K.E. Rosengren, L.A. Wenner, & P. Palmgreen (Eds.), *Media gratifications research: Current perspectives* (pp. 255-273). Beverly Hills, CA: Sage.

Bogart, L. (1995). *Communication culture: The media system and the public interest.* New York: Oxford University Press.

Boston Celtics. (1997). Boston Celtics limited partnership and subsidiaries. *Annual Report.*

Brown, R. (1996, June 17). NBC cable moves vex affiliates. *Broadcasting & Cable, 126,* p. 15.

Budd, M., Entman, R.M., & Steinman, C. (1990). The affirmative character of U.S. cultural studies. *Critical Studies in Mass Communication, 7,* 169-184.

Cantor, M.G., & Cantor, J.M. (1986). Audience composition and television content: The mass audience revisited. In S.J. Ball-Rokeach & M.G. Cantor (Eds.), *Media, audience, and social structure* (pp. 214-225). Newbury Park: Sage.

Carey, J.W., & Kreiling, A.L. (1974). Popular culture and uses and gratifications: Notes toward an accommodation. In J.G. Blumler & E. Katz (Eds.), *The uses of mass communications: Current perspectives on gratifications research* (Vol. 3, pp. 225-248). Beverly Hills, CA: Sage.

Carragee, K., Rosenblatt, M., & Michaud, G. (1987). Agenda-setting research: A critique and theoretical alternative. In S. Thomas (Ed.), *Studies in communication* (Vol. 3, pp. 35-49). Norwood, NJ: Ablex.

Chicago Professional Sports Limited Partnership and WGN Continental Broadcasting Company v. NBA. (1991). 754. F. Supp. 1336 (N.D. ILL.)

Chicago Professional Sports Limited Partnership and WGN Continental Broadcasting Company v. NBA. (1992). 961. F. 2nd 667 (7th Cir.)

Coe, S. (1995, March 27). On-air Jordan soars for NBC. *Broadcasting & Cable, 125,* 19.

Comisky, P., Bryant, J., & Zillmann, D. (1977). Commentary as a substitute for action. *Journal of Communication, 27*(3), 150-153.

Curran, J., Gurevitch, M., & Woollacott, J. (1982). The study of the media: Theoretical approaches. In M. Gurevitch, T. Bennett, J. Curran, & J. Woollacott (Eds.), *Culture, society and the media* (pp. 11-29). London: Methuen.

D'Alessandro, D. (1998a, June 12). Why it will end: Just call the Bulls' final chapter the summer of discontent. *Newark Star-Ledger*, pp. 55, 59.

D'Alessandro, D. (1998b, November 3). An imperfect union. *Newark Star-Ledger*, p. 51, 53.

D'Alessandro, D. (1999, January 10). Moving ahead . . . step by step. *Newark Star-ledger*, p. 8.

Danielian, L.H., & Reese, S.D. (1989). A closer look at intermedia influences on agenda-setting: The cocaine issue of 1986. In P.J. Shoemaker (Ed.), *Communication campaigns about drugs: Government, media and the public* (pp. 47-66). Hillsdale, NJ: Erlbaum.

Entman, R. (1993). Framing: Toward clarification of a fractured paradigm. *Journal of Communication, 43*(4), 51-58.

Gantz, W. (1981). An exploration of viewing motives and behaviors associated with television sports. *Journal of Broadcasting and Electronic Media, 25*(3), 263-275.

Gantz, W., & Zohoori, A.R. (1982). The impact of television schedule changes on audience behavior. *Journalism Quarterly, 59*, 265-272.

Ghanem, S. (1997). Filling in the tapestry: The second level of agenda-setting. In M.E. McCombs, D.L. Shaw, & D. Weaver (Eds.), *Communication and democracy: Exploring the intellectual frontiers in agenda-setting theory* (pp. 3-14). Mahwah, NJ: Erlbaum.

Goldaper, S. (1996). The first game: November 1, 1946. www.nba.com.

Grant, A.E., Guthrie, K.K., & Ball-Rokeach, S.J. (1991). Television shopping: A media system dependency perspective. *Communication Research, 18*(6), 773-798.

Horowitz, I. (1974). Sports broadcasting. In R. G. Noll (Ed.), *Government and the sports business* (pp. 275-323). Washington, DC: The Brookings Institution.

Hubbard, J. (1984, November 25). Q&A: David Stern. *The Dallas Morning News*, p. 20b.

Hunt, T., & Ruben, B. D. (1993). *Mass communication: Producers and consumers*. New York: Harper Collins.

Jhally, S. (1989). Cultural studies and the sports/media complex. In L.A. Wenner (Ed.), *Media, sports, and society* (pp. 70-93). Newbury Park: Sage.

Katz, E., Blumler, J.G., & Gurevitch, M. (1974). Utilization of mass communication by the individual. In J. Blumler & E. Katz (Eds.), *The uses of mass communication* (pp. 19-32). Beverly Hills: Sage.

Kline, F.G., Miller, P.V., & Morrison, A.J. (1974). Adolescents and family planning information: An exploration of audience needs and media effects. In J. Blumler & E. Katz (Eds.), *The uses of mass communication* (pp. 113-136). Beverly Hills: Sage.

Kosicki, G. M. (1993). Problems and opportunities in agenda-setting research. *Journal of Communication, 43*(2), 100-127.

Lane, R., & Midgett, W. (1993, December 20). Jock support: Endorsements take athletes to the top. *Forbes, 152*, 94-98.

Lasorsa, D.L. (1997). Media agenda-setting and press performance: A social system approach for building theory. In M.E. McCombs, D.L. Shaw, & D. Weaver (Eds.), *Communication and democracy: Exploring the intellectual frontiers in agenda-setting theory* (pp. 155-167). Mahwah, NJ: Erlbaum.

Lever, J., & Wheeler, S. (1993). Mass media and the experience of sport. *Communication Research, 20*(1), 125-143.

Lippmann, W. (1922). *Public opinion.* New York: Macmillan.

Livingstone, S.M. (1990). *Making sense of TV: The psychology of audience interpretation.* Oxford: Pergamon Press.

McAllister, M.P. (1998). College bowl sponsorship and the increased commercialization of amateur sports. *Critical Studies in Mass Communication, 15*(4), 357-381.

McChesney, R.W. (1989). Media made sport: A history of sports coverage in the United States. In L.A. Wenner (Ed.), *Media, sports, and society* (pp. 49-69). Newbury Park: Sage.

McClellan, S. (1997, November 17). NBA not quite a loss leader for NBC, Turner; networks will pay more than double current rights fees, and will profit less. *Broadcasting & Cable, 127*, p. 14.

McClellan, S., & Jessel, H.A. (1997, April 28). Going once, twice . . . ; bidding by TV nets for NFL, NBA and other big-league sports rights could be fierce. *Broadcasting & Cable, 127*, 14-15.

McCombs, M.E. (1976). Agenda-setting research: A bibliographic essay. *Political Communication Review, 1*, 1-7.

McCombs, M.E., & Shaw, D.L. (1972). The agenda-setting function of the mass media. *Public Opinion Quarterly, 36*, 176-187.

McCombs, M.E., & Shaw, D.L. (1993). The evolution of agenda-setting research: Twenty-five years in the marketplace of ideas. *Journal of Communication, 43*(2), 58-67.

McCombs, M.E., & Weaver, D.H. (1985). Toward a merger of gratifications and agenda-setting research. In K.E. Rosengren, L.A.

Wenner, & P. Palmgreen (Eds.), *Media gratifications research: Current perspectives* (pp. 95-108). Beverly Hills, CA: Sage.

McConnville, J. (1996, October 21). WGN-TV/NBA headed back to court in 6-year-old case; superstation will not be allowed to broadcast Bulls games during this round of litigation. *Broadcasting & Cable, 126,* 45.

McLeod, J.M., & Becker, L.B. (1974). Testing the validity of gratification measures through political effects analysis. In J.G. Blumler & E. Katz (Eds.), *The uses of mass communications: Current perspectives on gratifications research* (Vol. 3, pp. 137-164). Beverly Hills: Sage.

McQuail, D., & Gurevitch, M. (1974). Explaining audience behavior: Three approaches considered. In J.G. Blumler & E. Katz (Eds.), *The uses of mass communications: Current perspectives on gratifications research* (Vol. 3, pp. 287-301). Beverly Hills: Sage.

Miller, G.A. (1956). The magical number seven, plus or minus two: Some limits on our capacity for processing information. *Psychological Review, 63,* 81-97.

Newcomb, P. (Ed.). (2000, March 20). The power 100 fame and fortune. *Forbes, 165,* 161-244.

New York Knickerbockers. (1998). *Media guide.*

Newark Star-Ledger (2000, February 20). Putting up big numbers, p. 9.

Palmgreen, P., & Clarke, P. (1977). Agenda-setting with local and national issues. *Communication Research, 4*(4), 435-452.

Parente, D.E. (1977). The interdependence of sports and television. *Journal of Communication, 27*(3), 128-132.

Parks, B. (1999, February 7). Trying to cash in with a brand-new image. *Newark Star-Ledger,* pp. 1, 8.

Pluto, T. (1991). *Loose balls: The short, wild life of the American Basketball Association—as told by the players, coaches, and movers and shakers who made it happen.* New York: Simon & Schuster Trade Paperbacks.

Pluto, T. (1996, January 8). Out of their league. *The Sporting News, 220,* 22-26.

Protess, D.L., & McCombs, M.E. (1991). The public agenda. In D.L. Protess & M.E. McCombs (Eds.), *Agenda setting: Readings on media, public opinion, and policymaking* (pp. 1-4). Hillsdale, NJ: Erlbaum.

Rader, B.G. (1984). *In its own image: How television has transformed sports.* New York: The Free Press.

Rather, D. (1994). Courage, fear and the television newsroom. *Television Quarterly, 27*(1), 87-94.

Roberts, M. (1997). Political advertising's influence on news, the public and their behavior. In M.E. McCombs, D.L. Shaw, & D. Weaver (Eds.), *Communication and democracy: Exploring the intellectual frontiers in agenda-setting theory* (pp. 85-96). Mahwah, NJ: Erlbaum.

Rogers, E.M., Dearing, J.W., & Bregman, D. (1993). The anatomy of agenda-setting research. *Journal of Communication, 43*(2), 68-84.

Rosen, C. (1997, July). League of his own: Commissioner David Stern turned a sagging NBA into the world's most recognizable sports league. *Sport, 88,* 40-44.

Rubin, A.M. (1983). Television uses and gratifications: The interactions of viewing patterns and motivations. *Journal of Broadcasting & Electronic Media, 27,* 37-51.

Rubin, A.M. (1984). Ritualized and instrumental television viewing. *Journal of Communication, 34*(3), 67-77.

Rubin, A.M., & Perse, E.M. (1987). Audience activity and television news gratifications. *Communication Research, 14*(1), 58-84.

Ryan, B. (1985, May 21). When it comes to pros, don't let them con you. *Boston Globe,* p. 63.

Schiller, H.I. (1989). *Culture, Inc.: The corporate takeover of public expression.* New York: Oxford University Press.

Schlosser, J. (1998, June 22). Significant others. *Broadcasting & Cable, 128,* 32.

Schoenbach, K., & Semetko, H.A. (1992). Agenda-setting, agenda-reinforcing or agenda-deflating? A study of the 1990 German national election. *Journalism Quarterly, 69,* 837-846.

Semetko, H.A., & Mandelli, A. (1997). Setting the agenda for cross-national research: Bringing values into the concept. In M.E. McCombs, D.L. Shaw, & D. Weaver (Eds.), *Communication and democracy: Exploring the intellectual frontiers in agenda-setting theory* (pp. 195-207). Mahwah, NJ: Erlbaum.

Shaw, D.L., & Martin, S.E. (1992). The function of mass media agenda setting. *Journalism Quarterly, 69*(4), 902-920.

Shaw, D.L., & McCombs, M.E. (Eds.). (1977). *The emergence of American political issues: The agenda setting function of the press.* St. Paul, MN: West.

Sloan, L.R. (1989). The motives of sports fans. In J.H. Goldstein (Ed.), *Sports, games, and play: Social and psychological viewpoints* (pp. 175-240). Hillside, NJ: Erlbaum.

Spiegel, P. (1997, December 15). Jordan and Co. *Forbes, 160,* 180-206.

The Sporting News Official NBA Guide (1997-98 ed.). (1997). New York: NBA Properties.

Staudohar, P.D. (1996). *Playing for dollars: Labor relations and the sports business*. Ithaca, NY: ILR Press.

Stewart, L. (1989, November 10). NBC gets NBA for four years, $600 million. *Los Angeles Times*, pp. C1, C11.

Stroud, M. (1998, June 22). NBC investing in NBA futures. *Broadcasting & Cable, 128*, 50.

Sutherland, M., & Galloway, J. (1981). Role of advertising: Persuasion or agenda-setting? *Journal of Advertising Research, 21*, 25-29.

Swanson, D.L. (1987). Gratification seeking, media exposure, and audience interpretations: Some directions for research. *Journal of Broadcasting & Electronic Media, 31*(3), 237-254.

Takeshita, T. (1997). Exploring the media's roles in defining reality: From issue-agenda setting to attribute-agenda setting. In M.E. McCombs, D.L. Shaw, & D. Weaver (Eds.), *Communication and democracy: Exploring the intellectual frontiers in agenda-setting theory* (pp. 15-27). Mahwah, NJ: Erlbaum.

Trusdell, B. (1997, February). Life in the fast lane. *Sales & Marketing Management*, pp. 66-71.

Tutko, T.A. (1989). Personality change in the American sport scene. In J.H. Goldstein (Ed.), *Sports, games, and play: Social and psychological viewpoints* (pp. 111-127). Hillside, NJ: Erlbaum.

USA Today. (2000, May 1). www.usatoday.com.

Wanta, W., & Wu, Y. (1992). Interpersonal communication and the agenda-setting process. *Journalism Quarterly, 69*(4), 847-855.

Webster, J.G., & Lichty, L.W. (1991). *Ratings analysis: Theory and practice*. Hillsdale, NJ: Erlbaum.

Wenner, L.A. (1989). Media, sports, and society: The research agenda. In L.A. Wenner (Ed.), *Media, sports, and society* (pp. 13-48). Newbury Park: Sage.

Wenner, L.A. (1991). One part alcohol, one part sport, one part dirt, stir gently: Beer commercials and television sports. In L.R. Vande Berg & L.A. Wenner (Eds.), *Television criticism: Approaches and applications* (pp. 388-407). New York: Longman.

Wenner, L.A., & Gantz, W. (1989). The audience experience with sports on television. In L.A. Wenner (Ed.), *Media, sports, and society* (pp. 241-269). Newbury Park: Sage.

Williams, B.R. (1977). The structure of televised football. *Journal of Communication, 27*(3), 133-139.

Wright, C.R. (1986). *Mass communication: A sociological perspective* (3rd ed.). New York: Random House.

Zillmann, D., Bryant, J., & Sapolsky, B.S. (1989). Enjoyment from sports spectatorship. In J.H. Goldstein (Ed.), *Sports, games, and play: Social and psychological viewponts* (pp. 241-278). Hillsdale, NJ: Erlbaum.

Zucker, H.G. (1978). The variable nature of news media influence. In B. Ruben (Ed.), *Communication yearbook* (Vol. 2, pp. 225-246). New Brunswick, NJ: Transaction Books.

AUTHOR INDEX

A

Andersen, R., 13, *241*
Ang, I., 39, *241*
Associated Press, 183, *241*

B

Ball-Rokeach, S. J., xvii, 42, 43, 44, 46, 49, *241, 243*
Becker, L. B., 40, 41, 47, *241, 245*
Bellamy, R. V., Jr., xvi, *242*
Blumler, J. G., xvii, 38, 39, *242, 244*
Bogart, L., xvi, *242*
Boston Celtics, 160, 161*t*, *242*
Bregman, D., 37, 190, *246*
Brown, R., 80, *242*
Bryant, J., 2, 7, 29, 30, 192, *242, 247*
Budd, M., 39, *242*

C

Cantor, J. M., 43, *242*
Cantor, M. G., 43, *242*
Carey, J. W., 38, *242*
Carragee, K., 37, *243*
Chicago Professional Sports Limited Partnership and WGN Continental Broadcasting Company v. NBA, 10, 159, 160, *242*
Clarke, P., 36, *245*
Coe, S., 178, *242*
Comisky, P., 7, *242*
Curran, J., 43, *242*

D

D'Alessandro, D., 112, 167, 168, 175, 179, *243*
Danielian, L. H., 37, 190, *243*
Dearing, J. W., 37, 190, *246*
DeFleur, M. L., xvii, 42, 43, 44, 46, *241*

E

Entman, R. M., 35, 39, *242, 243*

SUBJECT INDEX

CPSIA information can be obtained
at www.ICGtesting.com
Printed in the USA
FFOW04n0510050915
16501FF

9 781572 734081